SHARP

SHARP

The Women Who Made
an Art of Having an Opinion

MICHELLE DEAN

Grove Press
New York

FIRST EDITION

Published simultaneously in Canada
Printed in the United States of America

First Grove Atlantic hardcover edition: April 2018

Library of Congress Cataloging-in-Publication data available for this title.

ISBN 978-0-8021-2509-5
eISBN 978-0-8021-6571-8

Grove Press
an imprint of Grove Atlantic
154 West 14th Street
New York, NY 10011

Distributed by Publishers Group West

groveatlantic.com

18 19 20 21   10 9 8 7 6 5 4 3 2 1

For every person who's ever been told,
"You're too smart for your own good"

Contents

Preface

I gathered the women in this book under the sign of a compliment that every one of them received in their lives: they were called sharp.

The precise nature of their gifts varied, but they had in common the ability to write unforgettably. The world would not have been the same without Dorothy Parker's acid reflections on the absurdities of her life. Or Rebecca West's ability to sweep half the world's history into a first-person account of a single trip. Or Hannah Arendt's ideas about totalitarianism, or Mary McCarthy's fiction that took as its subject the strange consciousness of the princess among the trolls. Or Susan Sontag's ideas about interpretation, or Pauline Kael's energetic swipes at filmmakers. Or Nora Ephron's skepticism about the feminist movement, or Renata Adler's catalog of the foibles of those in power. Or Janet Malcolm's reflections on the perils and rewards of psychoanalysis and journalism.

That these women achieved what they did in the twentieth century only makes them more remarkable. They came up in a world that was not eager to hear women's opinions about anything. It can be easy to forget that Dorothy Parker began publishing her caustic verse before women even had the vote. We often don't think about the fact that the second wave of feminism kicked up *after* Susan Sontag had become the icon she was with her "Notes on 'Camp'" essay. These women openly defied gendered expectations before any organized feminist movement managed to make gains for women on the whole. Through their exceptional talent, they were granted a kind of intellectual equality to men other women had no hope of.

All that personal success often put them in tension with the collective politics of "feminism." While some of the people in this book called themselves feminists, others didn't. Virtually none of them found themselves satisfied by working as activists; Rebecca West, who came closest, eventually found the suffragettes both admirably ferocious and unforgivably prudish. Sontag wrote a defense of feminism, then turned around and roared at Adrienne Rich about the "simple-mindedness" of the movement when challenged. Even Nora Ephron confessed to feeling uneasy about the efforts of women to organize at the 1972 Democratic convention.

The ambivalence here is often said to be repudiation of feminist politics, and occasionally it explicitly was that. These women were all oppositional spirits, and they tended not to like being grouped together. For one thing, some of them despised each other: McCarthy had no interest in Parker, Sontag said the same about McCarthy, Adler famously scorched the earth when she went after Kael. For another, they had little time for notions of "sisterhood": I can imagine Hannah Arendt haranguing me for placing her work in the context of her womanhood at all.

And yet, these women were received as proof positive that women were every bit as qualified to weigh in on art, on ideas, and on politics as men. What progress we have ever made on that front was made because the feminine side of the equation could lay claim to Arendt and Didion and Malcolm, among the others. Whether or not they knew it, these women cleared a path for other women to follow.

I wrote this book because this history has never been as well-known as it deserves to be, at least outside certain isolated precincts of New York. Biographies had been written of all of them and devoured by me. But as biographies do, each book considered these women in isolation, a phenomenon unto herself, missing the connections I felt I could see. The forward march of American literature is usually chronicled by way of its male novelists: the Hemingways and Fitzgeralds, the Roths and Bellows and Salingers. There is little sense, in that version of the story, that women writers of those eras were doing much worth remembering. Even in more academic accounts, in "intellectual histories," it is generally assumed that men dominated the scene. Certainly, the so-called New York intellectuals of the mid-twentieth century are often identified as a male set. But my research showed otherwise. Men might have outnumbered women, demographically. But in the arguably more crucial matter of producing work worth remembering, the work that defined the terms of their scene, the women were right up to par—and often beyond it.

Is there, after all, a voice that carries better through the ages than Parker's? You can practically hear the scratch of her voice in every verse. Or is there a moral and political voice whose reach exceeds Hannah Arendt's? Where would our vision of culture be without Susan Sontag? How would we think about movies without Pauline Kael to open the door to the celebration of popular art? The longer I looked at the work of these women laid out before me, the more puzzling I found it that anyone could look at the literary and intellectual history of the twentieth century and *not* center women in it.

I can't help thinking the reason people haven't is because being so bright, so exceptional, so sharp, did not always earn these women praise in their own time. More often people reacted badly to the sting. Broadway producers hated Parker and chased her out of a theater critic's post. Mary McCarthy's friends at the *Partisan Review* despised the parodies she wrote of them, feeling her haughty and unkind. Pauline Kael was criticized by the male cineasts of her era for being insufficiently serious. (Actually she's still criticized for that.) The letters to the editor were scathing when Joan Didion published her famous essay on central California, "Some Dreamers of the Golden Dream." When Janet Malcolm observed that journalists exploit the vanity of their subjects, newspaper columnists took to their pulpits to shame her for sullying the alleged honor of journalism.

Some of that criticism came from bald sexism. Some from plain stupidity. Quite a bit of it was some blend of both. But the key to these women's power was in how they responded to it, with a kind of intelligent skepticism that was often very funny. Even Hannah Arendt could roll an eye, now and then, at the furor her *Eichmann in Jerusalem* provoked. Didion once fired a simple "Oh, wow" at an intemperate letter writer. Adler had a habit of quoting writers' own words back at them, pointing out word repetition and philosophical emptiness.

Their sardonic ways sometimes became grounds to ignore these women, to deem them "not serious." Irony, sarcasm, ridicule: these can be the tools of outsiders, a by-product of the natural skepticism toward conventional wisdom that comes when you haven't been able to participate in its formulation. It is my view that we should take more notice of an attempt to intervene when it has that sort of edge to it. There is always intellectual value in not being like everyone else at the table, in this case not being a man, but also not being white, not being upper class, not being from the right school.

It was not so much that these women were always in the right. Nor that they are themselves a perfect demographic sample. These women came from similar backgrounds: white, and often Jewish, and middle-class. And as you will see in the following pages, they were formed by the habits, preoccupations and prejudices that entails. In a more perfect world, for example, a black writer like Zora Neale Hurston would have been more widely recognized as part of this cohort, but racism kept her writings at the margin of it.

But even so, these women were there in the fray, participating in the great arguments of the twentieth century. That is the point of this book. Their work alone is reason to acknowledge their presence.

I will cop to a secondary motive, one that shaped the kinds of questions I explored about these women. There is something valuable about knowing this history if you are a young woman of a certain kind of ambition. There is something valuable in knowing that pervasive sexism notwithstanding there are ways to cut through it.

So when I ask in the following pages what made these women who they were, such elegant arguers, both hindered and helped by men, prone to but not defined by mistakes, and above all completely unforgettable, I do it for one simple reason: because even now, even (arguably) after feminism, we still need more women like this.

1

Parker

Before she was the lodestar she later became, Dorothy Parker had to go to work at nineteen. That was not how things were supposed to go, not for someone like her. She was born well-enough-to-do in 1893 to a fur merchant. The family name was Rothschild—not *those* ones, as Parker reminded interviewers all her life. But still a respectable New York Jewish family, financially comfortable enough for Jersey Shore vacations and a large apartment on the Upper West Side of Manhattan. Then her father died in the winter of 1913, devastated by the deaths of two wives and a brother who sank with the *Titanic*. His children inherited almost nothing.

There was no impending marriage available to rescue then Dorothy Rothschild. She had no education to speak of either. She had not even graduated from high school, not that women of her background were generally educated to work. Secretarial schools, which would grant a host of middle-class women the power to make their own living by the midcentury, were only starting to open when she came of age. Parker had to turn instead to the only talent she had that could quickly prove remunerative: she could play the piano, and dancing schools were beginning to crop up all around Manhattan. Sometimes, Parker liked to say, she even taught the slightly scandalous new ragtime dances to the students: the Turkey Trot, the Grizzly Bear. She always made herself the punch line of the story. "All her men graduates, ever after, Lame-Ducked on the wrong foot," a friend remembered her telling him.

It was a good story, granted that it was also almost certainly an exaggeration. In all the annals kept by her friends and contemporaries, no one mentions Parker so much as sitting near a piano, not to mention doing any kind of dancing. Maybe she just gave it up. Maybe, as would happen to her later with writing, having to make money with her musical talents turned the whole activity sour. But perhaps, too, she exaggerated in the service of humor, because from the beginning humor provided a good escape. Her jokes would eventually give Dorothy Rothschild a legendary status as "Mrs. Parker," a kind of avatar of the good time. Mrs. Parker always had a cocktail in her hand and had just dropped a quip on the party like a grenade.

But just as the noise and glitter of a party often hide miseries and frustrations, the same was true of Parker's life. The stories that enchanted other people were carvings of a kind, taken from horrible experiences and offered up as fun. Even this jovial image of a piano-playing Parker sitting at the center of a bunch of people whirling to a beat hid anger and suffering. Parker clearly didn't mind telling people she had been left penniless, because there was a certain heroism in having built herself up from that. But she much more rarely talked about her mother, who had died by the time Parker was five, or the hated stepmother who had followed. She also tended not to mention that when she left school at fifteen, it was to stay home with her increasingly ill and disoriented father. It would be nearly five years before his death would spring her from that particular trap.

Later, in a short story she wrote about the last day of "The Wonderful Old Gentleman," Parker described the state of the (fictional) man thus:

There was no need for them to gather at the Old Gentleman's bedside. He would not have known any of them. In fact, he had not known them for almost a year, addressing them by wrong names and asking them grave, courteous

2

questions about the health of husbands or wives or children who belonged to other branches of the family.

Parker liked to present her father's death as a tragedy and could sometimes sound bitter about how she'd been left to fend for herself: "There was no money, you see." But the need for a job turned out to be a boon, the first time Parker would turn a bad experience into a good story. This was her gift: to shave complex emotions down to a witticism that hints at bitterness without wearing it on the surface.

After that experience, Parker apparently decided that all good fortune was a kind of accident. The business of writing happened by chance, she usually said. She wrote for "need of money, dear." That wasn't really the whole truth. Parker had composed verse from the time she was a small child, though it's unclear exactly when she got the idea. She wasn't a record keeper, and very few papers of hers survive. One of her biographers managed to lay hands on a few childhood notes to her father, which already had a budding writer's voice to them. "They say when your writing goes uphill, you have a hopeful disposition," she wrote to him once, referring to the slant of her handwriting. Then she added the sort of deflating remark that was to become her signature maneuver: "Guess I have."

Talent can be a kind of accident sometimes. It can choose people and set them up for lives they never would have dreamed of themselves. But that was really the only kind of accident that had any hand in making Dorothy Parker a writer.

The first person who gave Parker a professional chance was a man named Frank Crowninshield. He pulled her from a pile of unsolicited submissions sometime in 1914. He may have recognized something of himself in her, perhaps her oppositional spirit. Though already in his forties by then and born a Boston Brahmin, Crowninshield was not like everyone else in the New York high society. He never married—perhaps because he was gay, though there is no firm proof of it. To all interested parties, Crowninshield presented himself as merely devoted to a troubled brother who was addicted to narcotics. He was known about town chiefly for his pranks, and for his stewardship of the first iteration of *Vanity Fair*, a once staid and proper men's fashion magazine he was hired by Condé Nast to reinvent.

It was then still the early days of American magazines. *Harper's* and the *Atlantic Monthly* were kicking around. But no one had yet invented the *New Yorker*, much less dreamed of catering to an audience more cosmopolitan than "the old lady from Dubuque." Edward Bernays, a nephew of Freud's who is often credited with the invention of public relations, had only begun his career in the fall of 1913. Advertisers were only beginning to have some idea of their eventual power in America.

Having so few models to emulate, Crowninshield's *Vanity Fair* turned out something like its editor's personality: tart and impertinent, particularly in regard to the very rich. Something—perhaps the sufferings of his brother, perhaps the clear fact that Crowninshield's family had always possessed more prestige than money—had made him a critic of the well-off. But he was not much for fire-and-brimstone social criticism. His method, instead, was ridicule. Even his editor's note to the first issue of the revamped magazine was sardonic:

> *For women we intend to do something in a noble and missionary spirit, something which, so far as we can observe, has never before been done for them by an American magazine. We mean to make frequent appeals to their intellects. We dare to believe that they are, in their best moments, creatures of some cerebral activity; we even make bold to believe that it is they who are contributing what is more original, stimulating, and highly magnetized to the literature of our day, and we hereby announce ourselves as determined and bigoted feminists.*

This is the kind of irony that can easily fold back on itself and become confusing: Is this humor about feminism, then still a relatively new concept? Or is it humor in the service of feminism? Or is it empty ridicule, with no kind of political purpose? To me, it appears to be all three. One of the great pleasures of irony like this is being able to watch it refract in different directions. At least a few of those directions were paths women could walk down. When this first issue was published in 1914, women couldn't even vote. But because Crowninshield liked to poke fun, he needed writers with oppositional viewpoints, people who didn't quite fit into the recognized bounds of propriety.

A great many of that kind of writer also happened to be women. Anne O'Hagan, a suffragette, wrote about the alleged bohemianism of Greenwich Village. Clara Tice, an avant-garde illustrator who liked to claim she'd been the first woman ever to bob her hair, was an integral part of the magazine from the start. Marjorie Hillis, who by the 1930s had become an avatar of the single life for women everywhere, also published there in the early days of the magazine.

Parker would become the signature voice of the magazine, but it took a while to install her there. Crowninshield's eye was caught by a bit of light verse she'd submitted. The poem is called "Any Porch," and its nine stanzas present themselves as overheard remarks, the idea being they could be heard on "any porch" of the largely well-to-do and slightly well-informed. Stylized and relying on the moral prejudices of an early twentieth-century high society, it's a bit of a clunker to modern ears. But it already bore the marks of Parker's future preoccupations: her acid read of the confines of femininity and her impatience with those who spoke only in the clichés of received wisdom:

> I don't call Mrs. Brown bad,
> She's un-moral, dear, not im-moral . . .
> I think the poor girl's on the shelf
> She's talking about her "career."

Crowninshield saw something in this. He paid her five or ten or twelve dollars for the poem. (Her account, his, and those of others all differ on the amount.) This small success emboldened her to ask him for a job. At first he could not wrangle a job for her at *Vanity Fair* proper, so he found a place for her at *Vogue*.

It was not exactly an ideal fit. The *Vogue* of 1916 was a prim magazine for nice women with a lot of prim, nice writing in it. Parker wasn't much interested in fashion, never had been. Yet at this magazine she found herself with a job that required her to hold passionate, almost religious views as to the merits of one fabric over another, as to the length of a hem. From her first days at the magazine she could not muster the energy. Late in life she'd try to present her memories politely. But she could not hide that she'd been as much a critic of her coworkers as she was of anything else. She told the *Paris Review* that the women at *Vogue* were "plain . . . not chic." The compliments she had for them were never half so long as the insults:

> *They were decent, nice women—the nicest women I ever met—but they had no business on such a magazine. They wore funny little bonnets and in the pages of their magazine they virginized the models from tough babes into exquisite little loves.*

Vogue was driven by the demands of the fledgling commercial clothing industry, a business that mostly pandered to and trivialized its customers. There was, even in this early period, a kind of marketing gloss to every article in the magazine, the copy always demanding the tone of a catalog. And with an admirable and wicked kind of prescience—it was still more than half a century before women would begin to revolt over the confines of dress—every move Parker made at *Vogue* undermined the idea that a beautiful outfit was the height of feminine sophistication.

To be fair to *Vogue*, the couple of years spent marinating in a subject she so plainly felt beneath her focused Parker's wit. The writer of "Any Porch" wielded a pen like a hammer. The duress at *Vogue* made her sly and subtle. When, for example, she was assigned to write captions for the pen-and-ink fashion illustrations that took up most of the real estate in *Vogue*'s pages, she would thread a very fine needle. She might find the subject indescribably stupid, but her wit had to be wielded so subtly that the editor in chief wouldn't catch any hint of Parker's condescension to *Vogue*'s readers. This filigree work led to some truly brilliant captions—such as the famous one that affirmed that "brevity is the soul of lingerie." Others poked even lighter fun at the elaborate undercarriage fashion required:

> There is only one thing as thrilling as one's first love affair; that is one's first corset. They both give the same feeling of delightful importance. This one is planned to give something approaching a waistline to the straight sturdiness of the twelve-year-old.

Her editors noticed. Some of Parker's captions were rewritten when her disdain cut too clearly through the text. And even though Parker's manners were apparently impeccable, Edna Woolman Chase, the coolheaded editor in chief of *Vogue*, called Parker "treacle-sweet of tongue but vinegar-witted" in her own memoirs. It seems important that Chase also noticed the way Parker's bite was hidden in subterfuge, delivered with honey. It echoes the picture a later friend, the drama critic Alexander Woollcott, would draw of the young Parker: "So odd a blend of Little Nell and Lady Macbeth." Work simply poured out of Parker in those early years. She wrote almost as frequently for *Vanity Fair* as she did for *Vogue*, clearly angling for a job at the former. *Vanity Fair* just had more room for the kind of light, satirical, and more often than not forgettable verse that Parker seemed able to deliver by the gallon. She returned again and again to a form she called hate songs, light verse whose targets ran the gamut from women to dogs. Some of these could be quite funny, but mostly they took the form of raw complaint, and their harshness could grate. She did better when allowed to flesh out her talents at greater length in essays. Her vinegar wit did well when it was drawn out like that, a slow-acting acid eating away at the ridiculous subject. Her boredom, again, gave the pieces she was producing a finer edge.

In a November 1916 issue of *Vanity Fair*, Parker explained her singleness in a piece titled "Why I Haven't Married." It was send-up of the New York dating scene, apparently as hopeless in Parker's era as it is in ours. She sketched the "types" a single woman found herself dining with in terms that still seem apt. Of Ralph, a nice man of unfailing solicitousness: "I saw myself surrounded by a horde of wraps and sofa pillows . . . I saw myself a member of the Society Opposed to Woman Suffrage." Of Maximilian, a leftist bohemian: "He capitalized the A in art." Of Jim, a rising businessman: "In his affections I was rather third—first and second, Haig and Haig; and then, third, me."

Meanwhile "Interior Desecration," published in the July 1917 issue of *Vogue*, sent Parker out in the world describing a bewildering visit to a home decorated by one (possibly fictitious) Alistair St. Cloud. (This visit was itself possibly fictional.) One room, we are told, is decorated in purple satin and black carpet, and contains "infrequent chairs, which must have been relics of the Inquisition."

> *There was no other thing in the room, save an ebony stand on which rested one lone book, bound in brilliant scarlet. I glanced at its title; it was* The Decameron.
> *"What room is this?" I asked.*
> *"This is the library," said Alistair, proudly.*

She was getting better all the time, landing more punch lines, hitting her targets with greater precision. Her talent had been obvious from the start but her skill had needed the time to develop. It also needed, it seems, the stimulation of Crowninshield's admiration and attention. In the first years of her career Parker was more productive than she'd ever be again. The discipline of earning her own way—which she did even after she married Edwin Pond Parker II in the spring of 1916—suited her.

The man who gave Mrs. Parker his name was a young, blond Paine Webber stockbroker of good Connecticut stock, but like hers, the name implied more money than its holder possessed. Eddie, as he was known, was a person destined to come to us more through the lens of other people's impressions than his own telling. But we know that from the start he was a drinker, a bon vivant, far more than his future bride. When she met him, Dorothy was a near teetotaler. Over the course of their marriage Eddie would get her into gin.

"From beginning to end, the process of getting married is a sad one for the groom," Parker quipped in an article she wrote after her 1916 marriage. "He is lost in a fog of oblivion which envelops him from the first strains of the Wedding March to the beginning of the honeymoon." And though she seemed by all accounts to love Eddie, she mostly left him to the fog. When America entered World War I a few months after their wedding, Eddie enlisted in an army company and went away to training and eventually the front. There, he apparently picked up a morphine addiction to pair with his alcoholism.

Eddie Parker's problems made him a spectral presence in his wife's history, a ghost she dragged along to parties, someone she shoehorned into a story or two, without ever quite conveying what might have attracted her to him. Crowninshield was finally able to get Parker to *Vanity Fair* in 1918, and when he did it was her prose he wanted. P. G. Wodehouse had been the magazine's drama critic from the time of its rebirth, but he'd quit. Crowninshield offered Parker his job. She had never written a word about the theater, yet the drama critic of *Vanity Fair* bore a considerable burden for the magazine. In the early half of the twentieth century, fashionable, important people cared about theater reviews. Moving pictures were not yet ascendant forms of popular entertainment; live theater still created and nurtured actual stars. There was a lot of money and status to be toyed with, influenced, and considered—not to mention insulted—on the drama critic's beat.

Perhaps that explains why Parker's first reviews for the magazine were so tentative. The sure feet of the humor pieces suddenly lost their rhythm. She chatted nervously for the first few columns. In many of them, she spent little time describing the plays and musicals she was seeing at all. The very first, published in April 1918, devotes itself to a lengthy complaint about an audience member who spent most of the performance of a musical searching for a glove. It ends, abruptly: "So there you are."

Confidence came, but gradually. Long windups began to be more reliably punctuated by fastballs. Parker's aim improved, too. By her fourth column she was complaining about the "dog's life" of a theater critic who often found herself wanting to review shows that had closed by the time the magazine appeared on store shelves. By her fifth column she was casting aspersions on the theater's love of the trappings of war: "How will they ever costume the show-girls if not in the flags of the Allies?" Her barbs gradually took on her old elegant touch: "I do wish that [Ibsen] had occasionally let the ladies take bichloride of mercury, or turn on the gas, or do something quiet and neat around the house," she would complain of the inevitable gunshots in a production of *Hedda Gabler*.

One source of her growing confidence was that at *Vanity Fair* Parker found herself writing for friends. Crowninshield understood her, as did the other editors at the magazine. Humor depends on a measure of shared understanding. Even when a joke is outrageous or transgressive, it can be that way only if there is some kind of consensus between joker and audience for its teller to transgress. And for most of Parker's professional life, there was ready encouragement and approval from a circle of close friends and confidants. Almost all of them were men. Two *Vanity Fair* colleagues were particularly important. One was Robert Benchley, a maladroit newspaperman hired on as *Vanity Fair*'s managing editor shortly after Parker arrived from *Vogue*. The other was Robert Sherwood, a slimmer and quieter man whose reserve hid an equally devastating sense of humor. These three were an inseparable troublemaking trio at *Vanity Fair*.

They wrote their own legend, in every sense of the phrase. "I must say," Parker admitted much later with an obvious note of proud wickedness, "we behaved extremely badly." They liked pranks, especially ones that needled their bosses. A favored anecdote saw Parker subscribe to a mortuary magazine. She and Benchley loved morbid humor. They also loved how much Crowninshield flinched when he passed Parker's desk and saw the embalming diagram she'd ripped from one of the issues and pinned up. They took long lunches, were late and refused to make excuses for it, and when Crowninshield left for Europe on a business trip with Condé Nast they got worse. They were not dedicated employees.

Their lazy ethos naturally extended to the Algonquin Round Table, that storied clique of writers and other assorted glamorous hangers-on who briefly gathered at the Algonquin Hotel in Midtown Manhattan. The Round Table formally began in self-indulgence, when Alexander Woollcott, then the drama critic for the *New York Times*, held a lunch to welcome himself back from war in 1919. Attendees enjoyed the occasion so much it was agreed they would continue. The group's reputation long outlasted its actual existence, which was brief and ephemeral. The first references to the Round Table in gossip columns appear in 1922; by 1923 trouble is reported in the ranks, owing to anti-Semitic remarks by the hotel's proprietor; and by 1925 the phenomenon was declared over.

Parker later became ambivalent about the Round Table, the way she tended to become about virtually everything she'd done that had been a success. She was not, as is sometimes said, the only woman at the table; journalists like Ruth Hale and Jane Grant and novelists like Edna Ferber were often there sharing drinks with the rest. But Parker was undoubtedly the person whose manner and voice were most closely associated with it. Her reputation dwarfed those of most of the men who were there, most of whose names are forgotten now. And because her wit was so pithy, she was the one most frequently quoted by the gossip columnists.

Uncomfortable with all of it, Parker would sometimes snap at interviewers who brought up the Round Table. "I wasn't there very often," she would say. "It cost too much." Or she'd put the whole thing down: "Just a bunch of loudmouths showing off, saving their gags for days, waiting for a chance to spring them." She was undoubtedly affected by the contemporary press, which was skeptical about, even critical of, the Round Table's claims to literary might. "Not one [member] had given an impressive tone to literature nor had one fashioned a poem of consequence," sniffed one gossip columnist in 1924. "Yet theirs was an attitude of superiority over conventional minds."

Parker was perhaps protesting too much, selling her friends a little short. Their laughter at the hotel lunches and dinners was obviously a light prize, carrying little consequence. But it was a kind of fuel for other, greater things. The sort of willing audience Benchley, Sherwood, and the rest of the group provided was energizing for her. Never again would she write as much as she did during the *Vanity Fair* and Algonquin years.

Parker's congenital inability to accept people's self-images—as serious writers, as glamorous stars—haunted her as a critic. She was not a theatergoer who was easily satisfied; she was, in short, not a fan. Producers grew angry about the wounding remarks that appeared in Parker's columns. The offense caused was always disproportionate to the insult, but that rarely mattered. The producers were advertisers as well as critical subjects. They could wield a club.

Sometimes Parker managed to anger them without even trying. The column that broke Condé Nast's back was sadly not even one of

Parker's best. The show under review was a now-forgotten Somerset Maugham comedy called *Caesar's Wife*. Its star was one Billie Burke, of whom Parker remarked:

> *Miss Burke, in the role of the young wife, looking charmingly youthful. She is at her best in her more serious moments; in her desire to convey the girlishness of the character, she plays her lighter scenes rather as if she were giving an impersonation of Eva Tanguay.*

This was a subtler cut than usual. Yet it sent Flo Ziegfeld, the legendary Broadway producer and Burke's husband, flying to his telephone with complaints. Eva Tanguay, for one thing, was an "exotic dancer," or the 1920 equivalent. Billie Burke, meanwhile, had a squeaky-clean image. She is probably now best known for her role as Glinda the Good Witch in the 1939 MGM version of *The Wizard of Oz*. But the squalid implications may not have been what most offended Burke. She had just turned thirty-five when this review was published, and more than likely resented Parker's jabs at her age much more than any implication of stripperhood.

In any event, Ziegfeld was only the latest to complain about Parker's critical liberties, so Condé Nast insisted on a change. Crowninshield took Parker to tea at the Plaza and told her he wanted to take her off the theater beat. There is some quarrel over whether she resigned or was fired from the magazine entirely, the pendulum swinging back and forth depending on who you're reading. She said she ordered the most expensive dessert on the menu, stormed out, and called Benchley. He immediately resolved to quit as well.

Benchley had become the most important person, bar none, in Parker's life. It was his approval she wanted and his voice she emulated. Their friends wondered if they were having an affair but there seems to be no evidence of that. She was plainly just as important to him as he was to her, since he gave up that job while he had children to support. "It was the greatest act of friendship I'd known," Parker said.

They were less angry about leaving the magazine than their dramatic exit suggested. They chose their own successors. Parker had pulled a very young critic named Edmund Wilson from the slush pile not too long before she left. When Crowninshield tapped Wilson to take over managing editor duties as Benchley's replacement, she may have even been pleased. Her work would be back in *Vanity Fair*'s pages within a year of her being fired.

The handoff was smooth, punctuated with drinks at the Algonquin for the young and uninitiated Wilson, who was years from becoming the revered and "serious" critic of *Axel's Castle* and *To the Finland Station*. Though invited to Round Table gatherings, "I did not find them particularly interesting," Wilson wrote in his diaries. But he did find Parker intriguing, because of "the conflicts in her nature." He distinguished her from the other Algonquinites because she could talk to serious people "on an equal basis." Her "well-aimed and deadly malice" made her less provincial than the rest of the group. All this suited Wilson, who'd keep up their friendship for the rest of Parker's life, even when she was washed-up and penniless. Wilson, unlike many men of his background and circumstances, really liked the company of sharp women. He couldn't seem to resist the company of the truly clever.

Parker didn't need to hold a grudge against Condé Nast, anyway. Forging out on her own, she never lacked for work now that she had a reputation. A magazine called *Ainslee's* quickly hired her as its theater critic. Her light verse appeared almost weekly in newspapers and magazines all over town, the theater reviews monthly, and she was doing prose pieces besides. Throughout the 1920s she worked constantly. And though she'd say her verse never made her enough money to live on, she was managing to survive on her earnings and some form of contribution from Eddie; they were living apart by 1922, though they would not formally divorce until 1928.

So her work was certainly popular. But was it good? The poetry has suffered badly in that regard. The American appetite for light verse diminished, then disappeared by the 1930s, and admittedly its appeal is hard to see now. It seems clichéd, overwrought. Her usual subject was romance, too, which got her accused of sentimentality. Parker internalized the criticism and came to feel her poetry was worthless. But read carefully, and you can see flashes of brilliance in the verses that took on the world around her. Even her throwaway poems still pack punches, as in 1922's "The Flapper":

> Her girlish ways may make a stir,
> Her manners cause a scene,
> But there is no more harm in her
> Than in a submarine.

This was no random attack. Parker was taking quiet aim at her contemporaries. Her star had risen alongside that of F. Scott Fitzgerald, the chief mythologizer of flappers and flapperdom. His *This Side of Paradise*, a campus novel about a young student in love with a flapper, was published to huge sales and critical fanfare in 1919. It made him a star; it also made him, briefly, into a kind of oracle for his age. Parker knew Fitzgerald personally before he published the book, when he was still struggling. Still, after his success, the sort of figure he cut in the media irked her. In March 1922, Parker published a hate song called "The Younger Set":

> There are the Boy Authors;
> The ones who are going to put belles lettres on their feet.
> Every night before they go to sleep

They kneel down and ask H. L. Mencken
To bless them and make them good boys.
They are always carrying volumes with home-cut pages,
And saying that after all, there is only one Remy de
    Gourmont;
Which doesn't get any dissension out of me.
They shrink from publicity
As you or I would
From the gift of a million dollars.
At the drop of a hat
They will give readings from their works —
In department stores,
Or grain elevators,
Or ladies' dressing-rooms.

Rémy de Gourmont, now mostly forgotten, was an enormously popular French symbolist poet and critic of the day. But here he is clearly a cipher for Fitzgerald, who was the true patron saint of Boy Authors. When *This Side of Paradise* was published, Fitzgerald was only twenty-four. And his contemporaries couldn't help noticing him, and envying him. "It makes us feel very old," complained another member of the Round Table who read the novel.

Did Parker envy him? She never admitted to it—always called Fitzgerald a friend and said she loved his work. But there are other hints she felt competitive. In 1921, she had published a parody under the title "Once More Mother Hubbard," the idea being that this was the classic fairy tale "as told to F. Scott Fitzgerald," in the pages of *Life*.

Rosalind rested her nineteen-year-old elbows on her
nineteen-year-old knees. All that you could see of her,
above the polished sides of the nineteen-year-old bath-
tub, was her bobbed, curly hair and her disturbing gray

eyes. A cigarette drooped lazily from the spoiled curves of her nineteen-year-old mouth.

Amory leaned against the door, softly whistling "Coming Back to Nassau Hall" through his teeth. Her young perfection kindled a curious fire in him.

"Tell me about you," he said, carelessly.

This parody, like all good ones, was the product of close attention to its target's work. If there was jealousy here, there was also some pretty trenchant criticism. Fitzgerald did fetishize high-class "carelessness." He was indeed sentimental about the Ivy League ("Coming Back to Nassau Hall" was a Princeton fight song). He was also fond of putting certain kinds of beautiful but not altogether *together* young girls in his heroes' sights, most of them simulacra of his wife, Zelda Fitzgerald. Fitzgerald did not leave behind any response to the piece, but if he read it, he surely saw that some of its slings and arrows were well aimed.

That Fitzgerald's treatment of women caught Parker's eye was no accident either. Like a lot of Fitzgerald's friends, Parker wasn't particularly fond of Zelda. "If she didn't like something she sulked," Parker told Zelda's biographer. "I didn't find that an attractive trait." Perhaps there was a feeling of competition: there are rumors of a sexual affair between Scott and Parker, though no proof of that survived. It was also something about image, about the way Zelda so often appeared to embrace a role Parker often resisted, so willing to be the press's ultimate flapper. In the publicity wave that hit Scott after the publication of *This Side of Paradise*, Zelda was usually part of the package. She'd say in interviews that she loved Rosalind, the character based on herself. "I like girls like that," she'd say. "I like their courage, their recklessness and spendthriftiness." Parker, by contrast, thought the whole thing a sham, couldn't give quotes like that, couldn't relate.

Nonetheless, Parker and Scott Fitzgerald remained friends most of their lives. They were just too much alike, rarely solvent alcoholics who suffered from writer's block. Eventually, too, he would come to agree with her both about the weakness of his earlier work and about the emptiness of Jazz Age excess. By the time Fitzgerald published *The Great Gatsby* in 1925, he wouldn't fetishize carelessness anymore. The flappers and scions of fortune were by then the cankers in their respective roses. But people were drawn still more to the shimmering mirage of places like Gatsby's West Egg than they were to the reality that all the glitter was counterfeit. *Gatsby* was a commercial flop. People weren't ready to hear that message from Fitzgerald in his lifetime. It wouldn't become popular until it was revived by an armed services edition distributed free to troops during World War II.

Unlike Parker, Fitzgerald died young, only forty-four when the alcoholism conspired with a bout of tuberculosis to kill him in 1940. Parker lived almost thirty years longer than he did. When she went to see him in his casket she quoted a line from *Gatsby* at him: "That poor son-of-a-bitch." No one caught the reference. By the late 1920s, Parker could not escape her own persona. She was in every newspaper, every magazine, everyone wanting to publish a poem, or a quip. In 1927, she released a collection of poetry called *Enough Rope*. To her surprise, and everyone else's, it promptly became a bestseller. Her poems became so popular that their lines and rhythms morphed into commonplaces, things people would say to each other at parties to seem witty and impressive. "Almost anyone you know can quote, re-quote, and mis-quote at least a dozen of her verses," complained a dour reviewer in *Poetry* in 1928. "She seems to have replaced Mah Jong, the crossword puzzle, and Ask Me Another."

Her popularity was even more surprising because Parker's poetry was not exactly relaxing to read. People simply loved the way she shocked them. There was something about her technique that, although repetitive, managed to deliver every time. Edmund Wilson, who had by then left *Vanity Fair* to become an editor at the *New*

Republic, reviewed *Enough Rope*—it was not strange until relatively recently for literary friends to review each other—and gave an excellent summation of how a typical Parker poem worked:

> *A kind of burlesque sentimental lyric which gave the effect, till you came to the end, of a typical magazine filler, perhaps a little more authentically felt and a little better written than the average: the last line, however, punctured the rest with incredible ferocity.*

The strategy had its drawbacks. Leading up to the zinger, the poems often use what look like clichés, purple language, the tools of what Wilson called "ordinary humorous verse" and "ordinary feminine poetry." Reviewers often complained about Parker's rote images, and often called her derivative for that reason. But they were missing something. When Parker used clichés, it was generally with a sense of their insufficiency; their emptiness was usually the joke. Nonetheless, she absorbed that criticism of her work, and often repeated it herself. "Let's face it, honey," she told her *Paris Review* interviewer, "my verse is terribly dated—as anything once fashionable is dreadful now."

It bears mentioning this was not how Wilson, among others, saw her work at the time. In his review of *Enough Rope* he wrote that he noticed certain infelicities in the poems, but he also thought they had "the appearance of proceeding, not merely from the competent exercise of an attractive literary gift, but from a genuine necessity to write." He saw the poet Edna St. Vincent Millay's style in Parker's work, but he found little similarity in their philosophies. The "edged and acrid style" Parker employed was something entirely her own, he insisted, and he felt it justified a lot of the weaknesses in her poems. He was certain it was a voice worth listening to.

Parker's voice was self-hating, masochistic, but the abuse had a target beyond herself. You could call that target the confines of femininity, or the falseness of the myths of romantic love, or even, in poems like the world-famous "Résumé," the melodrama of suicide itself:

> *Razors pain you;*
> *Rivers are damp;*
> *Acids stain you;*
> *And drugs cause cramp.*
> *Guns aren't lawful;*
> *Nooses give;*
> *Gas smells awful;*
> *You might as well live.*

Though most of her readers didn't know it, this poem was a bit of self-satire. Parker had first attempted suicide in 1922. She had chosen razors for the first outing. She had been despondent over a breakup with Charles MacArthur, a newspaperman who'd go on to write *The Front Page*, the template for the 1940s hit film *His Girl Friday*. At the bitter end of their affair, Parker had had an abortion. She did not pluckily pick herself up and recover afterward. Instead she seems to have told the story, again and again, sometimes not to the most sympathetic of audiences. A case in point: one of the people she chose to tell was a very young, very green writer named Ernest Hemingway.

Like Parker, Hemingway is now so famous it seems his genius must have been greeted with instant recognition, his reputation established the moment he published his first line. But when Parker first met him in February 1926, he was the author of a single collection of short stories, *In Our Time*, published by a tiny press called Boni and Liveright. The book did not make great waves in New York. Parker would later describe its reception as about as stirring as "an incompleted dogfight on upper Riverside Drive." It was Fitzgerald who would suggest Hemingway to his own publisher, the richer and more prestigious Scribner's. It was the negotiations over that first truly major book deal that brought Hemingway to New York in the spring of 1926, a deal that would eventually see Scribner's publish Hemingway's first truly successful book, the novel *The Sun Also Rises*.

So Parker and Hemingway did not meet as professional equals. By any measure of public acclaim, she was better known than he. This seems to have bothered him. It no doubt also bothered him that, having heard all his tales of the delightfully cheap life of the expatriate writer in France, Parker decided to prolong their acquaintance and sail back to Europe on the same boat as Hemingway. Over the next few months, she ran into Hemingway more than once on the Continent, in France as well as in Hemingway's beloved Spain. And she clearly began to grate on Hemingway's nerves.

Exactly what happened on that ship, and later in Spain and France as Parker and Hemingway met and talked, is lost. One of Parker's biographers said she somehow insulted Hemingway by questioning the honor and suffering of the Spanish people, in that she had made fun of a funeral procession. Certainly, though, she also talked of MacArthur, and of her abortion. We know Hemingway resented these confessions, because he was so bothered by them he decided to memorialize his irritation in a poem he called "To a Tragic Poetess":

> To celebrate in borrowed cadence
> your former gnaw and itch for Charley
> who went away and left you not so flat behind him
> And it performed so late those little hands
> those well formed little hands
> And were there little feet and had
> the testicles descended?

The poem ends on what Hemingway plainly considered a devastating note: "Thus tragic poetesses are made / by observation."

Parker may never have heard "To A Tragic Poetess." She left behind no hint that she knew it existed. But her friends did. Hemingway read it aloud at a dinner party at Archibald MacLeish's apartment in Paris, which was attended by the Round Tabler Donald Ogden Stewart and his wife. All present were reportedly appalled. Stewart himself had been in love with Parker at one point. He was made so angry by the poem that he promptly severed his friendship with Hemingway. Still, Hemingway clearly didn't regret having written it. He kept a typescript of the poem among his papers.

Parker registered Hemingway's disdain for her, even if she never heard the poem. And she could not simply brush it off. While not yet famous, Hemingway had the approval of a literary set whose approval she wanted too. Her ambitions were not as small as other people thought. Hemingway became a flash point for her. She apparently had a habit of asking their friends if they thought he liked her. Then she wrote two articles about him, a book review and a profile, both published in the then still fledgling *New Yorker*—both admiring, but written with palpable anxiety.

"His is, as any reader knows, a generous influence," she wrote in the review. "The simple thing he does looks so easy to do. But look at the boys who try to do it." She wasn't normally that good with straight compliments. The profile, too, was filled with awkward and perhaps unintentional barbs. Parker kept remarking on Hemingway's seductive effect on women, blaming his author photograph. She said he was overly sensitive to criticism, but that it was justified because "his work has begot some specimens that should be preserved in alcohol." In the end she said he had surpassing bravery and courage, and praised him for calling that "guts," instead. The whole thing reads like an apology that has gone on too long, making its recipient uncomfortable instead of forgiving.

As always, Parker excelled at internalizing the criticism of others. No one could hate Dorothy Parker more than she hated herself. That was something Hemingway did not understand. The *New Yorker* was then helmed by Harold Ross, another Round Tabler, who'd founded the publication in 1925. The magazine was meant to be a statement of sophisticated, metropolitan tastes, seeking an audience beyond that "old lady from Dubuque." But Ross was never a particularly refined character. Though the staff of the *New Yorker* would eventually become devoted to him, he was rough around the edges. He couldn't decide what he thought of women. On the one hand, he married a woman named Jane Grant, an avowed feminist whose beliefs likely explained why, in the early years of the *New Yorker,* men and women were published in roughly equivalent numbers. On the other hand, James Thurber, who would join the magazine in 1927, records Ross as continually blaming the incapacities of men on the "goddam women schoolteachers." Parker enjoyed Ross's complete confidence, but then she had already established a reputation before she began writing for him. In fact, she was far more instrumental in making the magazine's reputation than it was in making hers.

For the first troubled years of the *New Yorker*'s existence she simply contributed the occasional short story or poem. It was only when Robert Benchley needed to bow out as a book reviewer for the magazine for a while, and Parker filled in, that she made the magazine a famous outlet. She wrote under Benchley's chosen sobriquet: Constant Reader.

As a book reviewer, Parker was the queen of memorable one-liners. Her jab at the treacle of A. A. Milne, "Tonstant Weader fwowed up," is still famous. But many of the targets of Parker's most memorable insults—"the affair between Margot Asquith and Margot Asquith will live as one of the prettiest love stories in all literature"—are now forgotten by the larger public and thus often seen as beneath her notice. On that point Joan Acocella compared her unfavorably with Edmund Wilson, who was covering less popular but ultimately more important writers. "The Constant Reader columns are not really book reviews," she wrote. "They are standup comedy routines." This is slightly unfair owing to the aims of the different magazines, for the *New Yorker* never aspired to be the home of serious intellectual criticism; it aspired only to good writing. And good writing would always be easier to do in the context of a negative review, where it was possible to power through on jokes.

The comedy had smarter, more self-aware barbs than it's typically given credit for. My favorite of Parker's Constant Reader pieces isn't really a book review at all. It's a column, dated February 1928, about what Parker calls "literary Rotarians." The objects of her ire are a class of people who hang around the literary scene in New York attending parties and speaking knowledgeably of publishers, and who may even be writers of a sort themselves. She identifies them as writing columns with names like "Helling Around with the Booksy Folk" or "Turns with a Bookworm." In other words, they are posers, people who want to wear the trappings of literature without exercising any judgment: "The literary Rotarians have helped us and themselves along to the stage where it doesn't matter a damn what you write; where all writers are equal."

That someone with as cutting a mind as Parker's might take offense at a literary Rotarian attitude can't surprise anyone. But she was doing something more complicated and less abstract than simply defending the use of judgment in evaluating literature. After all, what Parker is writing here will be published under the rubric of a column called Constant Reader. She herself is known as a girl about town, albeit one who is producing poetry of a well-known sort. She could still be describing several members of the Round Table here, many of whom wrote under cuter-than-cute column names. Most of all she is describing what she seemed later to come to fear was true about herself: that she and most of her friends were simply working at trifles.

"I *wanted* to be cute," she told the *Paris Review* in 1957. "That's the terrible thing. I should have had more sense." This feeling dogged

Parker more and more as she became more successful. The knife had traveled inward, and instead of urging her to do increasingly better work, it shredded her will to do it at all. Parker was hardly alone in hating the "sophisticated" aesthetic of the 1920s by then. An article in the October 1930 *Harper's*, for example, bade "Farewell to Sophistication," and sideswiped Parker as a leading proponent of empty, useless "sophisticated talk."

The disillusionment began to play out in earnest in 1929. Paradoxically, that year began with a career triumph: Parker published a short story that would win her the O. Henry Award, and prove her talent could be directed at fiction. But it plays like a parable of Parker's disappointment with herself. The story is called "Big Blonde," and the heroine, Hazel Morse, has hair a color Parker describes as "assisted gold." Indeed, nearly everything about Hazel seems artificial, an act. We meet Hazel in middle age, after a successful youth spent entertaining men as a "good sport." "Men like a good sport," the narrator tells us, ominously. But Hazel tires of her own act—"she had become more conscientious than spontaneous about it"—and, growing older and less able to command the attentions of rich men, or to keep up the "good sport" appearance, secures a number of veronal tablets (a barbiturate, the 1920s version of Ambien) and botches a suicide attempt.

"Big Blonde" has obvious autobiographical elements. Parker had also tried (and failed) to commit suicide the same way, and she and Eddie had parted in the same mood of ambivalence that characterized the breakdown of Hazel's marriage. The depth of Parker's anguish, though, wasn't entirely about Eddie Parker, or about men in general.

Neither Parker nor Hazel was man obsessed in the traditional sense. If anything, both the writer and her character were on the fence about men. They had an idea of what fulfillment would look like, and they thought men would be part of that. But in practice, men were disappointments. They offered only surface engagement and were looking only for "good sports" instead of whole human beings with desires and aspirations and needs of their own. The autobiographical resonance of the story isn't in the details, then, in the number of tablets of veronal taken, in Hazel's devotion to whiskey as succor, in the elements of the divorce that may have been drawn from Parker's abandonment of Eddie. It's in the overwhelming feeling of disappointment: in men, sure, but also in the world, and in herself.

That year Parker also received the first of several offers to go to Hollywood and fine-tune the dialogue in screenplays. As a noted wit, she was offered more than the going rate. She took an offer for three hundred dollars a week for three months. She needed the money, of course, but she was also longing for escape. And while she mostly hated Hollywood, found it as stupid as all her contemporaries did, she was reasonably successful there. She cowrote many successful pictures and even received a credit on the original 1934 version of *A Star Is Born* starring Janet Gaynor. For that she won an Oscar and made a lot of money. It bought a lot of gin and a lot of dogs—one of which was a poodle she called Cliché. Parker clearly took great comfort and enjoyment in the things this money bought, while they lasted.

The problem was that the work proved so lucrative it took up most of her time. She more or less stopped writing poetry altogether. Once in funds, she'd put out a short story. At first this worked well; she'd manage to publish a story every few months in 1931, 1932, 1933. Then it tapered off. Soon there were entire years between stories. She was given an advance for a novel at least once, but never finished it and had to return the money. She became the sort of writer whose communications with publishers consisted primarily of apologies. She could concoct the most charming "dog ate my homework" notes, as in this telegram from 1945 regarding some now-forgotten project she had going with Pascal Covici, an editor at the Viking Press:

This is instead of telephoning because I can't look you in the voice. I simply cannot get that thing done yet never

*have done such hard night and day work never have so
wanted anything to be good and all I have is a pile of
paper covered with wrong words. Can only keep at it and
hope to heaven to get it done. Don't know why it is so terribly difficult or I so terribly incompetent.*

There were a few soothing balms for her disappointments. First,
there was her second husband, a man named Alan Campbell, tall and
slim and actorly handsome, whom she married in 1934. He appointed
himself the caretaker in their relationship, controlling her diet. He
took such a strong interest in her outfits that others speculated about
his sexuality. (Be that as it may, friends and observers always said that
when the relationship was on, there was obvious physical attraction
between them.) The course of the relationship did not always run
smooth: the Parker-Campbells would divorce, then remarry, then
divorce again, and ultimately Campbell would commit suicide in
the small West Hollywood house they shared even in separation and
divorce. But when it was good, it was very good.

Parker also found herself in politics—though many of her admirers would have said she was lost there, too. The spark was the late
1920s protests against the execution of the Italian anarchists Nicola
Sacco and Bartolomeo Vanzetti. Known to the Boston police for
their anarchist political activities, Sacco and Vanzetti were arrested
on charges of murder and armed robbery—charges of which many
American literary and political elites insisted they were wholly inno-
cent. Along with the likes of the novelist John Dos Passos and the
Supreme Court justice Felix Frankfurter, Parker was a fervent advocate
for Sacco and Vanzetti's release. Ultimately the appeals of writers and
politicians were ignored, and the men executed. But not before Parker
was arrested at a march in 1927 and made numerous headlines before
being released a few hours later. She pleaded guilty to "loitering and
sauntering" and paid the five-dollar fine. When asked by the press if
she felt guilty, she said, "Well, I did saunter."

This first taste of protest gave her an appetite for more. In subsequent years Parker would attach herself to innumerable political and social causes. She began to have real sympathies with the ununionized, participating in a protest of the plight of service workers at the Waldorf-Astoria. She was constantly appearing on the masthead of some new Hollywood political organization: the Hollywood Anti-Nazi League, the Motion Picture Artists Committee to Aid Republican Spain, and eventually, too, the Screen Writers Guild.

Some found it hard not to question these newfound egalitarian convictions, given her frequent association with the glamorous and the rich. But whatever her present situation, Parker knew what it was like to have material comforts suddenly disappear. She could well have been drawing on her own occasional panics over finances in sympathizing with the plight of others. And no matter how much time she spent in the company of the rich, her eye for the ridiculous, honed all those years back by Frank Crowninshield, kept her from fully sympathizing with them.

Besides, her political ventures provided new avenues for self-criticism. Parker often used the seriousness of the social and political causes she now involved herself with to club her prior activities. She did so, for example, in an article she wrote for the *New Masses*, the journal of the American Communist Party, in 1937:

> *I am not a member of any political party. The only group I have ever been affiliated with is that not especially brave little band that hid its nakedness of heart and mind under the out-of-date garment of a sense of humor. I heard someone say, and so I said it too, that ridicule is the most effective weapon. I don't suppose I ever really believed it, but it was easy and comforting, and so I said it. Well, now I know. I know that there are things that never have been funny, and never will be. And I know that ridicule may be a shield, but it is not a weapon.*

As the Depression waned and the country moved toward World War II, her self-flagellation intensified. In 1939, Parker gave a speech to the American Writers Congress, an openly Communist group, in which she elaborated on her disillusionment:

> I don't think any word in the language has a horrider connotation than sophisticate, which ranks about along with "socialite." The real dictionary meaning is none too attractive. The verb means: to mislead, to deprive of simplicity, make artificial, to tamper with, for purpose of argument, to adulterate. You'd think that was enough, as far as it goes, but it has gone farther. Now it appears to mean: to be an intellectual and emotional isolationist; to sneer at those who do their best for their fellows and for their world; to look always down and never around; to laugh only at those things that are not funny.

There was some truth in this. "Sophistication" had its foibles, an obsession with surfaces, a casual quality. And yet the things Parker said and wrote turned out to be anything but ephemeral. People still send each other "Résumé." They quote Parker's criticisms of A. A. Milne and Katharine Hepburn. They remember that she said, in 1957, long after she thought she'd been wrung out as a writer: "As for me, I'd like to have money. And I'd like to be a good writer. These two can come together, and I hope they will, but if that's too adorable, I'd rather have money."

But after Hollywood, after politics, nearly everyone who knew Parker well seems to have counted her a failure. The movies she worked on were thought to be beneath her. Her embrace of political sloganeering seemed devastatingly earnest in someone whose special skill was making fun of everything. Her ambitions to be a good short story writer were thought to wane because she never managed to repeat the success of "Big Blonde." Perhaps worst of all was how these criticisms leaked into her assessment of herself: she was a successful writer by any standard, even a "good" writer, but it never sank in. By the mid-1930s, Parker seemed to believe herself as washed-up as anyone else. Her stories became halfhearted; she quit writing poetry altogether.

Others, without Parker's punishing self-monologue, were easier with their praise. Reviewing a new and apparently surpassingly ridiculous book about the Russian mystic Rasputin in 1928, a writer by the name of Rebecca West said it had to be written by an American humorist. She identified in it "traces of the unique genius of Dorothy Parker," whom she considered a "sublime artist." West had particularly liked "Just a Little One," a short story Parker published in the *New Yorker* some months before, a story about a woman who becomes so drunk in a bar she dreams of bringing a cab horse back to her apartment to live with her. West knew something of despair over men, and how to write about it.

2

West

Rebecca West was something like the English version of Parker, in that she was a woman writer who was greatly celebrated in her own time. But as a young person, West had steeped in Fabian Socialism and the experimental morals of the artists and writers, like Virginia Woolf and her sister Vanessa Bell, of the Bloomsbury set. She had a comfortable footing among the "serious people" of her world from the beginning, a kind of sureness that she belonged among them that had always eluded Parker. But then, West rarely suffered from a lack of self-confidence. If anything, her confidence was what often sent her to the brink of her ambitions.

West made her mark when she introduced herself to the novelist H. G. Wells by attacking him in a newsletter called the *Freewoman*. The episode marked possibly the only time in history that future lovers have met when one gave the other an abysmal book review. The very young West had read Wells's now-forgotten novel *Marriage* and hadn't liked it. The fact that Wells was among the most respected writers of his day did not frighten her. "Of course, he is the Old Maid among novelists," she wrote, taking direct aim at Wells's proud claims to sexual radicalism:

Even the sex obsession that lay clotted on [his novels] like cold white sauce was merely Old Maids' mania, the reaction towards the flesh of a mind too long absorbed in airships and colloids.

We now remember Wells best for his airships, the scientific romances like *The War of the Worlds* and *The Time Machine*. But by the time West met him, Wells's oeuvre consisted chiefly of books like *Marriage*: confessional, thinly veiled autobiographical novels about love and sex. The novel before that one, *Ann Veronica*, had told the story of a scandalous affair very like one Wells had just conducted herself. The plot details of these books are less memorable than the dim view of matrimony they took; wedded bliss was a kind of prison for Wells. Every story was meant to chip away at marriage's claims to bestow eternal comfort and happiness.

In theory, this should have made West and Wells natural allies. Certainly, Wells thought of himself as an advocate of equality for the sexes. He was a supporter and regular reader of the *Freewoman*. He was usually careful to frame his criticisms of marriage as being about the liberation of women as much as men. He thought marriage took women away from their most important and fulfilling pursuits. Somewhat undermining his sense of female personhood, though, was his apparent belief that most women were exclusively interested in interior decorating and fashion. West called him to task for it:

> *I wonder about the women who never come across any man who was worth loving (and next time Mr. Wells travels in the tube he might look round and consider how hopelessly unloveable most of his male fellow-passengers are), who are not responsive to the lure of Dutch clocks, and forget, as most people do, the colour of the dining-room wallpaper, who, being intelligent, can design a becoming dress in five minutes and need think no more about it. I wonder how they will spend the time. Bridge-parties I suppose, and possibly State-facilitated euthanasia.*

To Wells's great credit he was not offended. He did not write some glowering, condescending letter to the editor. Instead, he invited West to the rectory where he resided with his wife, Jane, in what was a thoroughly admirable display of maturity when faced with harsh criticism. West turned up there for tea by the end of the same month she'd publish the review. She made a good impression, possibly a better one than she intended. Somehow she was always at her most charming when she was disagreeing with someone.

West came by her combative spirit honestly. Partly it was the environment she grew up in. In the first years of the twentieth century, London was a more militant place than New York. Great Britain was not quite the cultural center of the world—that would have been France, or perhaps Germany—but it was the political and economic one. The preoccupations of its thinkers and writers were hard matters of votes and money, less suited to the kind of carefree jesting style that had come to annoy the hell out of Parker in New York. Societies of intellectual socialists, suffragette demonstrations: these were the things of an English writer's life, circa the 1910s.

But West had a romantic streak and didn't head straight for politics or writing. She had at first thought she might be an actress, inspired by several months she spent hanging out with an Edinburgh theater company when she was a teenager. The Fates, unfortunately, had other ideas for her. On the way to her audition for the Royal Academy of Dramatic Art in 1910, West fainted on the tube station platform. Three women helped her up. One of them could not hold her pitying tongue, West wrote to her disapproving elder sister: "Poor child—an actress! I'll pay for the brandy."

It was a bad sign. West did get into the school in the end, but she barely lasted a year. The fainting happened again and again, the result of a delicate constitution. And although pictures of West in the era show a young woman with large, expressive eyes and mounds of glossy hair, she always said she wasn't considered pretty enough to be an actress. It became clear early on that she would have to write her own place in the world, if she was to have one.

She was still going by her long-winded birth name then, Cicely Isabel Fairfield, a fussy name that evoked someone of the sort of meek, obedient disposition West never in her life possessed. Like Parker, West came from a shabby-aristocratic background that had bequeathed her a certain reflexive defensiveness. Her drifting father, Charles Fairfield, was the sort of paternal figure you find in Frances Hodgson Burnett novels: a dashing man, great fun, adored by his children. But only when he was around, and he wasn't around very often. In a novel based on her childhood, West would call him a "shabby Prospero, exiled even from his own island, but still a magician." This was more apt than she knew. Her father had a real talent for sleight of hand. He kept secrets of near-epic scope; a West biographer recently dug up a prison stay, prior to his marriage, that his wife and daughters never seem to have known anything about.

Fairfield's defects of character might have been easier to forget had he been a good provider. But he could not seem to concentrate on anything long enough to make a proper go of it. He had started out as a wayward journalist, then morphed into an entrepreneur. What little income he did make, he gambled away. In the last of his schemes, he went to Sierra Leone to try to make a fortune in pharmaceuticals. Within a year he was back in England, penniless. Too ashamed to return home, he lived alone for the rest of his life, dying in a squalid boardinghouse in Liverpool before his three daughters had left adolescence.

As an adult, West could be scathing about him. "I cannot say that my father went to the dogs, because there is something definite about a dog," she'd write. She took offense, too, on her mother's behalf. Isabella Fairfield had been a talented pianist before she married, a real catch, but her life was effectively ruined by the stress of Charles's adventures. She was haggard, worn. "It was an odd training to have such a mother," West continued. "I was never ashamed of her, but I was always angry about it." The whole thing had led her to believe that marriage was a tragedy, or at least a pitiable fate.

Another way of looking at it, though, is that her father's ruin defined his daughter in the best possible way. It taught her an unforgettable lesson about the necessity of self-sufficiency. You could not depend on men. Romance novels were full of lies. Before any ideal of a "liberated woman" really existed, West knew that women often had to earn their own keep. She never seems to have questioned that she would have to make a way for herself.

So West was attracted to the suffragettes for obvious reasons: she felt their mission was important, that it spoke to her experience. But their raucous style appealed to her too. West was raised a fighter, arguing incessantly with her two sisters. There was also room, in political activism, for use of her natural charisma. West quickly fell in with Emmeline Pankhurst and her daughter Christabel, who were at the time two of the most visible suffragettes. Their organization, the Women's Social and Political Union, was the standard-bearer of the movement by that time. The Pankhursts were celebrities, to the extent such a thing existed in their day. "Crusade That Stirs All England; Pretty Girl Commander-in-Chief," read one representative American headline. "Christabel Pankhurst, Who Is Rich, Besides Young and Comely, Was the Initiator and Is the Chief Organizer of Agitation for Female Suffrage."

West marched with them often and admired their work, but she never quite fit in to their world. The Pankhursts—particularly Christabel—were firebrands, fierce and earnest in the defense of the suffrage cause. West often admired this, especially in Emmeline:

> One felt, as she lifted up her hoarse, sweet voice on the platform, that she was trembling like a reed. But the reed was of steel, and it was tremendous.

Even as a teenager West had a more literary disposition. She had always read novels, and been interested in the ideas about sexual freedom nurtured in more artistic circles than the relatively prudish Pankhursts were willing to occupy.

Another suffragette, Dora Marsden, proved a more crucial influence. Marsden, unlike West, had been to university—a proletarian sort called Owens College in Manchester. She barely lasted two years working with the Pankhursts. As an escape plan, she proposed to West and some other friends that they start a newspaper together. It would be called the *Freewoman* (and later, after a reorganization, the *New Freewoman*), and it would be more ambitious than your average feminist newsletter, allowing its writers to pronounce more widely on the matters of the day. This, Marsden hoped, would get the real writers of the suffrage movement out of the shackled forms and clichés of propaganda. This all appealed to West, who was thrilled to have the *Freewoman*'s relative editorial freedom to air the kind of views on sex and marriage that would horrify her Scottish Presbyterian mother. And to protect the family name, West then chose the nom de plume she'd use the rest of her life.

She'd claim she picked Rebecca West at random, simply wanting to escape the "blonde and pretty," "Mary Pickford" implications of her old name. Indeed, she did pick a pseudonym that had a firmer sound. The source was an Ibsen play called *Rosmersholm*. In it, a widower and his mistress slowly descend into an ecstasy of guilt over the pain their affair has caused his dead wife. The mistress admits to having aggravated the suffering. Eventually, at the end of the play, both commit suicide. The mistress's name is Rebecca West.

The layers of potential unconscious meaning here could fill a book by themselves. There is the repudiation of the absent father; the gesture at early, if ambivalent theatrical ambitions (and why an Ibsen character); and then, its prescience, because West would eventually carry on a famous affair herself. But that she would reach for the name of an outsider, an outcast, and an eventual guilt-ridden suicide: that's a matter worthy of note.

West was known all her life as a woman unafraid of showing emotion in her work. She rarely equivocated in her writing, always wielding the first person to remind you that you were in the land of subjective authority. But a friend told the *New Yorker* that she had "several skins fewer than any human being, a kind of psychological hemophiliac." Her work cut very directly at what she thought, what she wanted, how she felt. She was not a self-deprecator like Parker. Her shield was different. West overwhelms you with her personality. Her work can be read as one long, run-on sentence punctuated only occasionally for want of money. That looks like confidence, but it was actually a very elaborate mask. She worried about everything: about money, about love, about just about every subject on which she delivered such deceptively assured opinions.

But assured they were, from the start. She had a knack for choosing targets. For her first piece under her new pen name, West took aim at the exceptionally popular romance novelist Mary Augusta Ward (Mrs. Humphry Ward), a woman who suffered from a "lack of honor" in West's young estimation. A man angrily wrote to the *Freewoman* with the somewhat inapposite accusation that she was defending industrialism. West's reply began by elegantly flipping off her interlocutor: "This is most damping." Her boldness always managed to pull out a laugh, at least on the page. It was around this time West fired her book review cannon at Wells, then went over for tea. Of the pair, West had the more insulting first impression, finding Wells odd looking, with "a little high voice." Wells would remember the young woman who arrived that day as bearing a "curious mixture of maturity and infantilism." It was only their intellectual attraction that struck flint on steel. Wells was not the sort of person who turned away from challenges, so that elusive quality drew him in: "I had never met anything quite like her before, and I doubt if there ever was anything like her before." To Dora Marsden, though, West confessed she was intrigued by his mind.

It turned out West had correctly diagnosed Wells's romantic style in that review. At first, he behaved toward her in exactly the old-maidish ways she'd seen in his work. Seduction was forged by intellectual discussion. But he refused to touch West, despite her advances. It was not out of deference to his wife Jane. The Wells's marriage was an open one, his affairs conducted with Jane's full knowledge. But Wells had another mistress on the go at the time, and his practical streak seems to have kicked in. Two mistresses would have been a lot even for a liberated man.

All that notwithstanding, his resolve to be good lasted only a few months. One day in late 1912, Wells and West kissed accidentally in his study. Between two ordinary people it might have been nothing, the simple rise of a needle already trending toward an affair. Between two writers, each of an unusually analytical cast of mind, some kind of wrenching conflict seemed necessary to consummate the attraction. But at first, Wells withdrew again, and West was sent into a nervous breakdown by the rejection.

The notion that so intelligent a woman might have been undone by romantic rejection is not palatable to the feminism of our era. But West was nineteen and Wells appears to have been her first real taste of love. She also managed, as ever, to fit her emotional distress into a beautiful piece of writing, albeit one she did not publish. We have it only as the draft of a letter, written to Wells but believed not to have been sent. It begins:

> *During the next few days I shall either put a bullet through my head or commit something more shattering to myself than death.*

The letter accuses Wells of an unfeeling nature. "You want a world of people falling over each other like puppies, people to quarrel and play with, people who rage and ache instead of people who burn." West can't abide this treatment:

> *When you said, "You've been talking unwisely, Rebecca," you said it with a certain brightness: you felt that you had really caught me at it. I don't think you're right about*

this. But I know you will derive immense satisfaction from thinking of me as an unbalanced young female who flopped about in your drawing-room in an unnecessary heart-attack.

If Wells ever knew she felt this way—either by reading the letter, or otherwise—he did not immediately come running. He appears to have written a reply to West, but in it he castigates her for being so emotional. He didn't understand. It wasn't merely Wells stopping the affair before it started that bothered her. It was that Wells used his emotional distance to mock her anguish, too.

West wrote this letter in June 1913 from Spain, where she had gone with her mother for a month to recover her senses. From there she still sent dispatches to what was now called the *New Freewoman*. In "At Valladolid," she produced a lengthy suicide fantasy that presages the mood, tone, and themes of Sylvia Plath's *The Bell Jar*. The narrator, a young woman, arrives on the grounds of a hospital having shot herself. The source of the narrator's trouble is a love affair too, and it echoes what we know passed (and didn't pass) between Wells and West: "For though my lover had left my body chaste he had seduced my soul; he mingled himself with me till he was more myself than I am and then left me."

It's worth mentioning that West knew Wells was still reading the *New Freewoman*. He, obediently intrigued, would write her letters about her pieces. "You are writing gorgeously again," read the first one, which as far as we know she didn't answer. Instead she wrote a review of his latest novel, *The Passionate Friends*. In it, she wrote that she agreed with him there may be some link between sex and creativity:

For it is true that men often turn willy nilly to the business of love-making as a steamer however urgent for far seas must call at the coaling station: for some great thing they have to do they need the inspiration of an achieved passion.

Then she insists that women who engage in such liaisons are not as wholly destroyed by these brief affairs as Wells imagines them to be in his fiction. The key, she agreed with him, was that the woman in question needed autonomy in her own sexual and romantic life:

The woman who is acting the principal part in her own ambitious play is unlikely to weep because she is not playing the principal part in some man's no more ambitious play.

Not only did West begin this affair with a book review, she also perhaps unknowingly argued for her passion in subsequent book reviews.

It got the job done. The signal was received. Within a few weeks of publishing the review in the fall of 1913, Rebecca began meeting Wells in his study for trysts. The flirting through book reviews quickly stopped; their letters descended instead into a kind of romantic patois. They called each other by feline names, usually Jaguar (for Wells) and Panther (for West, which she later gave to baby Anthony as his middle name). The baby-talkish tone of those letters doesn't really show these writers in their best light.

Soon, something like dramatic irony struck their fates. Their second time together, Wells forgot to put on a condom. West had already been writing angry screeds for a new British journal called the *Clarion* about the plight of unwed mothers, who were mostly pariahs in British society up and down the class ladder. She could not have been thrilled to become one herself.

Indeed, from the moment Anthony Panther West was born in a tiny cottage in Norfolk in August 1914, he represented a problem for his mother. Her ambivalence about motherhood marked him deeply, he'd later insist. She could not hide her impatience with him and with the limits he imposed on her. West took little pleasure in being locked up in a house, staying behind the scenes, and fussing over baby things:

> *I hate domesticity . . . I want to live an unfettered and adventurous life . . . Anthony looks very nice in his blue lambs-wool coat, and I feel sure that in him I have laid up treasure for the hereafter (i.e. dinners at the Carlton in 1936) but what I want now is ROMANCE. Something with a white face and a slight natural wave in the dark hair and a large grey touring car.*

Wells, it bears mentioning, did not have these characteristics (except perhaps the white face). Though he behaved as honorably as he could under the circumstances, setting West and the baby up in a home of their own, he was not around enough to satisfy West. He was still her lover and intellectual mentor, but she proved not particularly suitable for the gilded existence of a favored mistress. She was too interested in a life of her own.

So West kept writing, at a pace many new mothers might envy. She began a novel while Anthony was an infant. Articles appeared at all her usual haunts, and she got a new venue for her thoughts too: Wells had gotten himself involved with a new American magazine, funded by the Whitney fortune, called the *New Republic*. He invited West to write for it too. She would appear in the magazine's inaugural issue, published in November 1914, the only woman to write for it, with an essay titled "The Duty of Harsh Criticism."

This would become one of West's most well-known pieces. It was written with a solemnity uncharacteristic of all her *Freewoman* work, presenting itself as more of a bookish Sermon on the Mount. Instead of an "I," West speaks from a royal, disembodied "we." Her analysis is delivered from a commanding position:

There is now no criticism in England. There is merely a chorus of weak cheers, a piping note of appreciation that is not stilled unless a book is suppressed by the police, a mild kindliness that neither heats to enthusiasm nor reverses to anger.

Given that she was building a successful literary career on exactly the kind of criticism she had found lacking, West was perhaps overstating the case. Her flight into abstraction here is somewhat unusual. Generally, her work was built on personal anecdote, but this essay had none. It's possible her call for "harsh criticism" was related to her frustration with her own situation at that particular moment of her life. She was stuck, but could not write about it because of the taboo against having children out of wedlock. To export the problem to "criticism in England" was to write about the banality of her life without addressing it directly. "Decidedly we shall not be safe if we forget the things of the mind," she wrote, which is true as it goes and also has the quality, cast against her circumstances, of a reminder to oneself.

Yet even in her frustration her personal fame was growing. In advertisements for their new magazine, the *New Republic*'s editors listed her as an attraction, making an issue of her sex, calling her "the woman H. G. Wells calls 'the best man in England.'" She did not return the debatable compliment, taking his writing as one of the targets of "The Duty of Harsh Criticism." Wells was a "great writer." She also wrote that "he dreams into the extravagant ecstasies of the fanatic, and broods over old hated things or the future peace and wisdom of the world, while his story falls in ruins about his ears."

The relationship was, at that point, going well. But Wells, reading this, might well have seen a double implication: on some level "his story" included Rebecca and Anthony. The young boy would be a point of contention between his parents all his life. At first they didn't tell him, clearly, that they were his parents. They also fought, bitterly, about whether Anthony would have a formal place in Wells's will. Wells was unwilling to reassure West on that score. It soured things.

And perhaps sensing how odd it was to continue to review her lover's work in the pages of magazines even as she wrote him love notes dripping with sentimentality, West began to focus on other writers and started on a book-length critical study of Henry James. She began outlining her interest in him in an early column in the *New Republic*, when she described having spent an entire night's World War I air raid in the country reading James's essay collection *Notes on Novelists*. As sirens sounded overhead, she derived less and less comfort from James's extreme precision as a writer:

> *He splits hairs until there are no longer any hairs to split, and the mental gesture becomes merely the making of agitated passes over a complete and disconcerting baldness.*

As though reasoning with herself, though, West eventually comes around to James's exacting, but wandering tones. Passion, fire, seems suddenly overrated in context. The planes "circling above my head in an attempt to locate the lightless town for purposes of butchery," she writes, "were probably burning with as pure and exalted a passion as they could conceive."

She'd be changing her mind about that. In her book, the core of West's objection to James was his "passionless detachment"—a complaint you may now recognize as one of her signature issues with the writings of great men—that he "wanted to live wholly without violence even of the emotions." It was not that every book of his had this problem. She admired *The Europeans*, *Daisy Miller*, and *Washington Square*. But she hated *The Portrait of a Lady* because she found Isabel Archer, its protagonist, to be a "nincompoop." James's worrisome detachment became particularly acute, West complained, when it came to women:

> *One can learn nothing of the heroine's beliefs and character for the hullabaloo that has been set up because she has come in too late or gone out too early or omitted to provide herself with that figure of questionable use—for the dove-like manners of the young men forbid the thought that she was there to protect the girl from assault, and the mild tongues of the young ladies make it unlikely that the duel of the sexes was then so bitter that they required an umpire—the chaperon.*

James would die about a month before West published the book in England, which led to its becoming a popular subject for reviews, perhaps more than a critical study could ordinarily garner. In general, the reaction was positive: The *Observer* called it "rather metallically bright." And most American critics seemed to agree. But one *Chicago Tribune* books columnist—a woman named Ellen Fitzgerald—was downright insulted by the book's "breach of literary honor." "Very young women," she argued, "should not write criticism of novels, either. It is hard on the novelist."

It is hard to imagine that West would be wounded by such a review. Breaking the rules for "very young women" was, by this time, old hat for her. She did not worry about whether she was making the right impressions on the right people. She did not care about the pieties novelists might build up about themselves and their works.

In any event, West was not ignorant of the travails of novelists. She went on to write a lot of fiction herself, publishing ten novels. They received generally positive reviews: "so austerely veracious, so gravely and only beautiful, so triumphant in their exalted spiritual realism," went one representative observation about her first book, *The Return of the Soldier*, published in 1918. Generally, though, even in praise reviewers reported disappointment, because her reputation preceded her. "It falls short of that measure of perfection so able a writer as Miss West might easily have attained," a *Sunday Times* reviewer wrote of *The Judge*, published in 1920. No one was surprised to find she could write a good novel, but reviewers expected her to write a great one. "But for her wit and the warm flashes of beauty in her intricate, slow-moving style, one might easily run aground half-way through her book and give up the struggle with its psychological shallows," the novelist V. S. Pritchett complained of *Harriet Hume* when it appeared in 1929.

This was the price one paid for being such a well-regarded critic who wanted to be more than just that. People become accustomed to a certain writerly persona, and every bit of subsequent work gets measured against it. Parker battled this when she wanted to be better known for her fiction than her quips and verse, and she couldn't achieve it. West's intelligence in prose turned out to be something of a devil in fiction; readers of the novels wondered where her digressions had gone.

Certainly her journalism did a better job of paying her bills, which were only partially handled by Wells. The *New Republic* columns led to more work in the *New Statesman*, and in other, lesser magazines and newspapers like *Living Age* and the *South China Morning Post*. West was not picky about where she appeared. She needed the money and was rarely short on opinions.

Nor was she picky about topics. She tended to take off from a book and then land somewhere far afield. She wrote about George Bernard Shaw's war speeches. She wrote about the strains of Dostoevsky she found in a drunk she met on a night train. She complained about the way one of Dickens's earlier biographers kept interrupting chapters with weather reports. She complained about novels that took the lives of the rural poor as their subjects: "They always work out tedious and unauthentic." She was also frequently called upon to write about women, and as World War I raged on, about the place of women in war. In the *Atlantic*, she delivered another long, passionate sermon, this time on the ways in which wartime nursing had fulfilled the promises of feminism, making ordinary women a part of the war. "Feminism has not invented this courage, for there have always been brave women," she wrote. "But it has let it strike its roots into the earth."

She was presenting herself with confidence on the page but other parts of her life had begun to crumble. Things with Wells were in trouble. He was always adding new mistresses and though the philandering could not possibly have come as a surprise, it sometimes led to unpleasant scenes. The low point came when a dalliance with a young Austrian artist (by the memorable name of Gattenrigg) ended with that woman's arrival at West's flat one day in June 1923. The woman tried to commit suicide at Wells's own house later that day. West kept her composure for the press, telling a local newspaper, "Mrs. Gattenrigg however was not abusive and there was not a scene. She is a very intelligent woman, doing really beautiful work, and I feel very sorry for her."

She had begun to feel quite sorry for herself, too. In letters to friends and family she began openly complaining of Wells's "constant disturbance of my work." His commanding presence, which had once enchanted her, she now called "egotism." The student had learned whatever the master had to teach, and though she worried she would not have enough to live on without Wells's generosity—he, after all, had no legal relationship to either West or Anthony at the time—the situation was untenable.

The romance had served its purpose in her life, launching her into the career she'd dreamed of. She was, if anything, by then almost more famous than Wells, since she was more prolific and in her prime while his output was beginning to drop off. She did not need him anymore.

The chance of a clean break came in the form of an American lecture tour. West sailed in October 1923, leaving Anthony with her mother. In America she was a hot commodity, and the freedom of being outspoken and unmarried suited her, at least as far as her public image was concerned. The American press was clearly enchanted with her. She was an avatar for the new sort of independently minded woman. Even better, for a reporter, she was quite willing to answer questions about it. The *New York Times*, for example, asked her why the numbers of young women novelists seemed to be surging. Was it the war? West shook her head:

> *It is true that in the field of the novel the younger women are "carrying on" but it didn't need the war to swell their numbers. It didn't need the war to show them the open door of expression. It wasn't war fever or war relaxation that did it. It was something for which the English woman had fought for years. It was the spirit of freedom, of feminism, if you will. It was something more than a fight for the vote. Remember that always. It was a fight for a place in the sun, a right to grow in art, in science, in politics, in literature.*

She added, too, that she didn't think age should matter, that in fact it could only enhance her powers, using the examples of Virginia Woolf, G. B. Stern, and Katherine Mansfield. "The woman of 30 and over, you see, is coming into her own," she averred. "Life begins to mean something to her: she understands it."

West seemed to be talking about herself. She was already thirty by the time she said this, and indisputably in the sun. Massive public interest followed her everywhere she went in America. She was, like Parker, a celebrity writer. She lectured at women's clubs across the country. Her social calendar was full to the brim. She was less sure about America than it was about her: New York could "dazzle the eye with richness" but also "fatigue it with monotony," she'd write in one of her four *New Republic* articles about the trip. There were unqualified positives: she loved the American train system and the Mississippi

River. But in her letters she tended to be cutting, particularly on the subject of American women: "beyond all belief slovenly," "repulsive wrecks," "incredibly uninteresting even in their evening clothes."

The fame was of a very comfortable sort. It left her space to remain oblique about her personal life in public, though Wells's name often came up in tandem with hers. As cover she was sometimes characterized as his "private secretary." Neither Anthony's name nor his existence was mentioned. But the affair and the child were open secrets among the intellectuals and writers she met in America.

Among them were several members of the Round Table, including Alexander Woollcott. She met the Fitzgeralds too. It's not clear if she ever met Parker herself. Although the New York journalists and wits would seem obvious kindred spirits to a sharp young woman from London, West did not fit in. Only Woollcott became a friend, and memories of the others were fraught. A party was held to honor West at some point during the trip. Parker doesn't seem to have been there. But her friend the feminist writer, activist, and Round Tabler Ruth Hale was. Hale had made her name as a war correspondent, then became a frequent arts commentator. She had married Heywood Broun but kept going by her maiden name, and in 1921 made headlines by getting into a fight with the State Department over whether her passport must bear her married name instead. When the State Department wouldn't budge, Hale returned the passport and gave up a trip to Europe. She was a woman of principle.

Apparently, too, Hale was not afraid to speechify in private. As West reported it to a biographer, Hale approached her at the party and launched into a tirade:

Rebecca West, we are all disappointed in you. You have put an end to a great illusion. We thought of you as an independent woman, but here you are, looking down in the mouth, because you relied on a man to give you all

*you wanted and now that you have to turn out and fend
for yourself you are bellyaching about it. I believe Wells
treated you too darn well, he gave you money, and jewels
and everything you wanted and if you live with a man
on those terms you must expect to get turned out when
he gets tired of you.*

Usually the members of the Round Table had a subtler manner
of insulting each other, but Hale was not a humorist like the rest of
them. West was remembering the remarks thirty years after they
were made, and may have sharpened them in the telling. But Hale's
disappointment obviously stung. The confrontation was a bad note
amid so much praise, during a trip that on all professional accounts
was successful. But it was such a bad note she would never forget it.

People were often disappointed with West: her mother, her elder
sister Lettie, Wells, critics of her novels, her peers. No member of
that choir sang louder than her son Anthony. As he grew up, shuttled
between two parents whose ambitions lay only partly with his development, he grew resentful of their lack of attention. In what has become
a time-honored tradition, Anthony focused all his resentment on the
parent to whom he had greater access, which was West. He would
eventually act on his bitterness by excoriating her in both a novel (the
subtly titled *Heritage*) and a nonfiction book. So persistent was his
obsession with this subject that in an interview with the *Paris Review*
late in life, West could only bring herself to be dry about it: "I wish
he'd turn his mind to other problems than bastardy. Alas."

For almost everyone but Anthony, West's writing was, in some
ways, the problem. There was something about who West was in
prose that promised people something they then felt distressed not
to see materialize in person. Ruth Hale read West, saw the Platonic
ideal of a strong, independent woman, then was disappointed when
someone else appeared at a party. Even those clearly dazzled by West's

intelligence and talent sometimes had difficulty coming to terms with what they saw as a kind of flyaway personal style. "Rebecca is a cross between a charwoman and gypsy, but as tenacious as a terrier, with flashing eyes, very shabby, rather dirty nails, immense vitality, bad taste, suspicion of intellectuals and great intelligence," Virginia Woolf wrote to her sister in 1934. It was one-half insult, and one-half compliment.

Her inability to satisfy people confused her, though she was hardly averse to employing personal criticism herself. Her journalism is larded with personal barbs, women unflatteringly described as having "hair light and straight and stiff as hay" and "sharp-nosed" men. But she could not understand why so many people reacted badly to her. "I've aroused hostility in an extraordinary lot of people," she said at the end of her life. "I've never known why. I don't think I'm formidable." She wanted lovers, admirers, and friends, and she never thought of herself as not caring about what other people thought: "I should like to be approved of, oh, yes . . . I hate being disapproved of. I've had rather a lot of it." At the heart of her confidence was this fundamental insecurity, a tension between wanting to be heard and wanting to be liked.

After Wells, West cycled through multiple suitors, among them the newspaper magnate Lord Beaverbrook (William Maxwell Aitken). She seemed to be finished with affairs with other writers, or perhaps just with affairs that came with major dramatic complications. Her cap was set for businessmen, which perhaps did prove, as Ruth Hale suspected, that she valued financial security above all else. Later, remembering their first meeting, she'd call an investment banker named Henry Andrews "rather like a dull giraffe, sweet, kind and loving." Evidently that was what she was looking for. Within a year she married him, in November 1930, and they would be together until his death in 1968. There were infidelities on both sides. It didn't change things. Mostly it left West to derive her satisfaction from her friends, and from work.

Among them, in the 1930s, was a then still-unknown French writer by the name of Anaïs Nin. West came to know Nin through the first book she published, a slim volume on D. H. Lawrence with the subtitle "An Unprofessional Study." It was one of the first defenses of Lawrence's work—often viewed as misogynist—from a woman's perspective. West, who had known Lawrence, and at his death had complained in print that "not even among his own caste was he honored as he should have been," invited Nin to meet her in Paris, where West was vacationing with her new husband.

Nin was exactly the sort of person and writer West was not. She was gamine and elegant where West was imposing and brash. The persona Nin affected in prose was lacquered and fragile, the opposite of West's confident warrior. Nin's approach to art was all about articulating private desire, and that she did it in her diaries rather than in the pages of a newspaper gives a pretty good measure of the distance between their approaches to both writing and life.

So their first meeting in 1932 was not obviously an encounter between kindred spirits. Nin recorded the mixed result in her diary:

> Such brilliant, intelligent fawn eyes. Pola Negri without beauty and with English teeth, tormented, with a strained, high-peaked voice which hurts me. We meet on only two levels: intelligence, humanity. I like her full mother's body. But everything dark is left out. She is deeply uneasy. She's intimidated by me. Excuses herself for her hair being messy, for being tired.

Nin added that she could see West "wanting to shine exclusively, yet [was] too timid deep down to do so, nervous and talking far less well than she writes." But over time this unlikely pair warmed to each other. West began to flatter Nin, telling her she thought Nin's writing was much better than that of Henry Miller. She also told Nin that she found her beautiful, which set Nin to thinking of seducing

West. (There is no evidence the desire was ever consummated.) Nin even came to hope she'd be just like West. "Her tongue is sharp, and she does not suffer from naïveté," Nin wrote in her diaries. "At her age, will I be as sharp?" Very different women, as it turned out, could find much to admire in each other.

In the 1930s West's life grew more and more stable. There were problems with Henry's career in banking, but then the couple inherited a great deal of money from his uncle and became rich. Anthony grew up and though he was never easy with his mother, he became less of a logistical burden for her. She kept up a steady stream of book reviews and essays, though literary affairs had plainly begun to bore her, almost the same way Parker had grown bored with the New York scene. But West did not go to Hollywood. She went, instead, to Yugoslavia.

Yugoslavia was a patchwork country, cobbled together at the end of World War I by a movement determined to unite Slavic peoples in a single territory. It was a grand experiment in cosmopolitanism, blessed by the Allied powers. And by the 1930s, it was a grand experiment that had totally failed. There had been coups, ethnic nationalism was on the rise, and the country was squeezed on both sides by German and Italian Fascist movements. The country would ultimately survive multiple annexations in World War II and manage to hold itself together—with the help of authoritarian rule—right down through the 1990s.

In 1936, the British Council had sent West to Yugoslavia on a lecture tour, and though she fell dreadfully sick there, she also became enchanted with the place. For some time she had been yearning to write something about a country she didn't live in, and a country whose fault lines were as elaborate as Yugoslavia's appealed to her. So did the tour guide she had there, Stanislav Vinaver, though when he tried to make their mutual affection into a sexual relationship, she refused him. Evidently the rejection was amiable. She kept using him as her guide over five subsequent trips and five years' work on a book about the country, and she kept visiting even as Hitler was making incursions into Czechoslovakia. The book that resulted, *Black Lamb and Grey Falcon*, stretched to over twelve hundred pages by the time it was published in October 1941.

A recent biographer of West's called *Black Lamb* "masterful albeit somewhat rambling." This is a fair criticism, but it perhaps understates the way rambling was always key to West's appeal, the whole reason the reader could keep going through so many pages. By the 1930s West had become a master of unlikely connections, moving from one thought to the next in maneuvers unique to her. One read West to watch her brain work.

Intellectually speaking, West's theories about Yugoslavia have their faults. She was not a person afraid to psychoanalyze an entire nation, a practice now rightly thought of as reductive, at least in the absolute terms she used. Early on we are told that a group of four plodding obedient Germans on a train are "exactly like all Aryan Germans I have ever known; and there were sixty million of them in the middle of Europe." West believed that nation was destiny, that there were certain unavoidable differences between people that had to be understood and respected. It led her to some unabashedly racist lines of analysis. In one passage in the book she even makes the claim that a "cherry-picking dance" she had often enjoyed seeing performed in America by "a Negro or Negress" became "animalistic" when she saw it performed by a white person.

She could move between geopolitics and jokes with ease. In the midst of explaining the 1915 Treaty of London, which had nearly handed several Slavic territories to the Italians, West paused. She had just described the way Italian protofascist poet Gabriele d'Annunzio, a bald, waxed-mustachioed man, had marched soldiers into Fiume (now a part of Croatia) to prevent the Italians from losing it. Considering the chaos this caused, and the fuel it gave to Italian nationalists, she observed:

I will believe that the battle of feminism is over, and that the female has reached a position of equality with the male, when I hear that a country has allowed itself to be turned upside-down and led to the brink of war by its passion for a totally bald woman writer.

And then there is Henry, who at all times in the book is presented as a sensible foil to West's more alluring matters of pure sentiment. An illustrative episode occurs when at one point West and her husband get into a discussion of literature with a Croatian poet, who tried to insist that Joseph Conrad and Jack London were writers superior to the more traditional "literary" types like Shaw, Wells, Péguy, and Gide:

They wrote down what one talks in cafés, which is quite a good thing to do if the talk is good enough, but is not serious, because it deals with something as common and renewable as sweat. But pure narration was a form of great importance [the Croatian poet felt], because it gathered together experiences that could be assimilated by others of poetic talent and transmuted into higher forms.

Henry offers a wan rejection of this ("Conrad has no sense of tragedy at all"), but it is the poet's continuing opinions that West goes on to quote at length and, one might even suspect, adopt.

The reviews of *Black Lamb and Grey Falcon*, first serialized in the *Atlantic Monthly*, were to say the very least quite flattering. In the *New York Times*, it was praised somewhat curiously as "a most brilliantly objective travel book," even as the reviewer credited its genius specifically to the fact that it was written by "one of the most gifted and searching of the modern English novelists and critics." In the *New York Herald Tribune*, the reviewer wrote, "This is the only book I have read since the war began which is life size, which has a stature of its own comparable to the crisis through which the world is moving."

That last remark was important. When *Black Lamb and Grey Falcon* was published, Pearl Harbor was still a couple of months off; America was still feeling quite safe from the tumult of Europe. For most Europeans, the war was not something to be compared to a thrilling book. By the time *Black Lamb* appeared, it was the all-consuming fact of daily life.

West and her husband spent the war quietly in England. Henry had been working for the Ministry of Economic Warfare since the beginning of the war in Europe in the fall of 1939. The couple had bought a manor in the country to live at, partially because they thought that if the worst came they could possibly "live to some extent on what we can grow." From England she sent two dispatches to Harold Ross's *New Yorker*. In them she referred to herself repeatedly as a housewife. Her travails during the war were not the stuff of Gibbon, she admitted, but she would never have wallpapered the new house if the price of wartime paint were not so high. Her lampshades were unsuitable only because they "send out rays that might cost us our lives, for my house stands on the top of a hill and might easily catch the eye of a cruising Dornier." She was particularly attuned to the effect of the war on cats, beginning one piece with some remarks about her ginger tabby:

> This crisis has revealed cats as the pitiful things they are—intellectuals who cannot understand the written or the spoken word. They suffer in air raids and the consequent migrations exactly as clever and sensitive people would suffer if they knew no history, had no previous warning of the nature of warfare, and could not be sure that those in whose houses they lived, on whose generosity they were dependent, were not responsible for their miseries. Had Pounce found himself alone in the house and free,

*he would probably have run out into the woods and not
returned to the dangerous company of humans.*

Black Lamb and Grey Falcon had established West as a reporter
of the first rank. She could not really put her journalistic tools to use
until after V-day in Europe, but she then became the *New Yorker's*
chief correspondent on war trials. Trials were a good subject for West,
since they consider both the case in front of them and the general
principles of law, a move from specific to general not unlike the way
West generally reasoned in her essays.

The first she covered was that of William Joyce, a man who had
become known in England as Lord Haw-Haw. Joyce's backstory was
somewhat involved. He was born in America but spent his life in
Ireland and later England as a die-hard Anglo-Irish nationalist. He
joined Sir Oswald Mosley's Fascist movement in the 1930s, then
found himself in Germany in the fall of 1939. He became a propaganda broadcaster for the Nazis, whose broadcasts were played on
English airwaves to hurt morale in England. His nickname came
from the British papers; he was a reviled figure. Captured after the
war, Joyce was put on trial for treason in England. West was among
those who believed firmly that he deserved the death sentence he
would eventually receive. She was eager to connect what she considered Joyce's moral smallness with his physical stature: "He was
a tiny little creature and, though not very ugly, was exhaustively so."
By the time she witnessed his hanging she was interested no longer
in Joyce, but in what she thought were his victims: "An old man told
me that he was there because he had turned on the wireless when he
came back from seeing his grandchildren's bodies in the mortuary
after a V-1 explosion and had heard Haw Haw's voice."

The trials at Nuremberg, which West also covered for the *New
Yorker*, presented somewhat more difficult questions for her. It was
not that she liked the Nazis any better, but she used her pen to sketch
them as ultimately not very menacing. On seeing Rudolf Hess, the

deputy führer, she observed that he was "so plainly mad that it seemed shameful that he should be tried." She wrote that Hermann Göring, Hitler's designated successor, was "very soft." She was not quite making the argument, later made famous by Hannah Arendt, that certain of these officials were not evil in the traditional sense of the word. West was certain they were guilty of the crimes committed, she was not persuaded by the argument that these officials had only followed orders, and she said so quite directly:

It is obvious that if an admiral were ordered by a demented First Sea Lord to serve broiled babies in the officers' mess he ought to disobey; and it was shown that these generals and admirals had exhibited very little reluctance to carry out orders of Hitler which tended towards baby-broiling.

The question of collective German guilt for the atrocities of the Nazis, which was to become one of the great moral and political questions of the second half of the twentieth century, was not of great interest to West in these early postwar writings. She had little to say about the Holocaust beyond the fact that it deserved punishment. Even then, she believed the Nazis deserved punishment for their conduct of war in general, and lumped "what they did to the Jews" under the general category of Nazi criminality.

This was a serious moral oversight. In part, it happened because as the trials dragged on, West's attentions were turning away to Soviet Russia. She identified certain similar strains of thought in Nazism and Communism, and as early as the Joyce article she was sounding alarms:

There is a similarity between the claims of the Nazi-Fascists and the Communist-Fascists, and no less similarity between the methods of putting them forward. The claims depend on an unsound assumption that the man

who possesses a special gift will possess also a univer-
sal wisdom which will enable him to impose an order on
the state superior to that contrived by the consultative
system known as democracy: which will enable him, in
fact, to know other people's business better than they do
themselves.

Her preoccupation with Communism would take up much of the next forty years of her life and writing, although she did not keep to a single subject. She was sent to write about the king's funeral, Democratic conventions, the trial, Whittaker Chambers, South Africa. She was called upon to remember the dead, as in a 1975 reminiscence of the suffragettes, whom she remembered as "extremely good-looking." But the attention she could command had leveled out, stalled. Her alienation from leftist causes and her flighty style alienated her from the young up-and-coming writers of the 1940s and 1950s. She was a kind of crank to them, a relic from an earlier era.

Late in her life, West sensed this diminution of interest and felt it keenly. To a friend, she wrote, "If one is a woman writer there are certain things one must do—first, not be too good; second, die young, what an edge Katherine Mansfield has on all of us; third, commit suicide like Virginia Woolf. To go on writing and writing well just can't be forgiven.'" She would write in that same painterly, chatty way of hers until the day she died. Her books would still receive acclaim, and in her later years she became a regular guest on intellectual talk shows. She was one of the only women who were considered experts on grave matters of state. But she made mistakes. Her obsession with anti-Communism was just one of them.

3

West & Hurston

In 1947, the *New Yorker* sent West to cover a lynching trial in Greenville, South Carolina. The assignment was her idea. On the night of February 16, 1947, twenty-four-year-old Willie Earle had been abducted from the Pickens County jail, where he was being held on murder charges in the stabbing death of a white taxi driver. Circumstantial evidence had connected him to the killing. The taxi driver's coworkers formed a mob and took Earle from the jail. They beat, stabbed, and shot him to death.

While lynchings in the United States had never truly ended, by the 1940s they were relatively rare. Earle's case made headlines all over the Northeast. Newspapers eagerly reported gory claims about the condition of Earle's body to shock their readers. One said his head had been "blasted to bits." Another claimed the mob had ripped his heart from his body. There was perhaps something comforting to Northerners about reading these brutal details. Because they lived far away, they could use their shock as a form of self-congratulation. The savagery, they told themselves, was confined to the backward South.

Except as it turned out, the South was also conflicted about the death of Willie Earle. South Carolina then had a relatively new governor, Strom Thurmond, in office only a month. The Greenville lynching provoked a crisis for him. President Truman's Committee on Civil Rights was said to be watching the trial closely, though the

FBI ultimately declined to investigate. In the end, thirty-one men were put on trial.

West, like most of the white intellectuals of her era, was appalled by the lynching. She saw it as the product of deeply entrenched racism. "It would, of course, be sheer nonsense to pretend that the men, whoever they were, were not affected in their actions by the color of Willie Earle's skin," she wrote. But West was at pains to convey what she evidently felt were the nuances of the situation. She wrote that she didn't see a culture of white impunity in the face of black suffering. The defendants, by West's measure, were seriously afraid they would be convicted. She diagnosed Earle as having "developed a great hostility to white men." She wrote that the white men who had performed the lynching did not, evidently, enjoy it. She said they were moved by outraged friendship with the dead taxi driver rather than bloodlust. She quoted only one black person at length, and this black person made "a plea for the extension for the Jim Crow system."

> *"There is nothing I wish for more," he said, "than a law that would prohibit Negroes from riding in taxicabs driven by white men. They love to do it. We all love to do it. Can't you guess why? Because it is the only time we can pay a white man to act as a servant to us."*

Where she saw racism, it was mostly impersonal, institutional. The court seats were segregated. The black journalists who had come to cover the trial were criticized for sitting among whites in the press area, so much so that they ultimately moved to the black seating area. She speculated that the lynch mob must have been less afraid of being prosecuted for the death of a black man than for a white one.

Her outrage had more direct targets. When a defense attorney said he wished more men like Willie Earle were dead, then added, "There's a law against shooting a dog, but if a mad dog were loose in my community, I would shoot the dog and let them prosecute me," West could not help herself. "A more disgusting incident cannot have happened in any court of law in any time." Her offense at the proceedings, though, was an offense taken on the part of humanity. The words "racism" and "prejudice" do not appear in the piece.

West did recognize that the eventual acquittal of the defendants was unjust, that the celebrations of the defendants on hearing the verdicts were mere "rejoicing at a salvation that was actually a deliverance to danger." She worried that the verdict would bring lawlessness, though it was mostly the conduct of blacks she seemed nervous about. She thought they did not "know what they were doing." She also thought the trial in Greenville augured the end of lynching in the South, a prediction we now know to be wildly incorrect.

Perhaps the problem was West's inexperience with the subject. In Greenville, West had waded into waters that were already better covered and understood by others, mainly black writers. The writings of Ida B. Wells, the black journalist who spent her life advocating against lynching, may have been half a century old, but her name was still widely known. And there were other black writers of the time, black writers who frequently appeared even in white newspapers, who better understood the circumstances of the South. Among them was Zora Neale Hurston.

Hurston had grown up in Eatonville, Florida, a black enclave in a racist state. A rebellious tomboy, she had left school early and spent eighteen months of her twenties acting as a maid to a performer in a traveling Gilbert and Sullivan troupe. She would only receive her high school diploma at twenty-six, after which she attended Howard University. By 1925 she ended up, as many aspiring young black intellectuals did, in Harlem, where she quickly became a regular writer at black magazines like *Opportunity* and the *Messenger*.

Her breakthrough piece, "How It Feels to Be Colored Me," was published in 1928. Hurston had not realized she was "colored," she wrote, until she left Eatonville as a child. And she did not believe it tragic that she was. She could not join in the sorrow other black people felt on account of their race either, she said, for "I am too busy sharpening my oyster knife." But twenty years into living in the white world, "I feel most colored when I am thrown against a sharp white background." The intellectual situation in the America of her time, and for many years after, was a very white background. Newspapers and magazines were effectively segregated, even in the liberated North. Hurston's work was covered by the major white newspapers—her books were all reviewed by the *New York Times*—but she was clearly considered first and foremost a black writer. And black writers were not invited to contribute to the *New Republic*, or the *New Yorker*. Making a living solely as a literary journalist would have been impossible for her.

So Hurston studied to be an anthropologist, eventually getting her PhD from Barnard College at Columbia. There she became a protégé of the pioneering anthropologist Franz Boas, who had her measure skulls for him. Her work could then be called ethnography and supported by foundations. She would publish several folklore studies in her lifetime, most of them efforts to preserve black vernacular spoken in enclaves like Eatonville. Those voices would also surface in her most famous novel, *Their Eyes Were Watching God*. She also explored the voodoo traditions of Jamaica and Haiti and recorded her findings in *Tell My Horse*.

This burgeoning career, however, came to a screeching halt in 1948 when her landlady's son accused her of molesting him. After several months of proceedings, the boy recanted his accusation, but it hit the press, and the stress of it all made it difficult for Hurston to write. It didn't help that her interest in the lives of black people did not align with the priorities of editors of magazines and publishing houses. "The fact that there is no demand for incisive and full-dress stories around Negroes above the servant class is indicative of something of vast importance to this nation," she wrote in the 1950 essay "What White Publishers Won't Print" for the *Negro Digest*.

Before she fell into obscurity completely, though, there was one story she had left to write. In 1953, Hurston was sent by the *Pittsburgh Courier*, a black newspaper, to cover the trial of Ruby McCollum in Live Oak, Florida. She agreed, her biographer says, primarily because she needed the money. But evidently the facts of the crime drew her in too.

McCollum, who was black, was standing trial for the murder of a white man, Dr. C. Leroy Adams. There was absolutely no question that she had killed him. McCollum shot Adams in his offices in front of several of his patients. Then she turned around, went home, and waited to be arrested. The question at the trial was not whether she had committed the crime, but why. It turned out there was some connection between the doctor's services and McCollum's husband's bolita empire. (Bolita is a Spanish lottery game.)

It also turned out that one of McCollum's four children was fathered by Adams. At the trial, she claimed he had repeatedly raped her, but she was not allowed by the judge to elaborate on the circumstances. After McCollum's first trial, she was convicted of murder; at the second, she was permitted to enter a plea of insanity and spent several years of her life in a mental institution.

Hurston was able to attend only the first trial. Her editors at the *Courier* pumped up the drama of her pieces with sensational headlines, but she covered it with nuance and respect. She reported on the visions of the spectators, who told Hurston they saw McCollum's spirit wandering around town with the head of an eagle and "a flaming sword in her hand." When it came to McCollum's story, she reproduced the court transcript, sometimes with her own annotations. When the prosecutor claimed that McCollum's real reason for killing Adams was an unwillingness to pay her medical bills, Hurston repeated it.

The simple reprinting of the transcript does not make for inspiring reading. But Hurston seemed to be biding her time. After the trial was over, she produced a kind of short story about McCollum's interior life. Printed by the *Courier* in ten installments, the series undoubtedly took liberties with the facts. Hurston wove a story of a brave, rebellious McCollum, who had ultimately "ruled the lives and fate of two strong men, one white, the other colored." In her telling, McCollum was a woman not unlike herself: tomboyish, eager to be loved, lonely in a bad marriage to a man who cheated on her. Something about the case seemed to meld fact and fiction for Hurston; scholars have pointed out that Hurston even used lines she previously used in *Their Eyes Were Watching God* in the pieces.

The pieces are not Hurston's best work but they had a certain vitality that suggested that in another life, under other circumstances, she would have been able to provide reportage of a trial that would have had all the hallmarks of what was later called New Journalism: fact, emotion, and personal experience all welded together. She also would have been able to use those tools in applications to cases like the Greenville trial West so imperfectly covered. As it was instead, the *Courier* stiffed Hurston out of eight hundred dollars it had promised her for the pieces. She died in obscurity eight years later, in 1961. It took a revival in the 1980s, chiefly led by the black feminist writer Alice Walker, to get her widely read again, though Hurston is mostly now thought of as a fiction writer.

4

Arendt

Hannah Arendt did not become a public figure until she was over forty. The achievement that lifted her into the public consciousness was a nearly five-hundred-page political theory treatise on totalitarian politics, written in the thick prose by which great ideas must often be transmitted. It might therefore be easy to forget she began her thinking life as a dreamy young woman who wrote reams of poetry and floridly described herself as "overcome by fear of reality, the meaningless, baseless, empty fear whose blind gaze turns everything into nothing, the fear which is madness, joylessness, distress, annihilation."

But that is indeed what Hannah Arendt wrote to her professor, the philosopher Martin Heidegger, while home from university in the spring of 1925. They were sleeping together, an affair of great intensity and, as it turned out, historical consequence for both of them. When she wrote this autobiographical document, voiced in the "protective third person," the affair was barely a year old. She called it "Die Schatten," or "The Shadows," a title plainly meant to signal depression. In her early twenties, Hannah Arendt was really very concerned that she might never amount to anything:

More likely she will continue to pursue her life in idle experiments and a curiosity without rights or foundation, until finally the long and eagerly awaited end takes her unawares, putting an arbitrary stop to her useless activity.

The pointlessness of life and the abruptness of ends were things that came up a lot in Arendt's life—much as they had in West's and Parker's. Arendt was born to a bourgeois intellectual family in the Prussian city of Königsberg, her mother a strong-willed home-maker with a talent for the piano and her father an electrical engineer who also considered himself an amateur scholar of the Greeks and Romans, keeping his nose buried in books.

Arendt did not know her father very long. Paul Arendt had contracted syphilis as a young man, before he married. By the time his daughter was three his condition was deteriorating rapidly. The details of his descent are awful: He'd collapse on family walks in the park, overcome by the ataxia associated with late-stage syphilis. By the time Arendt was five, he had to be institutionalized. He would die about two years later, in 1913, after growing so ill he no longer recognized his daughter when she visited. After he died, Arendt rarely spoke of him. The biographer Elisabeth Young-Bruehl wrote that Arendt told friends her memories of her father's illness were limited to the sound of her mother playing piano, which had soothed her ailing father at night.

Arendt's mother simply had to get on with things. She would be remarried when Arendt was a teenager, to an established business-man. Materially, life was as good as it could be for a widowed Jewish woman and her daughter living in post–World War I Germany. The country was careening through its Weimar period, the era of severe inflation, artistic experimentation, and Hitler's rise to power. But life at home was not difficult. Arendt always insisted her mother protected her from any anti-Semitism she encountered. If anti-Semitic remarks were ever made in the classroom, the young Arendt came home and told her mother. Martha Arendt would write the teachers a scolding letter, and the problem would cease. No doubt this explained why Arendt never believed that anti-Semitism was, as she put it in *Origins of Totalitarianism,* "eternal."

Notwithstanding what she'd report to Heidegger in "The Shad-ows," to others the young Arendt was already relentlessly self-confident.

She smart-mouthed teachers at school, because she could learn as much studying at home as she could under their tutelage, and it pleased her to let them know it. Once, insulted by one of her teacher's remarks—the content of which is lost to history—she organized a boycott against him and got herself expelled. She ended up largely having to tutor herself through her qualifying exams for university.

In her late adolescence, Arendt got interested in philosophy and specifically in the writings of the ruminative Danish existentialist Søren Kierkegaard. Kierkegaard was one of the first great articulators of our concept of angst, of the sense that something is profoundly off-kilter with oneself and with the world. Arendt, in any event, picked up on it. It was during this period that she wrote a lot of poems, bad ones, the proof of a deeply romantic heart in someone who would later be accused of being too cold, too logical, by those who didn't read her carefully:

> Ah, death is in life, I know, I know.
> So let me, floating days, give you my hand.
> You will not lose me. As a sign I leave behind,
> For you, this page and the flame.

Hearing from an ex-boyfriend about the brilliant lectures given by a Professor Heidegger at the University of Marburg, Arendt enrolled there too, promptly signing up for Heidegger's class. It was 1924. She was eighteen. Heidegger was thirty-five, and married, with two sons.

It is difficult to do credit to Heidegger's complex philosophical ideas in short order, but his approach to philosophy was marked by his shaking off of prior thinkers' devotion to cold, hard logic. He was a man who thought, as Daniel Maier-Katkin once wrote, that "human experience and understanding both lie closer to the realm of feeling and mood that inheres in poetry (an idea with strong appeal to Arendt)." Heidegger took that attitude right into his pedagogical approach. By everyone's account, his lectures were performances, soliloquies designed for more than the straight delivery of information. Of the talk around campus, Arendt would later write:

> The rumor about Heidegger put it quite simply: Thinking has come to life again; the cultural treasures of the past, believed to be dead, are being made to speak, in the course of which it turns out that they propose things altogether different from the familiar, worn-out trivialities they had been presumed to say. There exists a teacher; one can perhaps learn to think.

After she spent several months learning to think, Heidegger approached Arendt after class one day in February 1925. He asked what she had been reading. She told him. Her answers were apparently so charming they elicited an immediate love note: "I will never be able to call you mine, but from now on you will belong in my life, and it shall grow with you." It began there.

Arendt and Heidegger often couched their affair in the abstract, as was to be expected of those who trafficked all their lives in ideas. Their manner of writing about loving each other lent them not just high drama, but the appearance of a kind of high-mindedness. Unlike the love letters West and Wells exchanged, theirs included little baby talk, no pet names. Instead, Heidegger, whose side of the correspondence was the only one that survived, would write things like:

> The demonic struck me. The silent prayer of your beloved hands and your shining brow enveloped it in womanly transfiguration. Nothing like it has ever happened to me.

Womanly transfiguration notwithstanding, the demon was fickle. Just three months after the affair began, Heidegger backed off. Suddenly his tone in letters was remote. He pleads the demands of his work. He also makes florid claims of future commitment at a time when he can return his attentions to the world. In short, he behaved like any man who'd realized he'd made a mistake with a woman much his junior, but who in his guilt still didn't want to foreclose the possibility of future sex.

To be fair to Heidegger, he wasn't exactly lying. In a small shed his wife had built for him on their country estate, he was indeed toiling away at what would become his breakthrough masterwork, *Being and Time*. But when he brushed off Arendt, he was two years from the end of the project, and still planned to teach that fall. In any event, the result was that Arendt spent the summer alone.

When both teacher and student returned to Marburg in the fall of 1925, Heidegger kept avoiding Arendt. He had started to outright stand her up by the spring of 1926. Frustrated, Arendt then began the long process—it would last all her life—of giving Heidegger up. She left Marburg. She began to study with a different philosopher, Karl Jaspers. She did keep speaking to Heidegger, but she could mostly reach him only by letter, sending him mournful missives. There would be brief assignations in small-town train stations, but nothing that sustained itself beyond the time allotted for the visit.

Brief and unsatisfying though it clearly was, the affair would be a signature event in both lives. Heidegger's influence on Arendt was obviously formative, and in that sense it was enormous. But she took something more like inspiration than marching orders from him, carving her own path in the subject matter and scope of her work. He stayed in philosophy; she moved on to political theory. He stayed in Germany; she left. By the time they finally met again after World War II, she was on the verge of becoming a famous thinker in her own right, and the ideas that had made her reputation, particularly those concerning Germany's actions in World War II, were developed outside his comment or control.

Their experiences of Germany could not, in any event, have been more starkly different. Not long after his affair with Arendt ended, Heidegger joined the Nazi Party. There have been many subsequent debates about how sincere Heidegger could possibly have been about this affiliation, but he undeniably had some amount of sympathy for the movement. The romanticism of the Nazi vision of the world—one in which races were locked in combat, in which good resided in the *Volk*—aligned, catastrophically, with his.

He didn't just quietly accept the Nazis; he actively worked with them. Almost as soon as he joined the party, Heidegger began leading an effort to remove Jews from the universities, even signing the letter that removed his own mentor, Edmund Husserl, from the ranks of the professorship. (For this, Arendt would call Heidegger a "potential murderer.") This made him a leading figure of what the Nazis called the *Gleichschaltung*, sometimes translated as "collaboration," the process by which most Germans, be they members of civic organizations or intellectuals, were brought in line with Nazi priorities.

Later, speaking of the *Gleichschaltung* abstractly, Arendt simply said, "The problem, the personal problem, was not what our enemies did but what our friends did." The depth of her relationship with Heidegger did not become public knowledge until after her death. But she must have been thinking of him. Under Karl Jaspers at the University of Heidelberg, Arendt wrote a dissertation titled *Love and Saint Augustine*. It may have been another sign of her frustration with Heidegger that what interested her there was not romantic love but neighborly love. She finished this dense and challenging piece of work in early 1929. It was a few months before the Wall Street stock market crashed, setting off the Great Depression and destabilizing the loans that had been holding Germany to the Treaty of Versailles. Hitler would earn his popularity from the spoils of economic disaster, but just then—the moment Arendt got her doctorate—he was not yet fully ascendant.

Arendt was, by then, living in Berlin. The city was full of young graduates trying to figure out what to do with themselves in a country that was still reeling from what many considered the insult of the Treaty of Versailles. Like everyone else in Weimar, Arendt went to the glittering parties that belied the glum mood of the time. One fateful gathering was held at the Museum of Ethnology in Berlin. It was a leftist fund-raiser in the form of a masquerade ball. Arendt was dressed as an "Arab harem girl." One longs for a description of what such a costume might have looked like in 1929, but evidently it did the trick. She saw a classmate with whom she'd long ago lost touch, a man named Gunther Stern. They reconnected.

He seduced her, he later wrote in a memoir, by telling her that "loving is that act by which something a posteriori—the by-chance-encountered other—is transformed into an a priori of one's own life." For some other woman, this might have seemed pretentious. For Arendt, it was apparent proof that their connection could be intellectual as well as emotional. By September she'd marry Stern. Still, when she wrote to Heidegger to announce the marriage, it was in the key of defeat. She was settling, she reassured Heidegger, for the comfort, however imperfect, of a home:

> *Do not forget how much and how deeply I know that our love has become the blessing of my life. This knowledge cannot be shaken, not even today.*

Heidegger hadn't quite made his Nazi leanings public when she wrote that letter.

The comfort of marriage did prove useful. It gave Arendt the space to work more intensely on a new project. It was a book that did not exactly take her inner life as its subject. Yet it was the closest she'd ever come to writing a memoir. A friend, finding the eighteenth-century letters and diaries of a Jewish *salonnière* at a rare bookseller's, had passed them on to Arendt. The life of Rahel Varnhagen soon became an obsession for Arendt. She began work on a biography, a book that would ultimately become half a statement of personal philosophy and half an homage to a woman she considered a role model. In this, she was nearly unique among thinking women of her era. Most were afraid to admit any clear debt to women.

Varnhagen was born in Berlin in 1771, the daughter of a prosperous merchant. Though she did not have much of a formal education, Varnhagen was interested in ideas from the time she was very young. As an adult she surrounded herself with the great artists and thinkers of her era, mostly the German romantics. Her salon made her a key figure in German intellectual history. Part of what drew Arendt to Varnhagen so passionately was that like her, Varnhagen was Jewish and deeply assimilated. But Varnhagen was somewhat ambivalent about being Jewish. In light of that, Arendt found Varnhagen's alleged deathbed words, recorded by her husband, unforgettable:

> *The thing which all my life seemed to me the greatest shame, which was the misery and misfortune of my life—having been born a Jewess—this I should on no account now wish to have missed.*

Arendt was so affected by that sentence she began her own book with it. The project had a mediumistic quality almost from the beginning. Arendt freely called Varnhagen her "best friend." Her approach to the book, she wrote when she was finally able to publish it some twenty-five years later in 1958, was "an angle unusual in biographical literature." In fact, Arendt described her aims as almost metaphysical:

> *It was never my intention to write a book about Rahel; about her personality, which might lend itself to various interpretations according to the psychological standards and categories that the author introduces from the outside . . . What interested me solely was to narrate the story of Rahel's life as she herself might have told it.*

The claim to be able to tell Varnhagen's story "as she herself might have told it" is, as the Arendt scholar Seyla Benhabib once put it, "astonishing." You can spend a whole life in someone's archives, and yet find it impossible to get a full grasp of her inner life. Arendt must have known this and even experienced it as she tried to write Rahel's life from her perspective. For one thing, it's simply impossible to speak in the voice of someone who has been dead for a century or more. But the emotional attraction she felt to Varnhagen's life eclipsed the rational considerations. She had found a mistress she wanted to apprentice herself to, and writing the book was a way of doing it.

What Arendt found most intriguing about Varnhagen was that Varnhagen had found a way to make being different a kind of boon. This Arendt connected particularly to Varnhagen's identity as a Jew. Varnhagen's husband had tried to transcend his Jewishness by acquiring more and more social status. For Varnhagen, this had never worked. She could not, she thought, erase the mark. So she embraced it. If her Jewishness had set Varnhagen apart from German society, Arendt concluded, it had also given her a certain individuality of perspective that ultimately proved to have its own kind of value. Seeing things differently was not just a matter of perspective; sometimes to see things differently was to see them more clearly.

Varnhagen, Arendt tells us, was thus a kind of "pariah." She didn't mean this in the negative sense we now attach to it. That gets clearer when in her later work Arendt salts the term with an adjective: "conscious pariah." A conscious pariah knows she is different, and knows she may never, at least in the eyes of others, properly escape it. But she is also aware of what her individuality gives her. Among those things is an instinctual sort of empathy, a sensitivity to the suffering of others that comes from having known it yourself:

This sensitivity is a morbid exaggeration of the dignity of every human being, a passionate comprehension unknown to the privileged. It is this passionate empathy which constitutes the humaneness of the pariah. In a society based upon privilege, pride of birth and arrogance of title, the pariah instinctively discovers human dignity in general long before reason has made it the foundation of morality.

While Arendt mostly limited her use of the term "pariah" to apply to the distinction of Jewishness, she hinted that she knew there was a wider application for the model. It seems no accident that Arendt chose a woman as a role model for the pariah here, though Arendt would have denied it made much difference. She would probably have said that Varnhagen's status as a Jew was far stronger a connection than the woman thing. Yet a lot of what Arendt discovered about Varnhagen could extend by analogy, and on some level she knew it. In an introduction she penned when she finally published her life of Varnhagen in the 1950s, she wrote:

The modern reader will scarcely fail to observe at once that Rahel was neither beautiful nor attractive; that all the men with whom she had any kind of love relationship were younger than she herself; that she possessed no talents with which to employ her extraordinary intelligence and passionate originality; and finally, that she was a typically "romantic" personality, and that the Woman Problem, that is the discrepancy between what men expected of women "in general" and what women could give or wanted in their turn, was already established by the conditions of the era and represented a gap that virtually could not be closed.

The statements are wondrous, in the history of Hannah Arendt's relationship with feminism. Arendt had no interest in the movement or its rhetoric. Her professional alliances were mostly with men. She never worried much about whether she belonged among her mostly male intellectual peers. She did not feel that patriarchy was a serious problem. In fact, asked about women's emancipation late in her life, she said the "Woman Problem" was never much of a problem for her. "I have always thought that there are certain occupations that are improper for women, that do not become them," she told an interviewer.

> It just doesn't look good when a woman gives orders. She should try not to get into such a situation if she wants to remain feminine. Whether I am right about this or not I do not know ... The problem itself played no role for me personally. To put it very simply, I have always done what I liked to do.

This sort of self-contradictory answer gave little room to retroactively anoint Arendt as a quiet crusader for women or even an advocate for equality of the sexes, per se.

And yet she thought one should do what one wants to do. Instead of writing a biography of, for example, Kierkegaard, she began her public career with an obsession about another woman. One who was "neither beautiful nor attractive," but who was nonetheless possessed of "extraordinary intelligence and passionate originality." And one whose outsider status was not a difficulty to be overcome but something to be dug into, mined for strength. It's possible, as some scholars have speculated, that the reason any kind of discrimination against women seemed invisible to her is that in her lifetime her Jewishness had simply been a far more explicit target. Hostility to women was far more diffuse than the Nazis' campaign against the Jews.

Arendt was still working on the book on Varnhagen when, in 1933, the Reichstag—the seat of the German parliament—burned down. It was arson, a crime whose perpetrator is still in some dispute, though a young Communist was arrested and tried as the immediate culprit and the German left was blamed for the resulting chaos.

Hitler had been sworn in as chancellor only a month or so before the fire. The tumult gave him the excuse to assume emergency powers. Gunther Stern, Arendt's husband, who had deep roots with anti-Nazi dissidents, left for Paris immediately. Arendt stayed.

It was not that the danger of the regime was lost on her. In fact, she said the fire was an "immediate shock," one that no longer left her with the impression she could remain a "bystander." The fact that former friends and allies were gradually falling under Nazi influence must have been clear to her before then, though. The fall before, after hearing rumors, she had written to Heidegger asking about his new politics. Specifically her concerns were about the rumor that he had become anti-Semitic, news she gathered from her husband and his friends. His reply was, to say the least, petulant. It listed all the Jewish students he had recently helped, then added:

> *Whoever wants to call this "raging anti-Semitism" is welcome to do so. Beyond that, I am now just as much an anti-Semite in University issues as I was ten years ago in Marburg . . . To say absolutely nothing about my personal relationships with many Jews.*
>
> *And above all it cannot touch my relationship to you.*

But it had touched the relationship. This is the last letter that passed between them for over a decade.

Some months after the Reichstag fire, Arendt agreed to help surreptitiously collect anti-Semitic statements from pamphlets held by the library that also housed Varnhagen's papers. The statements were then going to be used by friends in Zionist organizing abroad. But within days Arendt was discovered and reported to authorities. She was arrested, along with her mother, and spent a few nights in a holding cell. Her arresting officer liked her, even flirted with her: "What am I supposed to do with you?" Eventually, he let her go. She was very lucky. In the interrogation she just lied. She had not revealed who she'd been working with.

But after that incident it became clear she couldn't stay in Germany. At first, Arendt and her mother went to Prague. Martha Arendt went from there to Königsberg, and Arendt went to Paris. She brought the manuscript on Varnhagen with her. But a cloud came with her. The depth of the Nazi catastrophe was becoming apparent to her. In Berlin, the intellectuals she'd known were starting to cooperate with the Nazi regime. Heidegger had taken up his work as a university rector, wore a swastika pin, and even briefly tried to meet Hitler. She knew all about it.

So Arendt left thinking to herself, "I shall never again get involved in any kind of intellectual business." Her plan to estrange herself from intellectualism did not, as we know, pan out. But the betrayal left a permanent mark. No longer could she see a traditional life of the mind as salvation. Even great minds were susceptible to poor judgment. They could abandon common sense very quickly.

"I still think that it belongs to the essence of being an intellectual that one fabricates ideas about everything," she told an interviewer a couple of years before she died. She was saying that she thought it was a bad thing. "Today I would say they were trapped by their own ideas. That is what happened." Intellectuals—like Heidegger— weren't actively making a strategic choice when they joined the Nazi Party. They weren't doing it just to survive. They rationalized it, aligning themselves with the ideas of the party because it was anathema for them to be associated with a cause in which they did not fervently believe. And in so doing, they became Nazis themselves.

When she arrived in Paris in 1933, Arendt broke not just with her home country but with her professional career in philosophy. She barely published a word during the eight years she spent in France, completing the Varnhagen manuscript only because friends urged her to. Instead she worked. She took a post as an administrator for various charitable efforts aimed at helping the increasing numbers of emigrant Jews gathering in Paris. Something about the relatively bureaucratic procedures of pencil pushing was comforting, achievable, and lacked potential for the same disappointments her "life of the mind" had previously held.

Arendt briefly reunited with Gunther Stern in Paris, but he had gotten himself lost in the writing of an enormously complicated novel (one he would never quite manage to publish), and the marriage soon crumbled. By 1936, she'd met another man—Heinrich Blücher, a gregarious German Communist whose roots in the movement were deep enough that in Paris he lived under a fake name.

It's tempting to romanticize Blücher's evidently staggering projection of masculinity, and many an Arendt biographer has succumbed. Blücher was a larger man than Stern or Heidegger. He also had a loud voice and a ready laugh, and he was a man of the world because of his long involvement with politics. But he could also joust intellectually with Arendt, something she demanded in a partner. He expounded strong views on philosophy and history in his letters as well as ordinary dinner conversation. In one memorable letter to Arendt, he begins with consolations and observations about the death of her mother and then ratchets himself up to a full-scale polemic against the allegiances philosophers have to abstract truth:

> *Marx simply wanted to spread out the heaven of being over the whole earth, as did all those lesser ideologues too. And thus we are all on the verge of choking to death in clouds of blood and smoke . . . Kierkegaard used the fallen blocks to build a narrow cave in which he locked his moral self together with a God of a monstrous nature. To that one can only say: Well, good luck, and thanks a lot.*

As his brash prose style suggests, Blücher was not an academic like Heidegger or Stern. He had done a lot of reading but he was entirely self-taught. Though he had literary ambitions, he never wrote a book himself. He complained of lifelong writer's block, which apparently didn't apply to his letter writing. He lived his life as a rejection of the gentility of academic intellectual life, and this seemed to appeal to Arendt. In a letter she'd write to Karl Jaspers ten years after meeting Blücher, she credited her husband (the pair married in 1940, in part so that Blücher could get papers to leave Europe) with having brought her to "see politically and think historically." She liked that he lived and worked in the concrete world, a place that Heidegger, certainly, had little interest in.

A friend, the poet Randall Jarrell, called them a "dual monarchy." The point was less their imperiousness—though they could be imperious—than the fact that the Blücher-Arendts drew considerable strength in their relationship from their discussions. Neither seemed to be the master or mistress of the other, although Arendt was frequently the breadwinner in their years in America. The marriage operated on a kind of natural equality, a balance generally untroubled by Blücher's occasional infidelities.

Being in Paris around other writers and thinkers turned out to be good for her. It was easier to think in concert, Arendt came to find. She had befriended fellow German refugee Walter Benjamin, then a rather unsuccessful critic who was having trouble getting published. Editors quarreled with him, and he only reluctantly gave in to their demands. Benjamin was a classically romantic figure, having come from a prosperous family that found any overt displays of professional ambition quite vulgar. Though his father largely refused to support him, he insisted on a career that naturally led him to penury. As Arendt put it, reflecting on Benjamin's choice to be an *homme de lettres*:

> *Such an existence was something unknown in Germany, and almost equally unknown was the occupation which Benjamin, only because he had to make a living, derived*

from it: Not the occupation of a literary historian and scholar with the requisite number of fat tomes to his credit, but that of a critic and essayist who regarded even the essay form as too vulgarly extensive and would have preferred the aphorism if he had not been paid by the line.

Benjamin was among the friends who insisted that Arendt finish her Varnhagen manuscript. "The book made a great impression on me," he wrote to their friend Gershom Scholem, recommending the manuscript in 1939. "It swims with powerful strokes against the current of edifying and apologetic Judaic studies." She, too, was interested in helping him do his own work. To Scholem, she wrote, "I am very worried about Benji. I tried to procure something for him here and failed miserably. Yet I am more than ever convinced of the importance of securing him a living for his further work."

Benjamin was always more of a mystic than Arendt. His connections to the real world were extraordinarily tenuous. But in his aloofness, she later wrote, she found a kind of political principle worth sustaining. She distinguished his *homme de lettres* mode of living from that of the "intellectuals" she had come to disdain:

Unlike the class of the intellectuals, who offer their services either to the state as experts, specialists, and officials, or to society for diversion and instruction, the hommes de lettres always strove to keep aloof from both the state and society.

In the Europe of the late 1930s and early 1940s, the state was a thing worth keeping one's distance from. Anti-Semitic propaganda rose to a fever pitch in France, and the whole country, pressured by the Nazis to the east, began to fall apart. In late 1939 Blücher was sent to an internment camp in the south of France and only freed months later by an influential friend. In 1940, Arendt herself was sent to a camp in Gurs, near the French border with Spain, where she remained for a month before France surrendered to Germany and internment camps for Jews like Gurs were disbanded. The couple were eventually reunited and obtained a visa to the United States, arriving in New York in May 1941.

In the meantime, Walter Benjamin had also seen the writing on the wall. He arranged to travel to Lisbon to catch a ship to the United States in the fall of 1940. Benjamin had to go through Spain to get to Lisbon. But when he arrived at the Spanish border with a small group of other refugees who had been living in Marseille, they were informed that just that day the border had been closed to people like them who were *"sans nationalité."* This meant they would likely end up in a camp. Overnight, Benjamin overdosed on morphine. Before losing consciousness, he gave his companions a note that said he saw no other way out.

Arendt was one of the first friends to hear of what followed, evidence of what she would later, in a long, elegiac essay, call his "bad luck":

> One day earlier Benjamin would have got through without any trouble; one day later the people in Marseilles would have known that for the time being it was impossible to pass through Spain. Only on that particular day was the catastrophe possible.

This was an intellectualized lament for Benjamin's fate, a laying of ideas onto the tragedy, an attitude that might suggest a certain emotional distance. But Arendt was not distant from what had happened to Benjamin. On her way out of France, Arendt made a special point of stopping and trying to find her friend's grave. She found only the cemetery, which, she wrote to Scholem:

> faces a small bay directly overlooking the Mediterranean; it is carved in stone in terraces; the coffins are also pushed

into such stone walls. It is by far one of the most fantastic
and most beautiful spots I have seen in my life.

Just before Benjamin left Marseille he'd given her and Blücher a collection of his manuscripts, hoping that if he couldn't make it to New York himself she could deliver them to his friends there. One of them, Benjamin's "Theses on the Philosophy of History," the Arendt-Blüchers read aloud to each other on the ship to America. "Reflection shows us that our image of happiness is thoroughly colored by the time to which the course of our own existence has assigned us." The piece continued:

> *The kind of happiness that could arouse envy in us exists*
> *only in the air we have breathed, among people we could*
> *have talked to, women who could have given themselves*
> *to us. In other words, our image of happiness is indissolu-*
> *bly bound up with the image of redemption.*

But by the time they were on that boat to America, it was already clear that the war raging across Europe would leave very little chance at redemption. Most of what had formed them, including the Germany they had known, was simply gone.

In New York, things were difficult. The Arendt-Blüchers (and later Arendt's mother) lived together in a couple of dilapidated rooms in a rooming house. They shared the kitchen with other residents. Blücher took a series of odd jobs, the first of which saw him take on a kind of factory work he had never performed before. Arendt went first to a home in Massachusetts to learn English, then began again to earn money by writing, primarily for a small German-language newspaper called *Aufbau* and other periodicals aimed at émigré Jews. She sent Benjamin's papers to his friend Theodor Adorno, who was also in New York. But nothing immediately came of it. There seemed to be no plans to publish them.

The articles Arendt wrote in those years are halfway between academic treatises and modern newspaper editorials. Most of them betray a certain stiffness of pen and deadening repetition of theme. Reading them in order, one starts to feel harangued rather than moved. But one piece stands out, a 1943 item written for the *Menorah Journal*, titled "We Refugees." It was originally published in English, which may explain the simple register in which it was written; at that point, Arendt had known the language only two years.

But the boiled, stripped-down tone her third language forced upon her suited her elegiac yet polemical purpose: "In the first place, we don't like to be called 'refugees.'" Arendt described a population so beaten down by their experience in Europe that they have suppressed it. The atmosphere, she writes, makes refugees wander around in a daze, unable to speak honestly about what troubled them because no one wants to hear about the "hell" they encountered:

Apparently nobody wants to know that contemporary history has created a new kind of human beings—the kind that are put in concentration camps by their foes and in internment camps by their friends.

Never afraid to venture into the uncomfortable subject, Arendt was also critical of the prevalence of suicide among refugees—not so much of the people who chose it as the mode in which it was rendered. "Theirs is a quiet and modest way of vanishing," she wrote. "They seem to apologize for the violent solution they have found for their personal problems." This, she felt, was inadequate because the logic of the suicide had been provided by the political catastrophe of the Nazis, and even by American anti-Semitism: "In Paris we could not leave our homes after eight o'clock because we were Jews; but in Los Angeles we are restricted because we are 'enemy aliens.'"

This essay, written when Arendt was thirty-seven years old, was the first sign that she had any gift for outright polemic. It had taken her that long to convince herself of the uses of writing for the public. Her essay wraps up by calling on Jews to become "conscious pariahs"—Rahel Varnhagen is invoked, along with several other examples that Arendt would flesh out in later essays: Heine, Sholem Aleichem, Bernard Lazare, Franz Kafka, "or even Charlie Chaplin"—because it is the only way out of the deadening, suicide-inducing denial of their situation.

> *Those few refugees who insist upon telling the truth, even to the point of "indecency," get in exchange for their unpopularity one priceless advantage: history is no longer a closed book to them and politics is no longer the privilege of gentiles.*

Articles like that brought Arendt to the attention of wider leftist publishing circles in New York. The one most key to all her later activities was the small, prematurely dusty collection of ex-Communists and literary critics who circled around a journal known as the *Partisan Review*.

For most people the name of that magazine is obscure, its influence unknown. But to a small and influential set of Americans, most of them living or born in the middle of the twentieth century, the *Partisan Review* came to be emblematic of everything desirable and glamorous about intellectual life in New York. It was a relaunch of an older magazine, one that had been associated with the Communist John Reed clubs. The men at the helm of the second edition—Philip Rahv and William Phillips—had been rebel editors of the first.

The Communist Party of America, in those years, was splitting into factions. One faction believed that allegiance to the Soviet Union must be maintained at all costs for the Communist experiment to succeed. The other took a more skeptical view, particularly of Stalin and his cult of personality. Rahv and Phillips fell into the latter camp.

It was not that they had abandoned their leftist principles; it was only that they were unwilling to follow dogmatic party lines. They were—you could say—conscious pariahs of the Communist movement. Since Arendt's concerns already lay with an analysis of Fascism and its roots, she fit right in.

But the *Partisan Review*, as it developed, became better known as a journal of arts and letters than as a journal of politics. Arendt's first contribution, published in the fall of 1944, was an essay on Kafka. Arendt was not the only woman on the masthead—she was joined by the short story writer Jean Stafford, and the poet Elizabeth Bishop—but she was the only one who was writing dense intellectual pieces.

Her early pieces had all the flaws attendant to writing in a second language—she had had to abandon her "Stradivarius," Blücher wrote to her once, for a "beer fiddle." This was made all the clearer by the work she did for the *Nation*, one of the leading magazines of the American left at the time. The editor there was Randall Jarrell, the friend who would help Arendt make her work easier for Americans to read. Evidence of his influence was almost immediate: In 1946, for both the *Nation* and the *Partisan Review*, she would write essays on existentialism. But only the one edited by Jarrell had the appealing lead: "A lecture on philosophy provokes a riot, with hundreds crowding in and thousands turned away." He'd become one of the friends she turned to most frequently to do what she called "Englishing" her work.

As for existentialism, Arendt had known Jean-Paul Sartre a little in Paris. She pronounced herself impressed by Sartre's *La Nausée* and Albert Camus's *L'Étranger*. But she had the same concerns about them as she now had about all intellectuals, and their tendency, "symbolically speaking, [to] stick to their hotel rooms and their cafés." She worried too about their paralyzing retreat into absurdity. If they didn't get out in the world and act, she worried:

The nihilistic elements, which are obvious in spite of all protests to the contrary, are not the consequences of new insights but of some very old ideas.

Arendt had by then begun work on her own omnibus of "new insights," the book that would become *The Origins of Totalitarianism*. She was publishing her analyses of anti-Semitism and the plight of stateless people in the *Partisan Review* and a small constellation of other American leftist journals throughout the 1940s. As early as 1945, she'd persuaded an editor at Houghton Mifflin that the entire analysis deserved to be turned into a book. But it would take her another five years to finish.

The tripartite, unwieldy text she produced is difficult to describe succinctly. It has, as her biographer Elisabeth Young-Bruehl observed, no gentle introduction that might situate the reader. In the preface to the first edition Arendt began with a broadside against simplistic interpretations of history: "The conviction that everything that happens on earth must be comprehensible to man can lead to interpreting history by commonplaces." She also resisted an easy, causal relationship between good and evil, though of course she believed that totalitarianism was by any measure evil:

And if it is true that in the final stages of totalitarianism an absolute evil appears (absolute because it can no longer be deduced from humanly comprehensible motives), it is also true that without it we might never have known the truly radical nature of Evil.

The expansive, meandering quality of the book was the result of its long gestation. The means of its production were, alongside experience and research, many rambling late-night conversations with Heinrich Blücher. Throughout much of its writing he had been depressed and unemployed; his English was not good enough for clerical work and he had no PhD that might have allowed him to teach. He spent hours instead in the reading rooms of the New York Public Library, while Arendt went to her day job as an editor at Schocken Books, a publishing house founded by refugees from Nazi Germany. The products of those labors—his knowledge of history and her analysis—were then turned over in the couple's minds late into the evening. The book and its insights were ultimately hers, but his help was invaluable.

The linchpin of Arendt's analysis of totalitarianism was the concentration camp, which she described as the ultimate instrument of the "radical evil" of totalitarianism. It was the site of the main Nazi experiment: the total domination of humanity. The terror of the camps succeeded in reducing each person to a "bundle of reactions," one person interchangeable with the next. This Arendt connected with the feeling many people had that they were, in some sense, "superfluous." Their lives and their deaths didn't matter, at least not so much as political ideologies mattered.

Ideology was another of Arendt's insights. So much of totalitarianism depended on the simplistic promises of ideology, she wrote, its ability to reassure those feeling adrift that the past and the future could be explained by a simple set of laws. It was, in fact, the simplistic reassurances of ideology—even those promises it could never keep—that made it so powerful. Their promise of solutions meant that totalitarian politics would be a continual threat, in Arendt's analysis:

> *Totalitarian solutions may well survive the fall of totalitarian regimes in the form of strong temptations which will come up whenever it seems impossible to alleviate political, social, or economic misery in a manner worthy of man.*

The reviews of the book, when it was finally published in 1951, were effusive. They praised not just Arendt's analysis but her erudition in delivering it. (The text had had "Englishing" from the critic Alfred Kazin, and another friend named Rose Feitelson.) Many of them focused on the way Arendt drew a connection between Nazi totalitarian strategies and the Soviets. The subtitle of the *Los Angeles Times* review was "Nazi and Bolshevik Varieties Rated as 'Essentially Identical Systems.'" In fact, she had never used that phrase in *Origins* at all, only highlighted the similarities between the strategies of movement elites. Arendt was married to an ex-Communist. Many of her new friends in New York were current and former Communists. It was Stalinism and the Soviet form of totalitarianism that worried her, not Communism itself.

The acclaim was so loud and clamorous that Arendt became a household name and *Origins* sold very well. Even *Vogue*, not a magazine generally given to covering intellectual affairs, had listed her as an item "People Are Talking About" in mid-1951:

> The Origins of Totalitarianism, *by Hannah Arendt, who has written a freshly conceived, monumental but extraordinarily readable book in which she wrote, "What is remarkable in the totalitarian organizations is that they could adopt so many organizational devices of secret societies without ever trying to keep their own goal a secret."*

The use of that somewhat random quotation, which by no mean encapsulates the arguments of *The Origins of Totalitarianism*, was a good harbinger of what Arendt was about to become: an icon whose ideas were, for many of her admirers, secondary to the figure she cut in public life. To other women in her orbit, she had done something incredible. She not only had achieved equal footing with all the men who styled themselves public intellectuals, but had vaulted past them to put their ideas about the war—all their painstakingly dense articles about the function of human history—in the shadow of her towering analysis. She hadn't just joined the constellation of intellectuals who had settled in New York in that era. She had become the polestar, a person others flocked to. Some forty years after the book was published, a journalist named Janet Malcolm would write of being "flatteringly mistaken . . . for someone who might have been invited to Hannah Arendt's parties in the fifties."

Not everyone liked Arendt's new status. Many men, notably, reacted badly. Arendt belonged to the so-called New York intellectuals, a name not used until long after many of its members were dead. The name refers to a cluster of writers and thinkers who gathered in Manhattan in the 1930s and 1940s, who befriended and dated and married each other, and a majority of whom were incorrigible gossips. They built their own legends by writing incessantly to and about each other.

Still, we have no record of exactly what their first impressions of Arendt were. We do know that the poet Delmore Schwartz, who hung around the set, called her "that Weimar Republic flapper." The critic Lionel Abel was said to call her "Hannah Arrogant" behind her back. Even Alfred Kazin, who wrote that she was "vital to my life," added that he had "submitted patiently to an intellectual loneliness that came out as arrogance."

These men were no shrinking violets; they were all self-possessed, even prone to grand pronouncements. The degree to which they mistook intelligence for arrogance is no doubt impossible to parse, posthumously. But it would become a problem for Arendt in a way that it never did for Parker, who rarely touched serious subjects like war, history, and politics, and in any event stopped producing much criticism after the 1930s. It also became a problem for Arendt in a way it never did for West, who perhaps was less proximate to the narcissistic competitions the New York intellectuals liked to enter. Men with brilliant, world-encompassing ideas do not seem subject to the same accusations of egotism.

At least at this early stage, only a few people were put off by Arendt's brilliance and even fewer were willing to say so in print.

More prominent were men who could rightly be called fanatics. The literary critic Dwight Macdonald was positively reverent in a review of *Origins* for a small leftist magazine called the *New Leader*. He first likened Arendt to Simone Weil, the philosopher-mystic who left behind aphoristic writings on religion and politics. Then, perhaps sensing that Arendt was more worldly than Weil, he went in for a still more ambitious comparison:

> *The theoretical analysis of totalitarianism here impressed me more than any political theory I've read since 1935, when I first read Marx. It gave me the same contradictory sensations of familiarity ("Of course, just what I've been thinking about for years") and shocked discovery ("Can this possibly be true?") that Marx's description of capitalism did.*

This was not too far off the mark. *Origins* has ascended to classic status, a must read for historians and political scientists. Thick and somewhat opaque as it was, the way Arendt described the rise of Fascism in the wake of popular discontent is now widely accepted as the truth. She differed from Marx in that she saw no revolutionary solution to the problem she set out. Having become much more sensible, grounded, and jaded in her old age, having watched so many friends fall prey to currents of stupidity and violence, she shrank from simplistic resolutions. She had learned to rely only on herself, and her friends.

She would make a new friend, too, from the publication of *Origins*. One of the *Partisan Review* set wrote to Arendt not long after publication, describing it in potboiler terms:

> *I've read your book, absorbed, for the past two weeks, in the bathtub, riding in the car, waiting in line at the grocery store. It seems to me a truly extraordinary piece of work, an advance in human thought of, at the very least,*

*a decade, and also engrossing and fascinating in the way
that a novel is.*

Interestingly enough, and perhaps as a sign of respect, the letter
writer went on to offer "one larger criticism," suggesting that in her
enthusiasm for her own ideas Arendt had not sufficiently accounted
for the role of chance, of luck, in constructing the institutions of
totalitarianism. "I don't think I express this very well, and I haven't
the book to consult, having already lent it," the letter writer continued chattily, first veering off to criticize an obtuse reviewer as "terribly stupid," then adding postscripts inviting Arendt and Blücher
for lunch and raising the question of anti-Semitism in the works of
D. H. Lawrence, Ezra Pound, and Dostoyevsky.

The author of this simultaneously nervous and self-assured letter was the critic Mary McCarthy. Arendt and McCarthy had known
each other since 1944, having met—and quarreled—at one of the
never-ending *Partisan Review* parties.

5

McCarthy

All her life Mary McCarthy was a recognized expert at conversation, chattering just the way she did in that letter to Arendt. She and Parker had that knack for talk and parties in common. In reminiscences of McCarthy, particularly the memories of women, she is always seen from across the room, holding court. The poet Eileen Simpson, for example, remembered meeting McCarthy around the same time Hannah Arendt did:

> She stood in what I later recognized as a characteristic stance, right foot forward and balanced on a high heel. In one hand she held a cigarette, in the other a martini.

But she was not always sure-footed; she tripped into that friendship with Arendt, at first. The conversation was about the war. In passing, McCarthy remarked something to the effect that she "felt sorry for Hitler" because it seemed to her the dictator had wanted to be loved by the very people he tortured. Arendt lost her temper immediately. "How can you say this to me, a victim of Hitler, a person who has been in a concentration camp?" she exclaimed, then stormed out. She did stop first to harangue the *Partisan Review* editor Philip Rahv for allowing "this kind of conversation in your home, you, a Jew?" McCarthy, who was usually the soul of social graces, felt embarrassed if not quite ashamed. It was an inauspicious beginning to a friendship that would very quickly become the center of both women's professional and intellectual lives.

People have long liked to classify McCarthy as a "dark lady of American letters." This suggests a femme fatale type, one who was endlessly and even callously self-possessed. McCarthy wasn't like that. Just as in Parker's projection of a wisecracker, there were parlor tricks involved in McCarthy's maintenance of her image, sleights of hand. Her friend Elizabeth Hardwick hinted at this after McCarthy died:

> *Her indiscretions were always open and forthright and in many ways one could say she was "like an open book." Of course, everything interesting depends upon which book is open.*

It also depends on which page you begin. One story McCarthy told and retold was that of her strange Dickens-by-way-of-Horatio-Alger childhood. Born in Seattle in 1912 to the progeny of two rich, respectable families, McCarthy had a toddlerhood full of the comforts bestowed on rich children. But the finances of this idyll were unstable, based mostly on the generosity of McCarthy's paternal grandfather. Roy McCarthy, Mary's father, was an intermittent alcoholic who was constantly ill and rarely employed. The grandfather eventually tired of writing Roy checks and recalled him home to Minneapolis.

The family boarded a cross-country train in the late fall of 1918 amid a countrywide epidemic of influenza. While aboard, every single McCarthy was infected, succumbing one by one to delirium. That they even made it to Minneapolis was a miracle. From the haze of the illness came a story that the train conductor had tried to force the sick family off the train in the middle of nowhere, somewhere around North Dakota. In the cloudy retelling, McCarthy's father had brandished a gun. It's not clear this ever happened. In any event, that last stand was futile: within a few days of arriving in Minneapolis both of McCarthy's parents were dead.

Their grandparents did not care for children. It fell to other relatives to take on the daily care of McCarthy and her three brothers. Unfortunately, those available to raise them were somewhat reluctant custodians: an aging great-aunt and her ascetic husband, both of whom seem to have borrowed their opinions on child rearing from the functionaries who ran nineteenth-century orphanages. In their care, the four young McCarthys were fed a diet consisting chiefly of root vegetables and dried prunes. They had their mouths taped shut at night to prevent "mouth-breathing." They were sent into the freezing Minnesota cold to "play" in the dead of winter. Their amusements were limited, sometimes in bizarre ways:

> Reading was forbidden us, except for school-books and, for some reason, the funny papers and magazine section of the Sunday Hearst papers, where one read about leprosy, the affairs of Count Boni de Castellane, and a strange disease that turned people to stone creepingly from the feet up.

Punishments were frequent and severe. The cruelty was physical—beatings with hairbrush and razor strop—but also emotional. The great-aunt and uncle had a real flair for wielding humiliation as punishment; in one case McCarthy, having broken her glasses, was told she would simply not receive new ones. This sort of neglect and abuse continued for five years before McCarthy's maternal grandfather finally intervened, whisking an eleven-year-old Mary back to Seattle, while her younger brothers were farmed out to boarding school.

McCarthy liked to present herself as a skeptic in regard to the insights of psychiatry and psychoanalysis in particular. In her first book, *The Company She Keeps*, the main character, lying on a psychoanalyst's couch, thinks suddenly: "I reject the whole pathos of the changeling, the orphan, the stepchild." But she also knows that one "could not treat your life-history as though it were an inferior novel and dismiss it with a snubbing phrase." The fact was that a whole other possible future had evaporated when McCarthy's parents died, and she knew it: "I can see myself married to an Irish lawyer and playing golf and bridge, making occasional retreats and subscribing to a Catholic Book Club. I suspect I would be rather stout."

What McCarthy got in exchange for that lost other existence was the inquisitive detachment that became known as characteristic for her writing. Her manner in all her memoirs is the light touch of a black comic, even when she's writing about tape over the children's mouths. Having lived through a melodrama, she was somehow reluctant to let her feelings out in full force. A sense of how absurd it had all been made her more comfortable, perhaps. The character in *The Company She Keeps* mentions her sympathy with those who had "a sense of artistic decorum that like a hoity-toity wife was continually showing one's poor biography the door."

The new Catholic school in Seattle in which her maternal grandparents installed her might have looked strict to another child. It was a place of long-established routine, McCarthy wrote, the nuns "versed in clockwork obedience to authority." McCarthy longed to be popular and self-assured like some of the other girls there, but being nice didn't seem to garner her many friends. So she changed strategies.

"If I could not win fame by goodness," McCarthy wrote later, "I was ready to do it by badness." She promptly set the entire school aflutter by pretending she had lost her Catholic faith. It is an open question whether she had any natural religious feeling to begin with. Her background was a mishmash of indifferent Protestantism and a Catholicism focused largely on formalities. Her mother's mother was, in fact, Jewish. And as she told the tale in her memoirs, the young McCarthy plotted a precise time frame for the task:

If I lost my faith on, say, Sunday, I could regain it during the three days of retreat, in time for Wednesday confessions.

Thus there would be only four days in which my soul would be in danger if I should happen to die suddenly.

McCarthy found that she enjoyed setting off this sort of scandal, enjoyed garnering the approval of others through staged rebellions. It gave her the nuns' full attention; it also gave her the status she sought among her classmates, an identifying trait that made her stand out: "There went the girl that a Jesuit had failed to convince."

It also taught McCarthy that she had a talent for calculating the reaction of others and using it to her own ends. As an adult, McCarthy knew how manipulative she could be in that regard. In *Memories of a Catholic Girlhood*, she describes her young self, preparing for the episode, as surveying the convent with the "cold, empty gambler's mood, common to politicians and adolescents." She saw how they behaved; she saw what they wanted; she made it her job to understand the rules, and then to understand exactly how much she could bend them to her advantage.

This talent didn't always benefit her socially. Her canny appraisals of other people often came across as, well, harsh judgments. Elizabeth Hardwick once wrote:

There was a scent of the seminarian in Mary's moral life which for me was part of her originality and also one of the baffling charms of her presence. Very little was offhand; habits, prejudices, moments, even fleeting ones, had to be accounted for, looked at, and written in the ledger.

This habit of assessment and calculation would prove a great boon for a critic who wanted, ultimately, to make great theater of her passions and judgments. Obviously not everyone liked it. McCarthy's ability to size people up often came across as haughtiness. "She presented herself to the world as the most responsible of people but she was irresponsible really," Diana Trilling opined to one of McCarthy's biographers.

Trilling, one of the other women who were regulars at the *Partisan Review* parties, was something of a hostile witness. McCarthy didn't like her and let it be widely known. Trilling always felt marginalized as a mere "wife" in the *Partisan Review* set. She was married to the considerably more celebrated critic Lionel Trilling. And while she repeatedly claimed not to mind the way his towering reputation as a critic eclipsed her own book reviews and journalism, she also could never stop remarking on it. "People celebrate one member of a household but not two," she wrote in a memoir. "To celebrate two members of a single household doubles the strain on generosity." She was not incorrect about that, but McCarthy, Elizabeth Hardwick, and Hannah Arendt managed to find their way into the circle despite being "wives" themselves.

In any event, McCarthy was aware of her tendency to judge. "You use your wonderful scruples as an excuse for acting like a bitch," the heroine's husband in *The Company She Keeps* says. The heroine assures him that she tries not to be so. He doesn't believe her, and continues, demanding: "Why can't you be like anybody else?" But McCarthy was never destined to be like anybody else.

During her adolescence in Seattle, McCarthy always insisted on having friends who were different. She left the convent school for public high school, and there she met the friend who gave her a taste for the literary life. This was a black-haired young woman, fond of wearing vests and brogues, named Ethel Rosenberg (not that one). She called herself Ted—"later, I gather, she became an overt lesbian," McCarthy remarks in a memoir—and she came equipped with a pile of book recommendations. McCarthy already read quite a lot. But it was mostly trash—pulp novels and magazines with titles like *True Confessions* that chronicled salacious murders and rapes. It was not exactly Kafka.

It was Ted who showed McCarthy that sex could be found in more serious literary work too. It helped that Ted's taste tended to the aesthetes and the decadents, who had sensuality baked into their work: Aubrey Beardsley, Anatole France. Another young man had tried to introduce McCarthy to the heavier tomes of Melville and Dreiser. But they offered less pleasure. "*Moby-Dick*," she wrote, "was way over my head—that I had seen the movie, *The Sea Beast*, with John Barrymore, was more a hindrance than a help." It was also Ted who brought McCarthy into her first proper intellectual circle, a Seattle salon run by an older lesbian whose husband owned a bookstore.

Within a year, McCarthy was put back into the more genteel environs of a boarding school. But the bohemians had left their mark. McCarthy would keep writing to Ted; she'd also write, for her classes, stories and essays about prostitutes and suicide. She would keep experimenting with men, traveling through a series of boyfriends before landing on a steady one in the improbable person of Harold Johnsrud, a bald actor several years her senior. He was hardly her first. Another boyfriend had already taken McCarthy's virginity ("a slight sense of being stuffed," she'd described the encounter in a memoir). But he was the boyfriend who lasted, and the relationship followed her, ultimately, to Vassar in 1929.

For obvious reasons—writing a bestselling novel casts long shadows—there has always been some tendency to exaggerate the way Vassar "formed" McCarthy. Sometimes she encouraged this mythmaking. In a magazine essay from 1951, she wrote that a single teacher had inspired her to flee to college in the Northeast. This fabled woman—who did exist but was rather more complicated than this—had a "light, precise, cutting voice" and McCarthy found herself enchanted by the way she'd "score some pretension, slatternly phrase or construction on the part of her pupils." Vassar was supposed to make her just as sharp.

But if friends were the chief engines of an intellectual life, Vassar posed a problem. It provided no gas for the tank. To put it more bluntly: McCarthy's classmates at Vassar didn't like her very much. There were one or two exceptions but mostly her college friendships did not stick. Still, McCarthy took pride in being there. She made the standoffishness of the girls into a deliberate quality. "Vassar girls, in general, were not liked, she knew, by the world at large," one character thinks to herself in *The Group*. "They had come to be a sort of symbol of superiority."

Yet even on that scale, McCarthy came across as snobbish to her classmates. When they remembered McCarthy, they pointed to her intelligence and then slammed her with it. "One of the most discouraging things in the world was being in an English class freshman year with Mary McCarthy," one is quoted as saying in a later biography. "I found her remarkable and intimidating," said another. "And she absolutely destroyed one's own ego. Mary would not be rude to your face. It was just an air of superiority." It would be tempting to write off these bitter recollections as the product of jealousy of McCarthy's later success. But she too noticed that she didn't fit. "About college—it's all right, better than the [University of Washington] anyway," McCarthy wrote to Ted Rosenberg. "But there is too much smart talk, too many labels for things, too much pseudo-cleverness."

It was a strange comment for someone who would become known for her enjoyment of "smart talk." Perhaps the problem owed something to the strict hierarchies of social position in the Northeast. It's tempting to sentimentalize the upper-class women of the 1930s, sheltered as they were from the Depression, destined mostly for marriage, not careers. But that underestimates the persistence of intrafeminine social competition. The women who went to Vassar in McCarthy's era were shrewd characters; they were attuned to changes of status and quick to call out what they saw as social climbing. They were from a mix of backgrounds, wealthy and bourgeois. Some of them would see their situations get worse as fathers lost their fortunes in the Depression. McCarthy, arriving from the West without the very strict training in how Northeast society was conducted, was bound to cause friction. She had better luck with her professors. There were two—a Miss Kitchel and a Miss Sandison—about whom she writes in cadences more associated with what Anne of Green Gables called "bosom friends." She dedicated her memoirs to them, instead of to friends her own age.

In fact, these professors were far more involved in her intellectual and literary passions than the man she was dating—still Johnsrud, who flitted in and out throughout her time at Vassar. They spent a month living together one summer. It was a disaster. They were on-again, then off-again for her entire undergraduate career. McCarthy's love affairs, in this way, bore much resemblance to Parker's: the men were mostly background figures.

The truly lasting effect of Vassar on McCarthy's life came in the form of her very first association with a "little magazine." She formed a journal with several other literary young women, who included among their number the poet Elizabeth Bishop. Originally to be called the *Battleaxe*, the magazine was eventually given the name *Con Spirito*. For it McCarthy wrote what was to be her first book review, one in which she contrasted Aldous Huxley's *Brave New World* unfavorably with Harold Nicolson's now-forgotten *Public Faces*. She detoured to take shots at the modernists:

> One by one the literary demi-gods of the nineteen twenties were collapsing . . . Virginia Woolf was masking her new lack of hard thinking which was later to appear undisguised in the simple "pretty" femininity of The Second Common Reader, in a pretense of acute feeling and "experimentation with a new form."

Later McCarthy said this hatchet job demonstrated her "characteristic perversity." But she was proud enough of it that she took it to New York just before she graduated. She had it in hand when she presented herself to the then literary editor of the *New Republic*, a man named Malcolm Cowley. Cowley was something of a frustrated artist: he'd been in Paris with Hemingway and the rest in the 1920s, but he never had the big breakthrough they did. He'd turned to editing when it became evident he could not support himself solely on his writing. He'd spend the latter half of his career chronicling the triumphs of others.

Cowley was unimpressed with McCarthy. He told her he'd give her a review to do only if she was a genius or starving.

"I'm not starving," I said quickly; I knew I was not a genius and I was not pleased by the suggestion that I would be taking bread from other people's mouths.

Cowley wavered only slightly on the point. McCarthy was given a few very short reviews to write before finally she was assigned a now-forgotten journalistic memoir called *I Went to Pit College*. Authored by a Smith graduate who'd spent two years living undercover in a mining community in Pennsylvania, it had been favored by the American Communist Party. Cowley was an avowed Communist himself; in fact, his section was widely viewed as being a "megaphone for the Communist Party." So McCarthy figured it was part of the job to like the book and say so in print. "For the first time, and the last," she remembered later, "I wrote to order." But after she filed the review, Cowley pulled a fast one on her. He didn't think she had been hard enough on it, so he ran a second review as a humiliating correction. "It should never be taken for a gripping social document or even an unstudied and humanitarian gesture," the second reviewer, the magazine's film critic, wrote. After that, McCarthy did not appear in the pages of the *New Republic* for several years.

The *Nation* was more amenable to McCarthy's style. She disliked most of the books it assigned her, and dispatched them with curt ad hominem criticism. Of a collection of short stories by a then famous journalist, now forgotten: "It is hard to believe that these stories represent the peak of Mr. Burnett's achievement. It would be kinder to think that he had discovered the majority of them in an old trunk." In another review of five books: "There are but two qualities they share, and the first is a splendid, sickening mediocrity." There was always, in these reviews, a note of wickedness, a sense the writer knew she was testing the conventions of reviewing propriety. Her impertinence became a kind of calling card. Its value lay in its general claim to superior honesty. Never feeling obligated to genuflect to an established reputation gave the reviews a life of their own. As with Dorothy Parker's Constant Reader columns, it wasn't so necessary to have read the book yourself to appreciate the spirit.

The *Nation* was evidently delighted with McCarthy's bad attitude. Within three years, it decided to send her on a more ambitious outing. The project would evaluate all the book critics at all the magazines and newspapers of America, as a kind of state of the union of book reviewing. McCarthy did much of the work herself. But the *Nation*'s editor, a woman named Freda Kirchwey, insisted McCarthy share her byline with the deputy literary editor, a slightly older woman named Margaret Marshall. Age and experience, Kirchwey thought, would lend the series more credit. It's hard to say if her concern was valid. In any event, the pieces were a success. Called "Our Critics, Right or Wrong," the articles appeared in five fortnightly installments. The tone was polemical; the nation's critics were called to account for the way their reviews had "on the whole worked for the misunderstanding of works and art and the debasement of taste."

Such omnibus critiques appear every once in a while in the history of American book reviewing. Critics love to review each other, and they insist on doing it no matter how pointless the general public finds such debates. "Our Critics, Right or Wrong" stands out in the genre for its comprehensiveness. These pieces do not so much advance a coherent theory of reviewing as score zingers on every critic in the land, naming and shaming each and every critic then working. The editor of the *Saturday Review of Literature,* for example, was mocked for his doddering approach to his subject:

> *Literature stirs in him simply a number of vague, often undocumented associative thought processes. He is like an old gentleman wandering down a strange street who sees in the faces that pass only flickering resemblances to a dead brother-in-law or a long-forgotten second cousin.*

Naturally, this method offered McCarthy the chance to settle some scores. Malcolm Cowley got a sideswipe for reviewing one of his best friend's books in the pages of a now-forgotten periodical called *Books.* McCarthy also launched an indirect hit by devoting an entire installment of the series to the poor showing of Marxist critics in the pages of the *New Masses.* It poked fun at "the curious internal warfare between Marx and aestheticism, which gives to left-wing reviews of bad proletarian books such a hybrid party line."

As hoped, "Our Critics, Right or Wrong" provoked reactions, not necessarily negative ones, but reactions that professed surprise that women were being so, well, sharp. A *New York Times* reviewer who'd drawn fire himself devoted an entire column to McCarthy and Marshall. He even took the time to compose a condescending verse about them:

> *Oh, Mary McCarthy and Margaret Marshall*
> *Are two bright girls who are very impartial.*

He nonetheless thought they'd missed the mark by placing too much emphasis on formal apprenticeship, never once dropping the term "girls" as he addressed them. Others were more direct about their dislike. Franklin P. Adams, who'd been one of Parker's early fans, complained, "The girls remind us of what Old Hen Strauss used to say of some man whose name we forget: 'He's the most even-tempered man in Chicago; always mad.'"

There were a few critics McCarthy liked and she said so: they were "perspicacious," though "their faint catcalls have been drowned out by the bravos of the publishers' claque." One of them was Rebecca West. The others on the list were mostly men, and one of them was singled out for special praise for his ability to "relate what is valuable in modern literature to the body of literature of the past." The man was flattered. This was Edmund Wilson, Dorothy Parker's old friend, who had by now left *Vanity Fair* and become a prominent man of letters. He was forty by then, twice married, and had become heavy and bald. His first marriage produced a daughter and ended in divorce; his second ended when his wife died in 1932, just two years after their wedding. And very soon he would make McCarthy his third wife.

When McCarthy graduated from Vassar in 1933, she had married Harold Johnsrud. She always described the marriage as a curiously impersonal act. "To marry a man without loving him, which was what I had just done, not really perceiving it, was a wicked action," she once wrote, her embarrassment palpable. He considered himself something of a playwright, but one gets the impression he lived in his own world throughout their marriage. McCarthy never had much to say about him. Each was unfaithful to the other; by 1936, they'd called it quits. McCarthy embarked on a series of love affairs—the one that had nominally broken up her marriage lost its luster after the divorce—but no man stuck for long.

Her participation in Communist circles was similarly ambivalent, which was half the trouble for her with someone like Malcolm Cowley. At college, she'd met left-wingers but thought their activities "a kind of political hockey played by big, gaunt, dyspeptic girls in pants." McCarthy, who was undeniably pretty if not flashily so, felt she wasn't like them. She lacked any personal compulsion to serve a greater social good by joining any sort of political party. But literary and leftist circles overlapped significantly in the mid-1930s. Meeting for cocktails meant talking of Kafka and of the party and its travails. As time wore on, their impassioned speeches on these subjects impressed her. "They made me feel petty and shallow; they had, shall I say, a daily ugliness in their life that made my pretty life tawdry," she wrote.

This was McCarthy's contrarian streak talking. If people didn't like something she did, she often wanted to know why. Her curiosity then carried her into conviction. "The mark of the historic is the nonchalance with which it picks up an individual and deposits him in a trend," McCarthy wrote in her essay "My Confession." In it she explained her unlikely history as a Communist. But not every individual clutches that trend to her chest and marches on. Equanimity was never McCarthy's way, at least not in print.

McCarthy chose sides in the Stalinist-Trotskyist debate quite by accident. A novelist friend put her name on a list of members who supported a defense committee for Leon Trotsky without quite explaining to her what it would mean, and that was that. She was anointed a dissident. Flabbergasted at first, she wrote, she started to think about the problem and more or less talked herself into adopting the proper politics for it. It gave her a certain cachet on the social circuit:

> Jeweled lady-authors turned white and shook their bracelets angrily when I came into a soirée; rising young men in publishing or advertising tightened their neckties dubiously when I urged them to examine the case for themselves; out dancing in a night club, tall, collegiate young Party members would press me to their shirt-bosoms and tell me not to be silly, honey.

This was what Diana Trilling had meant when she said she found McCarthy's approach to politics "irresponsible." All of McCarthy's critics were certain that her uncertainty was a sign of unseriousness. Even someone like Isaiah Berlin, who claimed to admire McCarthy, told a biographer that "she was no good on abstract ideas. She was fine on life in general. People. Society. People's reactions."

Yet to have insight about people rather than about abstract ideas is part of having insight into politics. McCarthy was not a thinker of the type of John Stuart Mill, or Berlin himself. She did not spend her time articulating a full system of rights, or expound on the nature of justice. But insight into humanity is still a valuable skill for political analysis, as was what she would later call the "certain doubt of orthodoxy and independence of mass opinion." It was a particularly good skill for analyzing politics of the midcentury, in which large systems of abstract ideas—National Socialism, Communism, capitalism—brought humanity to disaster more often than not. In any event, it made her exactly the sort of person who could weather the intramural leftist warfare of the thirties. Standing outside any particular consensus had its value when the consensus holders were at each other's throats.

By the time she was tangled up with the Trotsky Defense Committee, McCarthy was living with Philip Rahv, one of the coeditors of the *Partisan Review*. She also sat on the *Review*'s board. Rahv was not a conventionally handsome man, but he had a dark, stormy sort of charm. He talked "pungently, harshly, drivingly, in a heavy Russian accent." He was also deeply steeped in Marxism, having come to New York during the Depression and stood on the bread lines. What McCarthy did not take seriously enough, Rahv more than made up for, and he was not afraid of insulting people as he made his convictions known. "He wasn't a particularly nice man," said Isaiah Berlin. He was "a pretty brutal guy in many ways," per Dwight Macdonald, another member of the *Partisan Review* set. But McCarthy saw him differently. When she gave his eulogy, she said she was drawn to Rahv because of a review he'd written in the *Daily Worker* of *Tender Is the Night*. While the review was mostly negative, McCarthy was struck by its "sympathetic insight" into Fitzgerald, chronicler of the rich. His treatment of the book had a "tenderness" she had not been expecting she said.

Rahv, McCarthy wrote later, had had to issue "a ukase on [her] behalf" to put her on the *Partisan Review*'s board. (A "ukase" was a proclamation made by the tsar in pre–Soviet Russia.) That is what it took to get a woman involved in the whole project. In the first issue, published in early 1934, McCarthy was the only woman on the masthead, and the only woman contributor. This mode of her intellectual arrival, she reported with some amusement years later, had made her nervous. The other men who ran the review were all rather more committed to those vociferous debates of politics than either she or they perceived McCarthy to be. The sour aftertaste of Communist Party discipline did not rescue the *Partisan Review* from all sorts of internal orthodoxies. Anxiety over ideological purity ran rampant.

> *The backer, a young abstract painter from a good old New York family, was so "confused" politically that one day he went into the Workers' Bookshop (Stalinist) and asked for a copy of Trotsky's* The Revolution Betrayed; *he was wearing spats that day, too, and carrying a cane, and the thought of the figure he must have cut made the rest of us blanch. "Did anyone recognize you? Do you think they knew who you were?" we all immediately demanded.*

As this episode indicates, the writers and editors who worked with the *Partisan Review* were all still relatively young, in their twenties and thirties. They were eager to prove their "little magazine" deserved a place in the world. Their anxiety often presented itself on the page as arrogance, and not the kind any of them had earned by some proper channel of apprenticeship. "Only in America, or rather in a tiny section of New York," of the 1930s, as McCarthy later put it, "could an air of supreme authority be assumed with so few credentials."

McCarthy was given the theater because the men doubted her. It was, in the lens of their youthful orthodoxy, a bourgeois art form, one they paid little attention to. "If I made mistakes, who cared? This argument won out." It proved a good match. She was largely left to her own devices, which meant she could teach herself to write. It helped that McCarthy tended to hate the things all the other critics liked, just as Parker had.

Overeager to prove her Marxist bona fides at the beginning, at first McCarthy evaluated plays by their politics, sometimes resorting to cliché when doing so. "It was a doctrinaire time, and everybody was engaged in 'smoking out' the latent tendencies in works of art, like F.B.I, investigators," she wrote. Reviewing an Orson Welles production of George Bernard Shaw's *Heartbreak House*, she noted his tendency as an actor to use "a kind of viscous holy oil with which he sprays the rough surfaces of his roles." Clifford Odets and John Steinbeck, meanwhile, suffered from "auto-intoxication," insofar as they "punctuated [their writing] with pauses for applause that are nearly audible." The one exception, the one play she actually liked, was Thornton Wilder's *Our Town*, "purely and simply an act of awareness, a demonstration of the fact that in a work of art, at least, experience *can* be arrested, imprisoned and observed."

In one of these reviews she was called to comment on a predecessor. The actress Ruth Gordon was putting on a play called *Over Twenty-One*, which was among the many attempts by playwrights to put a Dorothy Parker–like character on the stage. "The character of Dorothy Parker," McCarthy remarked, "belongs as firmly to the theatre as a character in Sardi's." The faint echo of Parker's wit, she thought, was the only reason an audience might enjoy the play.

McCarthy never met Parker, not really. She'd seen Parker up close only once, spotting her at a Communist event in New York. "I was disappointed by her dumpy appearance," she wrote. "Today television talk shows would have prepared me." In later years, as she grew older, people would insult McCarthy by remarking that she was stout, too.

McCarthy met Edmund Wilson for the first time in 1931, when he gave a talk at Vassar. She was not enthusiastic. "He was heavy, puffy, nervous, and a terrible speaker, the worst I ever heard, including a stutterer, years later at a New York meeting I chaired, who pronounced 'totalitarianism' in twenty-one syllables—someone counted." In 1937, he was being wooed by the editors at the *Review*, who all worshipped him and his criticism with a devotion peculiar to young intellectual men. Wilson was, by then, gracing the pages of just about every major publication in New York, usually as a book critic, sometimes as a journalist. His book-length study of symbolism, *Axel's Castle*—the book that brought him to Vassar—had made him into a proper public intellectual. The *Partisan Review* wanted a literary imprimatur to give a higher cultural status. Wilson could provide that.

McCarthy, ever the antagonist in the group, was not as liable to be impressed by him as her *Partisan Review* colleagues. Still, she was enlisted to go out to lunch with him, along with five other editors. He also asked that Margaret Marshall, the coauthor of "Our Critics," come along. Feeling the pressure, McCarthy became nervous and went for predinner daiquiris with another member of the board. Then she showed up for a dinner at which manhattans and red wine flowed like water. McCarthy became so drunk she fell asleep in a hotel suite with Wilson and Marshall, never telephoning Philip Rahv to tell him where she was until the next morning.

The episode was unfortunate. But somehow, she agreed to go out with Wilson a few weeks later. She ended up back at his house in Connecticut and succumbed to his advances on the sofa. Within a short time, McCarthy would leave Rahv and marry Wilson. She was always at a loss to explain this move. "I greatly liked talking to him but was not attracted to him sexually," she wrote in her memoirs.

Bad marriages are often mythologized in retrospect. An oft-quoted characterization of Wilson and McCarthy's claims it was a union of "two tyrants." Perhaps this overstates the case. The reasons the pair could not get along were, to say the least, complicated. Their son, Reuel, born in 1938, wrote a book about the couple in which he characterized the pairing thus:

Suffice it to say that Wilson, goaded by inner demons, was capable of boorish, cruel, and even violent behavior. McCarthy, who carried the stigma of childhood trauma— as a young orphan she was cruelly used by her guardians— reacted emotionally to her husband's frequent needling and criticism.

Before he ever met McCarthy, Wilson had been leading a rather chaotic romantic and sexual life. He liked very intelligent women—his first passionate affair was with Edna St. Vincent Millay, though she ultimately broke it off—but he had trouble maintaining relationships generally, including those with his children. He was financially unstable, his earnings coming only through freelance writing, and it was a source of continual stress. To add to all that, he drank too much.

When McCarthy married Wilson it was with the promise he would take her away from the city and she would live a quieter life. But whatever charms life may have offered in upstate New York, or Wellfleet, or Chicago—all places the Wilsons lived while they were married—they were somehow insufficient. She was unhappy. It surfaced in flashes of hysterical rage that Wilson's other child, then a teenager, characterized as "seizures." It was one of these fits, in June 1938, that saw her bundled off to the Payne Whitney psychiatric ward, where doctors diagnosed her with an anxiety disorder. In the second volume of her memoirs, *How I Grew*, McCarthy claims her fit was triggered when a drunken Wilson punched her. She was, at the time, two-and-a-half-months pregnant.

This is a shocking episode, and many have been daunted when they tried to sort out the details of it. One of Wilson's cousins, who had befriended McCarthy and seen much of the worst of it, told his biographer Lewis Dabney that to talk to the pair about their marriage was to hear "visions of reality [that] were as mutually exclusive as those of the characters in *Rashomon*." As in that film, there may ultimately be no way to reconcile the stories. In their divorce proceedings Wilson claimed he'd never raised a hand to his wife—"except once." Perhaps he was describing the incident that ended with the Payne Whitney. In any event, at the divorce hearing in 1945 seven years later, friends sided with McCarthy.

But there were two unquestionably good results of the marriage. One was her son, Reuel. The other was her transit into fiction. All her life, she would say that Wilson was the one who insisted she try her hand at writing it, feeling the work she'd been doing at the *Partisan Review* and elsewhere was too narrow for her talents. He lent material support too, hiring help so McCarthy could write even with the demands of a small child.

The stories McCarthy wrote while married to Wilson fit the compliment he'd given to Parker's work: they had the same quality of having been written by someone who felt an "urgent necessity to write." The first she'd publish was called "The Man in the Brooks Brothers Suit." It was the first tale of Meg Sargent, McCarthy's alter ego, which saw the character taking the train to Reno to divorce a first husband. On the train she meets a boring, married midwestern businessman. Ultimately she sleeps with him, but ambivalently, even with regret. Throughout the encounter, Meg Sargent is watching herself, evaluating her own actions. "It was true, she was always wanting something exciting and romantic to happen," she muses at the beginning. "But it was not really romantic to be the-girl-who-sits-in-the-club-car-and-picks-up-men." She does precisely that anyway, in part because she likes to make such exercises of her sexual power. Meg is pretty, but she is not precisely vain about it. She knows she is pretty only to a certain kind of American man:

> At bottom, she was contemptuous of the men who had believed her perfect, for she knew that in a bathing suit at Southampton she would never have passed muster, and though she had never submitted herself to this cruel test, it lived in her mind as a threat to her. A copy of Vogue picked

111

up at the beauty parlor, a lunch at a restaurant that was
beyond her means, would suffice to remind her of her peril.
And if she had felt safe with the different men who had
been in love with her it was because—she saw it now—in
one way or another they were all of them lame ducks . . .
Somehow each of them was handicapped for American life
and therefore humble in love. And was she too disqualified,
did she really belong to this fraternity of cripples, or was she
not a sound and normal woman who had been spending
her life in self-imposed exile, a princess among the trolls?

Rahv was presumably one of the "trolls" she meant, but he took no apparent offense. They knew the story would raise something of a scandal. Its explicitness was completely unusual for its time. That only whetted their appetite to publish it, and the payoff proved worth it. "I was at Exeter at the time," George Plimpton told one of McCarthy's biographers. "And it made almost as much an impression as Pearl Harbor." Men often complained that the portraits of themselves in McCarthy's fiction were too harsh. Though Vladimir Nabokov, who happened to be a friend of Wilson's, loved the eventual collection of Mary's stories: "a splendid thing, poetic, clever and new." A very young aspiring writer named Norman Mailer, still then at Harvard, loved it too.

Women tended to like the story because they related to Meg's independence of mind, to her self-assurance, as well as to her mistakes. "This was a feminist heroine who was strong and foolish," Pauline Kael remembered thinking at the time, when she read it as a struggling film writer on the West Coast. "She was asinine but she wasn't weak." The nuance was hard to capture. But the quality Meg had, of being opinionated and self-assured without quite being right all the time, was an uncommon combination in feminine archetypes. In films and books, women were only rarely permitted to be both brash and vulnerable.

The story was so successful that within a year of its publication McCarthy put out a whole book of stories about Meg called *The Company She Keeps*. It was her first book, and it met with some rapturous reviews, almost all of which made McCarthy out to be a kind of murderer by prose. "Its satire is administered as gently and as murderously as a cat administers death to a mouse," wrote the *New York Times* reviewer. The (male) books columnist of the *New York Herald Tribune* declared that he believed McCarthy had "a gift for delicate malice," though he also called Meg a "spoiled darling." At the *New Republic*, Malcolm Cowley himself took it on, at first seeming to dislike the tone of the book's first four episodes:

> Clever and wicked, but not quite wickedly clever; psychologically acute, but never seemed to go much below the surface . . . And the heroine who keeps such bad company is perhaps the worst of the lot—the most snobbish and affected and spiteful, the least certain that she has any personality of her own, or even exists outside the book that she keeps rewriting.

Reasonable people might differ as to whether Meg is snobbish or affected or spiteful, or merely young. Meg goes to see a psychoanalyst and discovers that most of her confusions and pretensions relate back to a horrific childhood—the "poor biography" she was always showing the door. She walks out of that office prepared to "detect her own frauds." Cowley saw, in a way other reviewers did not, how much this turned the whole book on its head:

> Miss McCarthy has learned the difficult art of setting everything down as it might have happened, without telling a single self-protective lie . . . "The Company She Keeps" is not a likable book, nor is it very well put together, but it still has the unusual quality of having been lived.

As Cowley may or may not have known, the book had, indeed, been lived. The autobiographical nature of the stories isn't really in dispute. Details were fudged, but not the essentials. Meg, like McCarthy, is a girl from the West. She has a dead parent and had a deprived childhood, but is trying to make her name in New York as a writer. Her marriage has fallen apart in the same manner McCarthy's first marriage did: there was another man in the picture. She has the same kind of first job, the same kinds of friends, and the same kinds of lovers as McCarthy did in her youth. "I don't think that she ever wrote anything else that was as true a confession," the critic Lionel Abel once said, though he was no fan of hers.

McCarthy was in any event up to something a little different. While nowhere near as self-lacerating as Parker's, her fiction tended to be critical. To the extent it reflected her own experiences, she was clearly standing outside them, evaluating them and evaluating herself, and then fictionalizing events according to the judgments she made. The self-awareness of the fiction was something entirely different from the tone of confessional work generally: something arch, aloof, honest but ruthlessly so.

Evidently, the technique suited her enough that she could apply it to more recent events. Another story she wrote while with Wilson and published in the *New Yorker*, "The Weeds," pried open certain painful parts of the marriage. The story begins with an unnamed woman ruminating in her garden about how and when she will leave her husband. She ultimately flees to New York City. The unnamed husband travels there and brings her back. The woman has a fit, and the narrator, in describing it, harshly analyzes her motives:

> *She was aware that she cut a grotesque and even repulsive figure, that her husband was shocked by the sight and the sound of her, but the gasping sobs gave her pleasure, for she saw that this was the only punishment she had*

left for him, that the witchlike aspect of her form and the
visible decay of her spirit would constitute, in the end,
her revenge.

The autobiographical elements of the story were self-conscious: McCarthy had shown an early draft to Wilson. He had no complaints about the way he'd been portrayed. After it was published in the *New Yorker*, he changed his mind. "And he was really quite mad. I said, 'But I showed it to you before.' And he said, 'But you've improved it!'"

In 1944, after seven years of fights and arguments that had inspired this series of brilliant stories, McCarthy finally left Wilson. A fierce divorce battle ensued, one that landed them in court. There were a lot of arguments over the precise size and shape of each spouse's respective wounds. As bad a marriage as it had been, even though it could have been called, emotionally, a catastrophe, it had somehow midwifed McCarthy's best work. It did not, in the sense of popular rhetoric, "make up" for anything. But it was the fiction, more than the reviews of plays long ago closed and novels forgotten, that would last. This brings us back to the party at Philip Rahv's in 1944, the one where McCarthy made the remark that angered Hannah Arendt. The stress in the background, the dissolution of the marriage, perhaps explains the flippant remark about Hitler. It was an unusual misstep for McCarthy, who was a seasoned hostess. In "The Weeds," the wife arrives in New York only to find her milieu changed; few friends return her calls. In real life, McCarthy had returned to New York in a position of strength. Her critically successful short stories made her a proper writer, far more an object of envy than her theater and book reviews in leftist magazines could possibly have done. Fiction, then as now, was viewed as the pinnacle of literary achievement. She was suddenly in demand and began to get offers to teach and took them up, at Bard and later Sarah Lawrence. She also swiftly turned around and found a husband who was much calmer, much less imperious than Wilson. This was a slender, dapper *New Yorker* writer with the alliterative name Bowden Broadwater, whom she wed in December 1946.

By this point, McCarthy had become a very particular kind of household name. She was known to the kind of person who followed literary journals and middlebrow magazines, but her books were not quite bestsellers. Still, suddenly people were noticing things like how she arranged her hair, her style of dress. "There was a period . . . when she seemed to me to be cultivating a sort of George Eliot plain look," one observer of such parties remembered. And her fame had begun to leak into the wider culture. *The Company She Keeps* was written up in *Vogue*'s "People Are Talking About" column. McCarthy was declared to write "like a brilliant harpy with a harpoon that she jabs around just for fun."

That argument—that McCarthy's style was pure malice—was everywhere. Reviewers always admitted she had a certain perceptiveness, a chiseled style. But they did not like what she saw when she looked at the world, or at least they found her somehow impolite for recording it in prose. They chose imagery that suggested they found her intelligence wounding, destructive, and perhaps catty. This was as true of people who knew McCarthy personally as of those who didn't. Her friend Alfred Kazin later called the book "deeply serious" but "as maliciously female as one chorus girl's comments on another."

Perhaps nothing about this is female. Perhaps nothing about it is malicious, in the traditional sense of the word. McCarthy's fictions had a satirical edge, but the characters based on herself were every bit as susceptible to her judgment and ridicule as the ones based on other people. They were, in other words, sharp. But they were not necessarily malicious, or off-putting.

There was one possible exception to prove the rule. After she married Broadwater, McCarthy began writing a novel, one that took as its subject the leftist-intellectual scene in New York, called *The Oasis*. It has a somewhat fantastical premise, sending a group of

Socialist-leaning intellectuals off to rural Pennsylvania to build a utopia. Naturally, the effort fails, in no small part because of the pretensions of the people who live in the colony. It is hard to see what exactly motivated McCarthy to write *The Oasis*, a project she dashed off quickly, in a matter of months. There was a fashion for political satire at the time, set off by Orwell's *Animal Farm*; perhaps that might have inspired her. In real life, McCarthy had just been through a disastrous attempt to organize, among American intellectual leftists, support for foreign writers. The whole thing had disintegrated in infighting. Perhaps *The Oasis* was meant as revenge.

"The whole story is a complete fiction," McCarthy argued years later, nonetheless. She meant the plot. The people in it, she admitted, were drawn from life. "I do try at least to be as exact as possible about the essence of a person, to find the key that works the person both in real life and in the fiction." Philip Rahv's essence was given form in a character named Will Taub. Taub is a leader of the group, but his bluster masks serious insecurities—over, among other things, his Jewishness. He is supported by a silent wife with whom he is "brusque and out-of-sorts . . . when she tried to think about social problems." (Rahv had by then married one of McCarthy's Vassar classmates, a woman named Nathalie Swan, who somewhat answered to that description.)

Abstractly, the novel is funny. Socially, it was self-sabotage. McCarthy poked virtually direct fun at many of her friends. A round of backbiting about the novel's apparent nastiness was set off among all the people who, through the years, had been connected to the *Partisan Review*. "The woman is a thug," Diana Trilling was said to complain. It is hard to understate the deep sense of betrayal many of those parodied felt. Rahv, in particular, was wounded. He held a meeting to discuss what to do, at which point many tried to talk Rahv off his high horse. But Rahv had his mind made up: he threatened to sue. He had a lawyer send a letter to its American publisher claiming the book "constitutes a gross infringement of his right to privacy, with such material that is utterly false, objectionable, and defamatory." Eventually he backed off, in part because his friends reminded him he'd have to prove he was recognizable as the silly character in McCarthy's novel in order to make the defamation claim. The prospect was unappetizing.

Worse, the book was not much of a hit. It referred to a world that was relatively insular, and certainly not one the general newspaper readership could possibly be expected to recognize. "Miss McCarthy's very accuracy is a drawback in writing a book for her particular set of concentric audiences," complained the *New York Times* reviewer:

> The inner circle is too small. The editor of a little magazine is not the Lord Treasurer of England. And readers outside that circle can get little from The Oasis except a vague sense of defamatory brilliance and a few fine scenes.

One person who read the book, knew the inner circle quite well, and still loved it was Hannah Arendt. A little while before, she and McCarthy had made up on a subway platform. "We think so much alike," Arendt apparently told her, five years after the fight at the party. And in a letter, she praised the book that everyone else had hated so much:

> I must tell you it was pure delight. You have written a veritable little masterpiece. May I say without offense that it is not simply better than The Company She Keeps, but on an all together different level.

One thing the book did, then, was bring the "characteristically perverse" McCarthy closer to the conscious pariah, Arendt.

It turned out to be a match made in intellectual heaven. They would remain friends, without interruption, until Arendt died. A long friendship between like-tempered women is not remarkable in and of itself. But the McCarthy-Arendt alliance had a distinctive tenacity. They were rarely in the same place, therefore much of the friendship took place in letters. These were gossipy letters, but the gossip was always tangled up with the intellectual matters they discussed, too, their views of friends' books, of each other's work. Ideas were all fine and good, but they were lived out in the world, and were tethered to the humanity of those who had them.

For much of the 1950s, McCarthy was living in various small New England towns with her son and Bowden Broadwater. She would write to Arendt to describe a visit from Rahv—he'd proved as quickly moved to forgiveness as he had been to anger over *The Oasis*—by remarking that "his Marxist assurance strikes me as antediluvian." Then she proceeds to talk about how "he made me horribly nervous, as if we were screaming at each other on the Tower of Babel. Not unfriendly, just estranged and mutually watchful. Probably it was my fault." She'd also complain about all the people who had cut her short at parties and talks. Meanwhile, from her apartment on the Upper West Side in New York, Arendt would write back with long, sympathetic disquisitions about those "burlesque philosophers." She'd add thoughts on Socrates, Descartes, Hobbes, Kant, Pascal, and of course, Heidegger.

They traveled across oceans to see each other, too. Arendt would join McCarthy in Europe while McCarthy worked on books about Florence and Venice. She'd ask McCarthy to "English" her work, as other friends of hers had done. After Arendt began living primarily in Europe, McCarthy would always stay in Arendt's flat in New York. They were, in spirit, inseparable.

Many of McCarthy's contemporaries hinted, or flat-out admitted, that they didn't know what Arendt saw in her. They were so different on the page, people thought: Arendt dense with complicated thought and McCarthy slicing and elegant. At least that was the nicest way it was ever put. Many thought McCarthy wasn't a thinker on the level of her friend. But Arendt didn't find her friend's intellect so obviously minor. She sent McCarthy manuscripts to consider and edit, as well as to "English," and their letters are laced not only with gossip and household reports but with arguments about what constitutes fiction, about the reach of Fascism, about individual morality and common sense.

As much as McCarthy and Arendt are retroactively lodged within this circle of men who explain things (the "boys," in the vernacular of the women's correspondence), the reality of the situation was more complex for them. They hadn't been accepted as "one of the boys." To the extent men admired their work, they were also hostile and defensive when confronted by criticism from Arendt and McCarthy. To be fair, neither one of the pair had much good to say about most of the men in their set. Of Saul Bellow, for example, McCarthy wrote to Arendt:

> *I hear that Saul is in poor shape again, attacking what he calls the American Establishment, meaning his crit- ics. He gave a lecture in London and the audience was asked to stay in its seats for ten minutes (or five?) after the lecture was over, so that no one would approach him for his autograph on the way to his getaway car.*

Of Kazin, who'd written an attack on McCarthy, Arendt wrote:

> *These people get worse as they get older, and in this case it is just a matter of envy. Envy is a monster.*

Of course, the formulation of these insults was not solely a mat- ter of feminine solidarity. Neither McCarthy nor Arendt would have accepted a definition of their friendship that took it as "feminist." They disliked other women in their set. They were eager to talk as women but would never have wanted to speak of their gender as a defining characteristic. Some of that had to do with the time they lived in. Some of it was the fact that neither fit in particularly well with anyone but the other. The bond between them was not built on a traditional sense of sisterhood. They were allies who often thought "so much alike," as Arendt remarked at the outset of their friendship. And that common way of thinking simply thickened into armor they could jointly use, whenever the world seemed to be against them.

6

Parker & Arendt

In the mid-1950s, after nearly two decades in which she published only intermittently and was consumed mostly with screenplay work, Dorothy Parker started trying to write seriously again. She always wrote for the same reason: because she was broke. But she was finding it harder, suddenly, to get work.

The trouble was political: Parker's name kept being knitted up with Communism. Parker's membership in the Communist Party is still a matter of some dispute. But she had written for Communist Party organs, and she had appeared at Communist Party functions. So just as the mood in America turned against Communism, her name kept coming up in government investigations. When the FBI first came to her door, in 1951, her dog kept jumping all over the agents. "Listen, I can't even get my dog to stay down. Do I look to you like someone who could overthrow the government?" she apparently told them.

Either they were charmed, or Parker was too daunting a target. The FBI never arrested her. Senator McCarthy threatened to call her up before the House Un-American Activities Committee, but he never did. The state committee in New York did call her up, and she gave polite testimony and took the Fifth on the question of whether she had ever been a member of the Communist Party. Ultimately, no formal punishment was dealt to her, by any level of the law. Nonetheless, the stain set in. Parker suffered for it, not so much with the public as she did in Hollywood. She suddenly lost what had been, for almost twenty years, a steady source of substantial income. Her personal life, too, became unstable. She had started to drink a great deal. She'd divorced Alan Campbell in 1947, then remarried him in 1950, then separated from him again in 1952. She'd eventually reconcile with him in 1961.

In the interim period, Parker, at loose ends, returned to New York. She set herself up in a hotel she liked called the Volney. She cowrote a play about lonely and increasingly elderly women like herself called *The Ladies of the Corridor*. She also began writing stories for the *New Yorker* again, though none approached the excellence of her earlier work.

There were hints she was losing whatever remained of her talent, and hints too that she knew it. One story, called "Lolita," published in the *New Yorker* in August 1955, appears to have been inspired by the Nabokov book of the same name, although it appeared weeks before the novel was published for the first time in France. Parker's "Lolita" also follows the events of a lonely single woman whose daughter is seduced by a male boarder named John Marble. Why this book so closely echoed Nabokov's forthcoming novel isn't clear; the best theory of scholars who study the matter is that Parker heard of Nabokov's manuscript from Edmund Wilson, who had read *Lolita* and disliked it. No explanation of this episode—either an extreme form of forgetfulness, or else her desire to compete with a rising intellectual Russian novelist—suggests that Parker was doing well when she wrote that story.

In any event, none of the things Parker was writing could hold the dimmest of candles to the popular success of her earlier work. She was no longer interested in or capable of writing the wisecracking items the public still expected from Dorothy Parker. She was, in short, depressed. Benchley had died of a heart attack in 1945. Alexander Woollcott had also died of one, two years earlier in 1943. New York was different from what it was in the twenties and thirties. Now, instead of being a bright young thing at a table of up-and-comers,

Parker was more of an éminence grise, a role she evidently found uncomfortable.

The only steady income she could arrange, in the end, was through a contract with a newly rejuvenated men's magazine called *Esquire*. She was a favorite of the managing editor there, Harold Hayes, and was offered a contract to write about books. It was the last bout of reasonably steady prose she'd produce in her life, sometimes missing deadlines but at least managing to file a few times a year. The resulting reviews don't quite have the concision of Parker's earlier Constant Reader work. They were more like meditations delivered from a wandering, elderly mind than the polished bullets of the earlier reviews. But traces of her humor remained. She used them, sometimes, to reminisce about her friends:

> *The late Robert Benchley, rest his soul, could scarcely bear to go into a bookshop. His was not a case of so widely shared an affliction as claustrophobia; his trouble came from a great and grueling compassion. It was no joy to him to see the lines and tiers of shining volumes, for as he looked there would crash over him, like a mighty wave, a vision of every one of the authors of every one of those books saying to himself as he finished his opus, "There—I've done it! I have written the book. Now it and I are famous forever."*

Her filing was intermittent, her editors sometimes complaining that there had to be a forceps delivery. But when she managed to write, she seemed to have fun. She praised old friends, like Edmund Wilson. She attacked old enemies, like Edna Ferber. When her editor asked her to look at James Thurber's *The Years with Ross*, published some years before, she wrote some of her finest sentences in years, remembering her old boss: "His long body seemed to be only basted together, his hair was quills upon the fretful porcupine, his teeth were Stonehenge, his clothes looked as if they had been brought up by somebody else."

She sometimes seemed to want to compete with the writers of the nonfiction books she reviewed; one sensed an eagerness in her to get out into the field and catalog its uncertainties again. One was a book about Aimee Semple McPherson by Lately Thomas, which she thought could have been much livelier:

> (His publishers admit that "Lately Thomas" is the pseud-
> onym of a West Coast journalist and writer. One is led into
> fascinating mazes of wonderment, seeking to consider
> whatever could have been the pen names he discarded.)
> Whatever his name, he has written a completely straight-
> forward and serious-faced account of a nationally—well,
> no, internationally—known case that might have caused
> him to go off at any moment into helpless laughter.

She also mocked, at length, the self-absorption of Kerouac and the beats. But once again she had a clear foothold in the glittering world. She was invited on television with Norman Mailer and Truman Capote to discuss the new young poets. She complained that the beat poets just went with a "deadly monotony of days and nights, round and round." She also averred that she was not really a critic, that at *Esquire* "I write what I think and hope to heaven there is no libel suit." A young *New Republic* writer named Janet Winn—eventually to become Janet Malcolm—caught the program and wrote it up:

> Miss Parker, who is no longer (if in fact she ever were) the
> "acid wit" of the stories about her, contributed little to the
> proceedings, but she made a very agreeable impression
> and reminded one vividly at times of Eleanor Roosevelt.

Parker continued to write the columns at *Esquire* until 1962. The last book she reviewed was Shirley Jackson's *We Have Always Lived in the Castle*, which she loved. It "brings back all my faith in terror and death. I can say no higher of it and her." These were Parker's last words as a reviewer. Alan Campbell, her husband, died suddenly, just a year after their final reconciliation. Parker began to seriously deteriorate. She wrote one last piece for *Esquire*, about the work of the artist John Koch.

> *To write about art now gives me a feeling of deep embarrassment which, in the long ago, I kept hidden under what was known then as "She's having one of her difficult days again, ma'am—screaming and spitting and I don't know what all."*

Parker would struggle on for another three years before dying in a New York hotel room in June 1967. She had had, by any measure, a brilliant career. All these years after her death, it is still so easy to identify her voice in a piece of prose or poetry; she was one writer who could never help sounding exactly like herself. In her will, she left her literary estate to the NAACP. But it was her "deep embarrassments" that have often been called her legacy.

In September 1957, a single photograph dominated most newspapers. It showed a fifteen-year-old black girl trying to walk to school in Little Rock, Arkansas. This girl wears a white dress and sunglasses, clutching notebooks to her chest, her face determined. She's being followed by a mob. Behind her a white girl's mouth is set in an angry jeer, as though she is midway through yelling a slur.

The young black woman's name was Elizabeth Eckford, and she was one of the Little Rock Nine, sent to integrate Little Rock Central High School after the decision in *Brown v. Board of Education* amid a national crisis provoked when the governor of Arkansas threatened to block desegregation. There was no telephone at Eckford's home, so she'd missed a message telling her that the other students planned to meet and walk together, with an escort, into the school that day. Instead, Eckford simply walked through the mob, alone.

Hannah Arendt saw that photograph and was moved. "It certainly did not require too much imagination to see that this was to burden children, black and white, with the working out of a problem which adults for generations confessed themselves unable to solve," she'd write later. But out of that concern for the child in the photograph, Arendt somehow developed an objection to school desegregation in general. She wrote her argument in a piece that a young editor named Norman Podhoretz commissioned for a new then-left-leaning Jewish magazine called *Commentary*.

When Arendt submitted the draft, though, her argument was disturbing enough that the editors began fighting among themselves about whether to publish it. First, they commissioned a reply by the historian Sidney Hook, and proposed to run that alongside Arendt's article to soften the blows of her controversial argument. But upon receiving Hook's draft they became indecisive again, and held the article. Arendt angrily withdrew it. Sidney Hook claimed later she was afraid of his critique. But as the fight over school segregation dragged on through 1958, she sent the article to *Dissent*, which published it in early 1959.

To understand the nature of Arendt's objection to school desegregation, you must also understand that by 1959, her political theory took a tripartite view of the world. At the top was politics, in the middle was society, and at bottom was the private sphere. In the political sphere, she conceded, it was not only acceptable but imperative to legislate against discrimination. But Arendt was convinced that the private sphere needed to be protected at all costs from any kind of government intrusion. She was equally certain that the social world should be left relatively alone by the government, so that people could manage their own links and associations with each other.

Somewhat incredibly to a modern eye, Arendt therefore argued that discrimination was intrinsic to a functioning society. When people discriminated in the social world—when they kept to their "own" while shopping or working or going to school—they were simply adopting a modified version of freedom of association, she thought. "In any event, discrimination is as indispensable a social right as equality is a political right," she'd write in her article.

Horrific as it sounds, she meant it out of a kind of myopic kindness. You can connect Arendt's approach with her notion of the "conscious pariah," though she didn't use that term in this article. Clearly what had bothered her about that photograph was the pathos of the girl walking alone to join a group that made it eminently clear it did not want her. This, to Arendt's thinking, was the wrong strategy. Rahel Varnhagen would never have submitted herself to that walk to school. Varnhagen would have been comfortable holding herself apart from the imperatives of a society that demanded she assimilate. And Arendt evinced clear anger at the parents she saw as forcing the child to make this doomed walk alone.

It was a shortsighted way of looking at the desegregation issue. And Arendt's argument did not go unchallenged in her time, to say the least. In fact, Arendt had made such a clearly objectionable argument that the article appeared with an editor's note in a box at the top of the page:

> We publish [this piece] not because we agree with it—quite the contrary!—but because we believe in freedom of expression even for views that seem to us entirely mistaken. Because of Miss Arendt's intellectual stature, the importance of her topic, and the fact that an earlier opportunity to print her views had been withdrawn, we

feel it is a service to allow her opinion, and the rebuttals to it, now to be aired freely.

The two rebuttals were by mostly forgotten academics. One, a political science professor, was very temperate in his criticism of Arendt, though he thoroughly disagreed with her argument. The other, the sociologist Melvin Tumin (who Philip Roth has repeatedly said inspired the character of Coleman Silk in his later novel *The Human Stain*), began with a cri de coeur: "At first one thinks, this is a horrible joke." Tumin continued in much the same horrified tone for the rest of his critique, which mostly marveled at the idea that a mind as fine as Arendt's could be arguing against desegregation. His arguments were forgettable, but it is remarkable, given how often she'd come up against tone arguments herself, how much he got under Arendt's skin. "Of my two opponents, Mr. Tumin has put himself outside the scope of discussion and discourse through the tone he adopted in his rebuttal," she began in the space *Dissent* had given her to reply to her critics.

Or perhaps, despite her reputation for rarely apologizing, Arendt was beginning to change her mind already. She would eventually have an interlocutor she could not help listening to: Ralph Ellison, the essayist and critic most famous as the author of *Invisible Man*. His first challenge to her came in a riposte to an essay by someone else, *Dissent*'s then editor, Irving Howe. Arendt shared with Howe a kind of "Olympian authority," Ellison remarked, that he would make clear neither white writer had earned. He would elaborate on his problem with Arendt's argument in an interview with Robert Penn Warren:

I believe that one of the important clues to the meaning of [American Negro] experience lies in the idea, the ideal of sacrifice. Hannah Arendt's failure to grasp the importance of this ideal among Southern Negroes caused her to fly way off into left field in her "Reflections on Little Rock," in Dissent magazine, in which she charged Negro parents with exploiting their children during the struggle to integrate the schools. But she has absolutely no conception of what goes on in the minds of Negro parents when they send their kids through those lines of hostile people. Yet they are aware of the overtones of a rite of initiation which such events actually constitute for the child, a confrontation of the terrors of social life with all the mysteries stripped away. And in the outlook of many of these parents (who wish that the problem didn't exist), the child is expected to face the terror and contain his fear and anger precisely because he is a Negro American. Thus he's required to master the inner tensions created by his racial situation—and if he gets hurt, then his is one more sacrifice. It is a harsh requirement, but if he fails this basic test his life will be even harsher.

The ideal of the pariah, who could withdraw from society and survive that way, was not available to a black person facing a racist South. Staying with one's own, drawing strength from that difference, was not quite so possible in the context of the African American experience.

It was a convincing argument, convincing enough that Arendt wrote to Ellison herself. She conceded his point: "Your remarks seem to me so entirely right, that I now see that I simply didn't understand the complexities of the situation." In an irony that Susan Sontag would later write about in a completely different context, Arendt had made the classic mistake of a person who looks at a photograph. She assumed the picture of Eckford told her enough about the civil rights struggle for her to launch a whole critique of its tactics.

After writing "Reflections" and a second piece that argued along similar lines, "Crisis in Education," Arendt seemed to recognize that she had to back down, at least a little, but she also kept reexamining the subject. She wrote that letter to Ellison. She also wrote to James Baldwin, after one of his essays from *The Fire Next Time* was first published in the *New Yorker*, to argue with him about the nature of politics. (She was "frightened," she wrote, of his "gospel of love," though she also said she wrote "in sincere admiration.") At least one black scholar still maintains that Arendt was "paternalistic" even in her curiosity. It does not appear she had any black friends, or that she was particularly immersed in the civil rights battle. At that point her star as an intellectual was already so high that when she pronounced on something, it was always with Olympian authority. Arendt would keep that authority for the rest of her life. She'd remain someone who typically pronounced from above. But there was this chink in the armor, and one that was about to get, by some lights, bigger.

7

Arendt & McCarthy

In 1960, Arendt wrote to her old mentor Karl Jaspers that in spite of how busy she'd become, her life filled with travel from one teaching appointment to the next and never having enough time to spend visiting friends, she was trying to clear a swath of time to go to Israel and watch a trial. "I would never be able to forgive myself if I didn't go and look at this walking disaster face to face in all his bizarre vacuousness, without the mediation of the printed word," she wrote. "Don't forget how early I left Germany and how little of all this I experienced directly."

"This walking disaster" was a man named Adolf Eichmann. In May of that year, he had been kidnapped in Argentina by the Mossad, the Israeli intelligence service, and brought back to Israel for interrogation and trial. Eichmann was such an important Nazi war criminal that the then–prime minister of Israel, David Ben-Gurion, had decided not to rely on formal extradition procedures to retrieve him. Eichmann had been a high-ranking SS officer in charge of the department that administered the Final Solution, but after the war, he vanished. Using forged papers, he fled to Austria, then used those papers to get the Red Cross to give him a passport. He had been living in Argentina, using an assumed name, since 1950.

Eichmann's capture was an international media sensation from the beginning, the drama of a kidnapping making for dramatic headlines. But it also came at a moment when the West was finally beginning to reckon with the Final Solution. At the war crimes tribunals in Nuremberg, the Final Solution was repeatedly referenced, and Eichmann's name often came up. But there was a feeling that Nuremberg had not fully reckoned with the monstrosity of the Nazis' specific crimes against the Jews, and it was felt particularly acutely in Israel. When Eichmann was charged with fifteen different offenses under Israel's Nazis and Nazi Collaborators (Punishment) Law is 1950, it was seen as a chance to rectify that wrong. The rhetoric ran high. When the prosecutor rose to give his opening statement, he claimed to speak on behalf of the dead. "I will be their spokesman," he promised, "and in their name I will unfold the awesome indictment."

There was very little doubt that Eichmann was, at a minimum, responsible for what the Israelis said he was responsible for. They had interrogated him for several months before the trial. They had hundreds of pages of documents. But still, Eichmann pleaded "not guilty in the sense of the indictment." His argument was that he had only been following orders when he had coordinated the logistics that murdered millions of people. In fact, when called to testify, he claimed that "I never killed a Jew, or a non-Jew, for that matter—I never killed any human being." In sum, he claimed that his bureaucratic distance from the actual gore of killing was enough to remove his guilt.

His trial would last five months. Arendt was there on its first day in April 1961. By then, Parker's old friend Harold Ross had died, and his successor as editor of the *New Yorker* was a short, retiring man named William Shawn. Arendt had gone to him to ask if she could write about this trial. With Shawn she was much less loquacious than she was with Jaspers. She simply said she had been "very tempted" to go, and wondered if Shawn might be interested in an article or two. She had obviously gone in to the proceedings with the sense that the defendant had a "bizarre vacuousness." And as she watched, and later read transcripts for the portions of the trial she missed, Arendt was only more confirmed in that opinion. The emptiness of Eichmann fascinated her, and it was that emptiness that led her to what is now perhaps her most famous and controversial thesis: this notion of the "banality of evil."

Perhaps the best way to understand that phrase is first to accept Arendt's vision of Eichmann, an interpretation of his gestures and actions that later became controversial. But, to her, he was a puzzle, some lethal combination of pompousness and ignorance. She was fascinated by the excerpts of his memoirs that a German newspaper published, in which he related his origins and his position in what can only be called a most self-unaware manner. A representative passage primly claimed that "I myself had no hatred for Jews, for my whole education through my mother and father had been strictly Christian; my mother, because of her Jewish relatives, held different opinions from those current in S.S. circles." The tone of these passages both bewildered and amused Arendt. She complained that the comedy of these passages stretched right past the absurd into horror. "Is this a textbook case of bad faith, of lying self-deception combined with outrageous stupidity?" she asked. "Or is it simply the case of the eternally unrepentant criminal . . . who cannot afford to face reality because his crime has become part and parcel of it?"

In spite of all her bewilderment, in her "Eichmann in Jerusalem" *New Yorker* articles—published in 1962—and her subsequent book of the same title, Arendt made it clear she believed that Eichmann was monstrous. But she also believed that Eichmann's breed of self-deception was a general condition in Nazi Germany, an element of the mass delusion that made totalitarianism so powerful. The contrast between the grand evil and the small man was what struck her:

> *For all this, it was essential that one take him seriously, and this was very hard to do, unless one sought the easiest way out of the dilemma between the unspeakable horror of the deeds and the undeniable ludicrousness of the man who perpetrated them, and declared him a clever, calculating liar—which he obviously was not.*

Arendt had certainly put her finger on something, as far as the difficulty of coming up with a coherent theory of Eichmann's personality was concerned. In the half century since *Eichmann in Jerusalem* was published, his character and personal history have inspired a library shelf's worth of arguments, all in the name of litigating Arendt's claims about him. Proving Arendt wrong about Eichmann, by reference to the historical record, became a kind of crusade for many people. It has proved such fruitful soil because there is no clear answer. Silliness is in the eye of the beholder. The criticism was always motivated by a question that pressed just as hard as Arendt's argument, though: was Arendt somehow diminishing Eichmann's culpability for the Holocaust by suggesting he had not been clever or calculating?

The mainstream reviews argued that yes, she had diminished Eichmann's culpability. In the *New York Times*, the editors had asked one of the witnesses at Eichmann's trial—the judge Michael Musmanno—to review the book. He accused Arendt of "sympathizing with Eichmann." He claimed she was making a case for his innocence: "She says it was a terrible mistake to punish Eichmann at all!" She did not do either of these things, as most of the book's readers would admit. Her friends rushed to the letters pages to support her. Among them was the poet Robert Lowell, who wrote that he knew there would be better "point-by-point refutations" than he could provide but that he wanted "to say merely that my impression of her book is almost the reverse of [Musmanno's]."

Intellectuals tended to attack the book on different grounds. Arendt wrote a sentence in the book in which she observed that "the whole truth was that if the Jewish people had really been unorganized and leaderless, there would have been chaos and plenty of misery but the total number of victims would hardly have been between four and a half and six million people." She was referring to the Judenräte, the councils the Nazis set up in the ghettos they forced Jews to live in. Judenräte structure and duties varied from place to place, but among the duties they performed was keeping lists of Jews for the Nazis. Sometimes, they even directed the police how to round Jews up for transportation to concentration camps.

In the early 1960s, scholars had only begun to write proper histories of the Holocaust. It took until 1961 for Raul Hilberg's *The Destruction of the European Jews,* still a widely used text, to be published. Hilberg was focused on the administrative machinery that had helped implement the Final Solution; accordingly, his book contained a detailed account of the Judenräte. It also contained a portrait of Eichmann as a very ordinary bureaucrat. Arendt read that book as she reported on the trial, and the facts it conveyed clearly had a deep effect on her. Hilberg's work was in her thoughts as she wrote that line about the number of victims that "would hardly have been."

But not everyone had read Hilberg's book, and Arendt's summation of it shocked many readers, particularly Jewish ones. They thought her too casual, and cruel; in our own time, she might have been said to be "blaming the victim." Arendt's view was more complex than her line allowed, of course. Even in *Eichmann* she went back and forth about it. She did refer to the "role of the Jewish leaders in the destruction of their own people" as "undoubtedly the darkest chapter of the whole dark story." But she had also written that questions of shared responsibility for the Final Solution were "cruel and silly." She was reaching for a position that reconciled both of those views, but she didn't explicitly connect them.

It caused problems. Arendt discussed these questions of responsibility because they came up at Eichmann's trial, but all her observations on the issue became far more explosive and controversial than anything said in the courtroom. Her critics accused her of wholly recalibrating the scales, of being too kind to Eichmann even as she was too hard on the Jewish people. Norman Podhoretz, now the editor of a new magazine called *Commentary,* wrote his review in tones of thunder:

Thus, in place of the monstrous Nazi, she gives us the "banal" Nazi; in place of the Jew as virtuous martyr, she gives us the Jew as accomplice in evil; and in place of the confrontation between guilt and innocence, she gives us the "collaboration" of criminal and victim.

Podhoretz was overstating the case. But his sense that Arendt had become morally distracted by the issue of the Jewish councils was widely shared. Another of Arendt's evergreen critics, Lionel Abel, writing in the *Partisan Review*, fastened on this argument too. The problem, as Abel put it, was that Arendt had found Eichmann "aesthetically" interesting and the Jewish councils, much less so. (In fact, she'd spent a great deal of her manuscript addressing the councils.) "If a man holds a gun at the head of another and forces him to kill his friend, "Abel wrote, "the man with the gun will be aesthetically less ugly than one who out of fear of death has killed his friend and perhaps did not even save his own life." All Arendt's interest in Eichmann, Abel argued, boiled down to his being a more interesting, fuller character for her book. It weakened her argument.

But it wasn't only Arendt's traditional foes who felt this way. Abel and Podhoretz were gesturing toward an argument about tone that her old friend Gershom Scholem would make to her outright. Scholem had known both Arendt and Walter Benjamin in Berlin, but he had become a committed Zionist and had moved to Israel in 1923. There he became a scholar of Jewish mysticism, especially of kabbalah. He maintained an occasional friendly correspondence with Arendt but when he wrote to her in 1963 it was in extreme disappointment. The problem he identified was, in large part, a tone problem. He felt the mood of the Eichmann book was too flippant. "To the matter of which you speak it is unimaginably inappropriate," Scholem wrote to her in a letter that was initially a private correspondence. In essence, he asked her to have a heart, and some loyalty to the Jewish people.

In her reply to him, Arendt surrendered little ground. She could not accept her critics' view that she lacked some essential compassion, what she would often refer to in her letters to Scholem or others as a lack of "soul." She also could not accept his premise that as a Jew she owed her people the duty that Scholem had implored her to accept. "I indeed love 'only' my friends and the only kind of love I know of and believe in is the love of persons," she argued. "I cannot love myself or anything which I know is part and parcel of my own person."

Scholem, who had asked if he could publish the exchange, surprised Arendt by handing it to *Encounter*. She had assumed he meant to publish it in Israel. But instead it appeared in a journal that was widely read by Anglo-American intellectuals. *Encounter* had significant funding that as it would later turn out could be traced back to the CIA's anti-Communist effort. Thus, as Arendt put it to Karl Jaspers, with whom she was back in touch, the Scholem letter "infect[ed] those segments of the population that had not yet been stricken by the epidemic of lies."

Arendt was not an easily wounded person. She could look at the avalanche of criticism with some bemusement and even detachment. Of Abel's review, she wrote to Mary McCarthy: "This is a piece that is part of the political campaign, it is not criticism and it doesn't really concern my book." McCarthy agreed. But she too viewed the occasion as one for political alignment, immediately volunteering to write a loyal rebuttal despite not quite having read Arendt's book yet.

The personal element in all of this was hard to escape. "What surprises and shocks me most of all is the tremendous amount of hatred and hostility lying around and waiting only for a chance to break out," Arendt told McCarthy. There is indeed little indication in Arendt's letters that she knew some of her set found her haughty and imperious, that Abel and perhaps others called her Hannah Arrogant behind her back, that Saul Bellow chose to express his distaste by

insisting that Arendt looked like "George Arliss playing Disraeli."
But Arendt was shrewd. All her writing, and all her theorizing, was
grounded not so much in abstract logic as in personal observation.
Very little got by her, especially when it came to the darker human
exercises of jealousy, pettiness, and cruelty. That people would let such
insecurities run roughshod over intellectual honesty could hardly have
been a surprise to the person who wrote *The Origins of Totalitarianism*.
For McCarthy, 1963 also began in a triumph that rapidly soured. However, McCarthy was much more inclined than the stubborn Arendt
to be devastated by it. Since the 1950s, she had been working on a
long novel. The project was repeatedly interrupted. But suddenly in
late 1962 the publisher William Jovanovich had become so obsessed
with the idea of the book that he offered her a large advance to finish it. McCarthy seized the opportunity and in September 1963, the
book, with its cover image of a chain of daisies, promptly became the
bestseller its publisher expected.

This novel was *The Group*, which follows eight women through
the 1930s as they make their way in New York as wives and career
girls in the brave new world that the decade was for this sort of
well-educated-but-not-quite-liberated woman. The famous Barbizon
Hotel, a residential dormitory for young women working in New
York, was established in 1927 in part to host the young women who
were suddenly filling the city's clerical ranks. To these women a job
was still a kind of finishing school, a place to wait until marriage
struck. McCarthy's chronicle of eight such women, worldly and yet
not sophisticated, was among the first books to tell these stories.
The Group's characters all fit types: the plain Dottie Renfrew; the
sophisticated Lakey Eastlake; the "rich and lazy" Pokey Prothero.
It follows them through romantic mishaps, births, triumphs, and
losses until 1940, when one of the group commits suicide. This
character, Kay Strong, shares a few biographical facts with McCarthy.
Many of the other characters shared traits with some of McCarthy's
Vassar classmates.

The Group does not quite work as a novel. The tone of the book is arch but uncritical; the clear intelligence of its narrator and the rather psychologically uncomplicated view it takes of its characters make for an uneasy marriage. Gone was all the acute self-examination that appeared in the early short stories and *The Company She Keeps*, and gone was the satirical, biting edge that had made McCarthy famous. Almost none of McCarthy's intellectual and literary friends could abide the soapy qualities of the book, its occasional flights into melodrama, and its relative earnestness. Robert Lowell prophetically wrote to Elizabeth Bishop that "no one in the know likes the book, and I dread what will happen to it in the *New York Book Review*."

Lowell was referring not to the *New York Times Book Review*, but rather to the then nascent *New York Review of Books*. In January 1963, Lowell and his wife, Elizabeth Hardwick, had paired with friends of his, the editor Jason Epstein and his wife, Barbara, to create it. They had very little capital to start a literary magazine, but at the time, New York was in the throes of a newspaper strike that saw the *New York Times*, the *New York Daily News*, the *New York Post*, and a host of other publications suspend operations for months. Their book reviews disappeared with them. The *New York Review of Books* came at the right moment to fill the gap.

No one in New York intellectual circles had been very fond of the books coverage the *Times* churned out, anyway. Like McCarthy some years before, and Rebecca West before both of them, Elizabeth Hardwick had once written a long critique of the state of book criticism. Published in *Harper's* in 1959, it has often been read as a kind of manifesto for the *New York Review*. Hardwick wrote:

> The flat praise and the faint dissension, the minimal style and the light little article, the absence of involvement, passion, character, eccentricity—the lack, at last, of the literary tone itself—have made the New York Times *into a provincial literary journal, longer and thicker, but not*

much different in the end from all those small-town Sunday Book Pages.

McCarthy obviously agreed with this view; over twenty years before she'd articulated a similar attitude in her *Nation* articles on "Our Critics, Right or Wrong." So when Hardwick and Lowell asked her, McCarthy volunteered her services to the fledgling magazine in early 1963, writing for no fee in the first issue about William S. Burroughs's *Naked Lunch*. Somewhat improbably, she was a fan, calling it the "first serious piece of science fiction."

It would be, however, the last piece she'd contribute for several years. For when *The Group* came out, the *Review* devoted two pieces to it. One was a relatively straight review, by Norman Mailer. The other was a parody, written under the pen name Xavier Prynne.

It can be difficult now to imagine the kind of position Norman Mailer occupied at this stage of his career. He had had precisely one big commercial success: his first novel, *The Naked and the Dead*, which was published in 1948. Then, after languishing for several years with novels both the critics and the public hated, he published a kind of essay-collection-pace-autobiography called, without a bit of irony, *Advertisements for Myself*. The book expounds at length about Mailer's personal desire for fame and a larger readership. "If there is anything in Mailer's new book which alarms me," Gore Vidal wrote in the *Nation*, assessing it, "it is his obsession with public success." The Norman Mailer of 1963 was, in fact, somewhat famous. But he was probably best known to the public for having stabbed his wife at a party in the fall of 1960, and consequently pleading guilty to assault.

He had had a personal run-in with McCarthy, too, in the fall of 1962. In theory, he was an admirer. He had read *The Company She Keeps* in college, and it had fitted with his own views of how a writer ought to behave on the page. "She was revealing herself in ways she never did again," he told one of McCarthy's biographers late in his life. "She was letting herself be found out." But he also said he never felt at all close to her until they both attended the Edinburgh writers' festival in August 1962. That year the festival was notably raucous. "The most striking fact was the number of lunatics both on the platform and in the public," McCarthy wrote to Arendt. "I confess I enjoyed it enormously." In the middle of the insanity, Mailer, in a pugilistic mood, had challenged McCarthy to a debate on the BBC. She declined, and he became angry.

So when the editors of the *New York Review of Books* commissioned him to review *The Group*, they must have known what to expect.

> *She is simply not a good enough woman to write a major novel; not yet; she has failed, she has failed from the center out, she failed out of vanity, the accumulated vanity of being over-praised through the years for too little and so being pleased with herself for too little; she failed out of profound timidity—like any good Catholic-born she is afraid to unloose the demons; she failed out of snobbery— if compassion for her characters is beginning to stir at last in this book, she can still not approve of anyone who is incapable of performing the small act exquisitely well; she failed by an act of the imagination; she is, when all is said, a bit of a duncey broad herself, there is something cockeyed in her vision and self-satisfied in her demands and this contributes to the failure of her style.*

McCarthy was not surprised that Mailer would dislike the book. She was far more worried about what exactly had been going on in the minds of Elizabeth Hardwick and the *Review*'s managing editor, Robert Silvers, who were the two people she knew had commissioned the review. The week before the Mailer review, in fact, the *Review* had printed that Xavier Prynne parody of *The Group*, which had taken McCarthy to task for the same sins as Mailer. The details of the parody are best left to those who read *The Group* with a fine-tooth comb, as evidently Prynne did. The important thing to remember is what eventually McCarthy discovered: that Xavier Prynne was in fact Elizabeth Hardwick.

Hardwick was slightly younger than McCarthy. She was originally from Lexington, Kentucky, and when she arrived in New York in 1939, it was as a graduate student. Like McCarthy, she had a reputation for carrying extreme politeness with devastating malice. This was not the only thing they had in common. Not long after she began to fraternize with the *Partisan Review* crowd, Hardwick found herself becoming Philip Rahv's lover. Many of Hardwick's accomplishments have that quality, of coming later to something McCarthy had achieved first. But at least until this episode of Xavier Prynne, McCarthy does not seem to have regarded Hardwick as any kind of rival. They exchanged long, friendly, happy letters, right up to the breach.

Writers often critique each other's work in the ordinary course of friendship. Nary a volume of letters has ever been published that did not record some disagreement between writers, otherwise friendly, who simply didn't like a given story or poem. Nonetheless, in the history of twentieth-century writing, this move by Hardwick has few parallels. It is even stranger to consider that Hardwick had already written to McCarthy privately praising the book, if in somewhat guarded terms:

> *What I want to say is Congratulations. I'm so happy to have this wonderful book finished and so happy that you will make money on it as we all "knew you would!" ... It's a tremendous accomplishment, Mary.*

But while writing that letter Hardwick must have known what she was about to do. The parody was published less than two months later. "I find it strange that people who are supposed to be my friends should solicit a review from an announced enemy," McCarthy wrote to Arendt. "As for the parody, they have never mentioned it to this day, perhaps hoping that I would not notice it." She was especially troubled because apparently, throughout this time, the editors of the *New York Review* had been pestering her to contribute, and had she done so, one of her essays might have appeared alongside this condemnation of her work. Hardwick tried to apologize. "I am very sorry about the parody," Hardwick wrote a few weeks after it appeared. "That is what I wanted to say. It is hard to go back to the time it was done, but it was meant as simply a little trick, nothing more." It was not enough. For four years after, McCarthy didn't speak to Hardwick, or contribute to the *New York Review*.

This all raises an obvious question: could McCarthy not take what she dished out? A story also lingers in her biographies about Fred Dupee, one of the *New York Review* set, a now rather forgotten critic. He and McCarthy were at a party together, and Mary told him she'd heard he didn't like the book. As Gore Vidal told it:

> Fred, who was exquisitely polite, decorous, and noncombative, said, "Well, Mary, I don't like it." Then she made the second mistake. "Why don't you like it?" And he said, "Well, that's too much to go into, but you who have set such intolerably high standards for others must be ready to accept them as applied to you." With which she burst into tears.

McCarthy took at least some of the other criticism of her book in stride, telling her *New Yorker* editor that a letter full of criticism of *The Group* had actually pleased her: "I love you for taking all these pains to tell me the truth." It was, too, a giant bestseller. Hollywood came calling and made the book into a film just a few years later. It made McCarthy a truly famous writer, and it rescued what had been for many years quite regrettable personal finances.

But she also told friends she was sure the book had ruined her, that she even regretted writing it. She knew that to sell well was to inspire jealousy among the struggling polemicists and poets of her set. She also had a capacity for being wounded that belied all the formidable writing on the page. The poet Elizabeth Bishop may have been right about an observation she made after reading a first chapter of *The Group*, as well as an excerpt from Randall Jarrell's satirical campus novel *Pictures from an Institution*, which has a character based on McCarthy:

> *Oh poor girl, really. You know, I think she's never felt very real, and that's been her trouble. She's always pretending to be something-or-other and never quite convincing herself or other people. When I knew her well I was always torn between being furious with her and being very touched by her—because in those days her pretensions were so romantic and sad.*

And there was, after all, another novel published by a woman in the fall of 1963 that was getting all the proper intellectual laurels McCarthy had been used to getting herself. This was an avant-garde bit of work, whose resistance to the conventions of plot and character development made it the very antithesis of *The Group*. Its title was *The Benefactor*, and its author, fairly new to New York, was a woman named Susan Sontag.

8

Sontag

The very serious young Susan Sontag could not have made a more idiosyncratic debut as a writer. A *Times* reviewer called *The Benefactor* "a picaresque anti-novel," which though meant as a compliment could not have much helped its sales. The book follows a sixty-year-old male narrator, Hippolyte, as he wanders through a kind of bohemian life in Paris. His voice is digressive, self-absorbed. In her notebooks, later, Sontag said she had been trying to depict the "reductio ad absurdum of aesthetic approach to life—i.e. solipsistic consciousness," but perhaps in depicting solipsism she'd only managed to get too far inside her own head.

Not all readers can find their way into that kind of mind-set, which was likely the reason that *The Benefactor* was not a commercial success. Still, when Sontag's publisher sent it to Arendt to get her impressions, Arendt wrote with high praise:

> *I just finished Miss Sonntag's [sic] novel and I think it is extraordinarily good. My sincere congratulations: you may have discovered there a major writer. Of course, she is quite original and she has learnt to use her originality in the French school. Which is fine. I especially admired her strict consistency, she never lets her fancy go wild, and how she can make a real story out of dreams and thoughts . . . I really was delighted! And I shall be glad to come to the publication party.*

It's not clear how much of Arendt's work Sontag had read by then. She did not list *The Origins of Totalitarianism* or in fact any of Arendt's work among the books she intended to read in the notebooks she kept. Still, in the archives Sontag donated to UCLA, there is a marked-up copy of *Rahel Varnhagen*, the margins full of the penciled exclamation: "HA!" (Sontag was perhaps the only person in history who found Arendt's prose persona funny.) She had become an admirer of Arendt's by the time the two met. In fact, by 1967, Mary McCarthy was teasing Arendt about the way Sontag was hoping to drum up a friendship:

> When I last watched her at the Lowells', it was clear she
> was going to seek to conquer you. Or that she had fallen
> in love with you—the same thing. Anyway, did she?

The observation was playful, but McCarthy and Sontag were destined to be set up as rivals. An oft-repeated story has McCarthy referring to Sontag as "the imitation me." In its most dramatic form, the tale has McCarthy approaching Sontag at a party in those early years of the sixties, and saying something like: "I hear you're the new me." It is not clear whether this ever happened. Sontag wrote of hearing this story herself, but also said she didn't remember McCarthy saying it to her directly. She told McCarthy's biographers she never could pin down where or when McCarthy was supposed to have said this.

In a 1964 entry in her journals, Sontag simply left a neutral sketch of her elder, and not in terms that suggested real antagonism, at least not at first:

> Mary McCarthy's grin—grey hair—low-fashion red + blue
> print suit. Clubwoman gossip. She is [her novel] The Group.
> She's nice to her husband.

This first meeting, Sontag said later, must have been at the Lowells'. What she remembered of the encounter was one simple exchange, neither quite complimentary nor quite insulting. McCarthy observed that Sontag was clearly not from New York.

"No, actually I'm not. Although I've always wanted to live here, I feel very much I'm not from here. But how did you know?" Sontag said she replied.

"Because you smile too much," McCarthy said.

One can only imagine this remark brought an end to the subject. "Mary McCarthy can do anything with her smile," Sontag wrote in a notebook. "She can even smile with it." But she was, at least at the beginning, somewhat kind to Sontag. In 1964, McCarthy wrote to her friends, including Sonia Orwell, to introduce Sontag to intellectual sorts in Europe. She frequently had Sontag over for dinner in New York; extending further social niceties must have seemed only natural to McCarthy. Still, after one such dinner she included a postscript that must have lightly reminded Sontag that in the world of New York intellectuals, a world Sontag had long wanted to join, she was still an upstart:

> P.S. I realize I misspelled your name in the letter I wrote Sonia [Orwell]. With two n's. So please ask for Sonntag too at American Express.

McCarthy had been partly wrong about Sontag's origins, as it happened. Sontag was born in New York in 1933, and as a child lived on Long Island for some time with her grandparents. Her mother, Mildred Rosenblatt, had been staying with them when she gave birth to Sontag because she did not want to give birth in China, where her husband, Jack Rosenblatt, was working.

Like Dorothy Parker's father, Jack Rosenblatt worked in furs. He had a moderately successful manufacturing partnership in Shanghai. As a young man, however, he had caught tuberculosis, a disease that would kill him before Sontag was five. It took a year before Mildred Rosenblatt could bring herself to tell Sontag and her sister, Judith, that their father was dead. He consequently became a figure of great pathos to Sontag, so much so that in a short story she confessed, "I still weep in any movie with a scene in which a father returns home after a long desperate absence, at the moment when he hugs his child. Or children." Mildred, on the other hand, was if anything a suffocating presence. At some point, she became an alcoholic, one who was heavily dependent on her elder daughter for validation and support. One of Sontag's early journal entries catches her, at fifteen, preoccupied with her mother's happiness to an exorbitant degree: "All I can think of is Mother, how pretty she is, what smooth skin she has, how she loves me."

By then her mother was married again, this time to a decorated army pilot named Nathan Sontag. Both Sontag and her sister, Judith, took on his name, though he did not adopt them. The family lived first in Tucson and then in Los Angeles, where Sontag attended North Hollywood High School. It is fair to say that Susan Sontag, even as an adolescent, did not feel cut out for the wide spaces and long idling hours of the West. In almost every autobiographical fragment she left behind, published or unpublished, her restlessness is apparent. "I felt I was slumming in my own life," she once wrote. She did not fit in.

In Los Angeles, she sought out the one reasonable bookstore on Hollywood Boulevard, the Pickwick bookshop. Reading was her first means of escape. In her prose she would often give books the qualities of travel. She sometimes called books "spaceships." The comfort she took in reading quickly bloomed into pride, and then into a kind of self-defeating superiority: all her reading gradually alienated her from the people she had to deal with daily, her classmates and even her family. In "Pilgrimage," her one straightforward autobiographical essay, she says that Nathan Sontag often told her: "Sue, if you read so much, you'll never find a husband."

I thought, "This idiot doesn't know there are intelligent men out in the world. He thinks they're all like him." Because

isolated as I was, it never occurred to me that there weren't
lots of people like me out there, somewhere.

But the wider world, too, held disappointments. In "Pilgrimage" even a visit to the great Thomas Mann, whom Sontag deeply admired and who was then living in the Pacific Palisades, had "the color of shame." He liked Hemingway, a writer she could not really admire. He "talked like a book review." She was looking for ever higher states of exaltation and had trouble finding them. For Sontag, this would become a theme.

In search of the mecca where people spoke only of ideas and high art, Sontag began to read the *Partisan Review*. As the child of people who'd never been much interested in those subjects, Sontag had to go about learning a second language. A friend of Sontag's told a biographer that Sontag hadn't understood any of the essays in the first issue she purchased. In her later life Sontag was often characterized as intimidating or, as some people called it, pretentious. (Her friend the scholar Terry Castle recorded her as prone to bragging about loving the "lesser-known Handel operas.") But she had worked hard to acquire the fluency she would later have in avant-garde art. It had not come to her naturally, and perhaps that was the reason she prized it so highly. Her experience suggested that anyone who read enough could become enlightened.

Asked later to name people whose work had made her the kind of writer she was, she'd always name Lionel Trilling. Other inspirations would pile up later: Walter Benjamin, Elias Canetti, Roland Barthes. All Sontag's heroes wrote prose thick with allusions and references, every essay stuffed with proof of prior study. Their style entailed the projection of scholarship.

Perhaps, given all that, it isn't surprising that the single person Sontag always insisted she wasn't influenced by at all was Mary McCarthy. On this point Sontag was frequently emphatic: McCarthy was "a writer who had never mattered to me." One can imagine why.

McCarthy's writing was rarely about exaltation; it was usually tethered to social realities, social realities that Sontag never seemed to feel very comfortable either living with or writing about. But also, without quite saying it directly, Sontag was flagging that in the world of intelligent men she was seeking to join, she wasn't particularly worried about her status as a woman. In fact, she never seemed to worry much, in those early years, about how those serious intellectual men might receive her. She had traveled far enough already.

University would be the first chance she'd get to step out of her "slumming" life. She planned it carefully, graduating from high school early to get out as soon as possible. Sontag had wanted to attend the University of Chicago from an early age; it had a Great Books program that fitted her budding self-image as an intellectual. But her mother, perhaps not ready to cut the cord, insisted instead that for a transitional semester she try Berkeley, where sixteen-year-old Sontag arrived on campus in 1949. There, at the textbook exchange, Sontag met a tall young woman named Harriet Sohmers who would become a key figure in Sontag's young life. And Sohmers's pickup line was the kind of thing that would attract any young woman of pretension: "Have you read *Nightwood?*"

Shortly before she left high school Sontag had begun to worry that she was attracted to women. She had worked to suppress this impulse, dating men, professing attractions where she didn't feel them. It would be Sohmers who would introduce her to the active lesbian scene in San Francisco in those few short months at Berkeley, and Sohmers who would be the first woman she would really sleep with. She recorded the experience as nothing less than a liberation:

> *My concept of sexuality is so altered—Thank god!—*
> *bisexuality as the expression of fullness of an individual—*
> *and an honest rejection of the—yes—perversion which*
> *limits sexual experience, attempts to de-physicalize it,*
> *in such concepts as the idealization of chastity until the*

"right person" comes along—the whole ban on pure physical sensation without love, on promiscuity.

Opening herself up to sensuality, Sontag had a long affair with Sohmers, then one with another woman. She scrawled in the pages of the journal that she felt reborn. She reproached herself for having hesitated at her mother's suggestion of Berkeley, thinking she would have gone without these experiences had she not come to San Francisco.

For the rest of her life Sontag would date women and men, sometimes being coy about the precise label for her sexuality even though most of her important relationships were with women. This was a personal mode of liberation, a private one. She was always a private person, writing few memoirs. Even the "I" of her work, her recognizable voice, is not fleshed out as a person, the way Rebecca West's was. Her voice is a force of nature but one without any specifically personal experiences to report. There was much disappointment with Sontag for never coming out publicly as bisexual, or as a lesbian. But her reluctance to do so may never have wholly been about concealing queerness. She simply didn't share much in her public-facing work.

Eventually an acceptance letter from the University of Chicago came to Sontag at Berkeley, complete with the promise of a scholarship. Sontag was still determined to try out its rigorous program and arrived there in the fall of 1949. There were many professors Sontag admired at Chicago. She fell for Kenneth Burke, who as a literary young man had once shared an apartment in Paris with Hart Crane and Djuna Barnes. ("You can imagine what that did to me," Sontag told an interviewer.) But it was a man she'd meet in her second year there, Philip Rieff, whom she'd marry, just days after their first date.

If this seems an unlikely plot twist coming after those queer affairs in San Francisco, it was one Sontag tried to claim she'd chosen freely, out of love. There were plainly other motivations, though. In her first months in Chicago she had been reading a treatise by one of Freud's pupils, which in its opening pages claimed:

> *Our investigations thus far have repeatedly shown us that in the case of homosexuals the heterosexual path is merely blocked, but that it would be incorrect to hold that the pathway is altogether absent.*

And in a letter she tucked among her journals, Sontag told a high school friend that her mother's money from her father had run out, her uncle having squandered the business. "He needs all his money to keep from going to jail—there is no more for us." She was also likely to have to go to work unless she could find some other way to financially sustain herself as a college student.

Philip Rieff was eleven years older than his new wife. He had trained as a sociologist, and was working on a dissertation about Freud. He was said to be an enchanting lecturer, but he had a melancholy cast of mind. Sontag never said much about whatever degree of physical attraction struck up between them. But the intellectual bond was transformative. When first he asked her to marry him, she would tell an interviewer, she replied, "You must be joking!" He wasn't. The force of his desire led her to agree. "I marry Philip with full consciousness + fear of my will toward self-destructiveness," she wrote in her notebooks. It wasn't exactly the sort of thing written by a typical young bride, but then the whole thing was obviously a compromise.

At first, the partnership worked. The Rieffs simply "talked for seven years." Conversations continued through the day and into the night, out of the bedroom and into the bathroom. They began working together on his Freud book; Sontag would eventually claim that she had written every word of it. Meanwhile she completed her bachelor's degree and followed Rieff to Boston, where he had a job at Brandeis. She began a master's degree in philosophy, first at the

University of Connecticut. Then she went on to doctoral studies at Harvard. She also gave birth to a son, David, in 1952, before she'd even turned twenty.

In a reversal of the situation between Rebecca West and H. G. Wells—whose son was also born when his mother was merely nineteen years old, and just getting her sea legs—the marriage to Rieff was good for Sontag, at least at first. She was on track to academic stardom. Her professors raved about her brilliance. She was ranked first in her class at Harvard. And a few years into what appeared on the outside to be a kind of intellectual idyll, the American Association of University Women offered her a fellowship to Oxford for the academic year of 1957 to 1958, which she accepted with Rieff's blessings—at first.

By then, the stability of life with Rieff had begun to chafe Sontag. She published virtually nothing when she was with him, just a limp review of a new edition of Ezra Pound's translations for the *New Leader*. Later, in her novel *In America*, Sontag's narrator would describe her realization, at eighteen, that she'd married a simulacrum of Edward Casaubon. Casaubon was a character in George Eliot's *Middlemarch*, the elderly husband of the novel's heroine, Dorothea Brooke, and her life is hobbled by her early attachment to him.

"Whoever invented marriage was an ingenious tormentor," Sontag wrote in her journal in 1956. "It is an institution committed to the dulling of the feelings." What had once seemed a marriage of true minds now became a kind of prison. Rieff himself was possessive, in her estimation, an "emotional totalitarian." Sontag felt she'd lost herself. To Joan Acocella, Sontag recounted one lonely memory of going to a movie theater to see *Rock Around the Clock*, a schlocky, enjoyable commercial film made to capitalize on the success of the song of the same name, a hit in 1956. She loved it, but she suddenly realized she had no one to talk to about it.

"It took me nine years to decide that I had the right, the moral right, to divorce Mr. Casaubon," the narrator of *In America* reports.

The year at Oxford was the end for the Rieffs. Sontag went alone; David was sent to his grandparents. After four months at Oxford, Sontag threw in the towel on academia and went to Paris instead to study at the Sorbonne and to experience French culture. There she met and took up with Harriet again, and through her met the Cuban playwright María Irene Fornés. By the time Sontag returned to Boston in 1958, her sense of self was sufficiently fortified to let her tell Philip Rieff at the airport that she wanted a divorce. She retrieved David from his grandparents, and moved to New York.

Fornés joined them there. One day the couple were sitting in Le Figaro Café in Greenwich Village, where they both discussed how they wished to write, but could not figure out how to begin. In Sontag's telling—there are a few versions of this story—Fornés said to her: "Well, why don't you start your novel right now?"

I replied, "Yes, I'm going to." And she said, "No, I mean right now."

That apparently motivated Sontag to leave the café, go home, and write the first three pages of what became *The Benefactor*. It was, she said later, a kind of "blank check." She typed for the next four years, she'd say, often with David in her lap. The composition process would long outlast the relationship with Fornés. By the end, David was ten, and Sontag liked to boast that he would stand by her and light her cigarettes as she typed.

Though it did not bring her riches, or even really good reviews—one of the odder compliments was that the book exhibited a "shrewd, serene, housewifely confidence"—merely publishing a novel made Sontag more confident in New York. At a party, she met one of the *Partisan Review*'s two editors, William Phillips. She asked him if she could write for the magazine. He asked her if she would like to write a theater column. "You know, Mary used to do it," he apparently said. Sontag had no interest in the theater, but she had a great interest in being published in the *Partisan Review*, so she said yes. She wrote two reviews, both of which digressed from their stated subject into her actual passion, the movies, before she found she couldn't continue. She really wanted to be a novelist, she told people. But the writing was on the wall. Dwight Macdonald told her that "no one's interested in fiction, Susan."

But people very quickly became interested in Sontag's essays. Her first big success was "Notes on 'Camp,'" originally published in the *Partisan Review* in the fall of 1964. "Many things in the world have not been named," it began. "And many things, if they have been named, have never been described." Camp, she argued, was a sensibility devoted to artifice, where style was slyly valued over content. The insouciant, winning tone of the essay matched the subject matter perfectly, and it caught on. Sontag had managed to define a trend, and that trend would in turn come to define Sontag.

Her star had been on the rise since *The Benefactor*: she had won a merit award from *Mademoiselle*, had published a short story in *Harper's*, and had been suddenly asked to write book reviews for the *New York Times Book Review*. But nothing had attracted the sort of attention the essay did. Sontag was elevated to the status of pop-cultural soothsayer. The notion of camp became so widely discussed it inspired a backlash. By spring, a writer for the *New York Times* had even managed to find an anonymous professional willing to denounce the phenomenon:

> *"Basically, Camp is a form of regression, a rather sentimental and adolescent way of flying in the face of authority,"* an anti-Camp psychiatrist told a friend recently. *"In short Camp is a way of running from life and its real responsibilities. Thus, in a sense, it's not only extremely childish but also potentially dangerous to society—it's sick and decadent."*

This sense of threat seems quaint now. The notion of camp has now become so mainstream and commercialized it is difficult to capture the radicalism of speaking of it outright in 1964. The New York intellectuals, for all their Communist politics, had made little room in their ranks for serious cultural outlaws. They were not fans of the beats; they had little to say about Allen Ginsberg. Queer culture was just about invisible to them. All that resistance was probably best summed up in a letter Philip Rahv sent to Mary McCarthy in April 1965, after *Time* magazine had favorably summarized the "Camp" essay, giving it a currency almost no little-magazine piece ever enjoys:

> *Susan Sontag's "Camp" style is very much in fashion, and every kind of perversion is regarded as avant-garde. The homosexuals and the pornographers, male and female, dominate the scene. But Susan herself, who is she?—In my opinion, above the girdle the girl is a square. The faggots love her because she is providing an intellectual rational for their frivolity. She, in turn, calls me a conventional moralist, or so I am told.*

"Notes on 'Camp'" was a reckoning with popular culture the likes of which had rarely been seen before. All the phenomena Sontag lists therein as "part of the canon of Camp" are high pop items: *King Kong*, *Flash Gordon* comics. The spirit of the essay was essentially democratic, liberating people from having to classify their own taste as either good or bad. Camp allowed for bad taste to be good, or in other words, it allowed people to have fun. "It's embarrassing to be solemn and treatise-like about Camp," Sontag writes. "One runs the risk of having, oneself, produced a very inferior piece of Camp."

The coyness there now is plainly calculated, but it's easy to forget that this younger Sontag was not the imperious, officious writer of her later essays. She was still figuring out her specific style, and in fact, put next to later pieces on Walter Benjamin or Elias Canetti, or to the book-length works of cultural criticism she'd later produce, "Notes on 'Camp'" doesn't sound like her at all. Perhaps that is one reason why, as her friend Terry Castle would remark, Sontag came to dislike the essay. Castle argues for deeper reasons, too: that Sontag's affinity for camp was too obviously queer, too revealing of her sexuality, for the later Sontag to be comfortable with it. And this concealment was something of a puzzle to the gay and lesbian people who read "Camp" in 1964, and could see what she saw in their community, for she wasn't truly fooling anyone.

"Against Interpretation," the other of Sontag's major first essays, would appear in the *Evergreen Review* some months later. At first glance it reads like a refutation of the task Sontag would spend the rest of her life working out. "Interpretation," it claims, "is the revenge of the intellect on art." This sounds like simply another way of phrasing an old idea, that critics criticize because they can't make good art. But the phrasing has a more palatable seductiveness to it, insisting finally that "in place of a hermeneutics we need an erotics of art."

Many draw a false conclusion from this, believing that Sontag meant to attack all writing about art. But certainly she did not quit writing about art herself in an attempt to live up to such a principle. The argument, she would say later, that she was trying to make was about the interaction of form and content in art, the way the rules of any given medium also impinge on "what it means." A simpler way of putting this might have been to say that for Susan Sontag, the acts of thinking and writing were erotic, sensual experiences in and of themselves. She tried to convey this by writing sentences that layered back on themselves, and she could make use of high-flying terms like "antitheses" and "ineffable" with alacrity, making them seem accessible, even beautiful. This was her chosen substitute for the chumminess of an "I" more willing to take a personal tone.

After both "Notes on 'Camp'" and "Against Interpretation" made waves, Farrar, Straus and Giroux, which had published *The Benefactor*, saw an opportunity and collected these critical essays into a book, published in 1966. The book, *Against Interpretation*, took its title from Sontag's celebrated essay. It was far more widely reviewed than her novel and gave the mainstream press a new opportunity to marvel at her. As an unsigned *Vogue* item put it, her work was "bickered over" as "either history-making or a daring sham." In the mainstream press, most of the reviewers felt that Sontag was a sham. One reviewer called Sontag "a sharp girl, a kind of undergraduate Mary McCarthy clawing her way through contemporary culture," just before panning the book. Another offered the following observation in the *Washington Post*:

> *As the author of these essays, Susan Sontag is hardly a likable person. Her voice rasps and is rude and strident. And there is nothing in this book to indicate that she cares very much what we think of her tone or her manners.*

Not all the reviews were like that; in the *Los Angeles Times* and the *New Leader*, the critics rather appreciated Sontag. But these personal comments were rarely mere asides. More often than not, the critic's entire opinion would be predicated on his or her personal image of Sontag. And as a result, from then on, Sontag's personality would become as much an issue as what she wrote. That vague property, her "image," would become as much a part of her literary reputation as her writing. Her publishers were often shrewd about this, making what they could of Sontag's undeniable, dark-eyed attractiveness. On the mass-market paperback cover for *Against Interpretation*—which had become an unlikely bestseller—the image was simply a photograph of Sontag, by the photographer Harry Hess. She is looking over her shoulder, off to the side.

It is difficult to overstate how much writing about Sontag is concerned with her appearance. Even in the most serious essays about her there is usually some remark about her looks. The mountains of ink may be summed up as follows: she was exceptionally good-looking. But I think she had a more complicated relationship to beauty than the raptures of bystanders and the fineness of her photographs suggested. Her notebooks are filled with self-exhortations to bathe more; contemporaries observed that she often looked unkempt, her hair usually swept away from her face but otherwise unstyled, fly-away. This was true even in media appearances; in one interview, her uncombed hair and lack of makeup contrast strikingly with the film director Agnès Varda's sleek bob.

Sontag also dressed exclusively in black, the standard strategy of those who don't want to have to think about what they are wearing. In later years, she was known to lift her shirt and show people her surgical scars. Though attractive people often have the privilege of not thinking about what they look like, there was something about Sontag's indifference that was genuine, unstudied. She liked that her looks got her places, but that was about as far as it went.

From the beginning, too, she worried about the image her pub-licists were trying to project. The photographs began to overwhelm the person. A British publisher offered to put out a limited edition of *Against Interpretation* featuring reproductions of Rauschenberg photographs, but Sontag nixed the idea:

> Is this the kind of ultra-chic occasion—me and Rauschenberg—that's bound to be written up in LIFE and TIME + will confirm that image of me as the "with it" girl, new Mary McCarthy, queen of McLuhanism + camp, that I'm trying to kill?

Fortunately or unfortunately, Sontag's resistance to It Girl sta-tus didn't win out. Her interviews repeated someone's quip that she had become "the Natalie Wood of the U.S. avant-garde." She would publish a second novel, *Death Kit*, but its reception wouldn't man-age to eclipse her growing fame as an essayist. Like *The Benefactor*, *Death Kit* has very little by way of plot; a Pennsylvania businessman spends much of the novel wondering if his memory of killing a railroad worker is true or false. The book is densely allusive, following a style then fashionable in France. Gore Vidal, reviewing the book for the *Chicago Tribune*, put his finger on exactly why it didn't work:

> *In a strange way, Miss Sontag has been undone as a novelist by the very thing that makes her unique and valuable among American writers: her vast reading in what English Departments refer to as comparative literature . . . This acquired culture sets her apart from the majority of American novelists, good and bad, who read almost nothing, if one is to admit as evidence the meager texture of their works and the idleness of their occasional commentaries.*

Critics as interested in the avant-garde as Sontag were few and far between. Instead, the press coverage stuck to the easier subjects. "If there were any justice in this world, Susan Sontag would be ugly, or at least plain," a female *Washington Post* reviewer remarked. "No girl that good-looking has any right to have all those brains." The feminist academic Carolyn Heilbrun, commissioned by the *New York Times* to interview Sontag, was so overcome that she produced an article without a single quote in it—"I must not quote her, for those words, too, crystalized, wrenched from the conversation which evoked them, become simplified, false." In theory this was flattering. The interview became a kind of prose poem about what Sontag was like, in the heightened rhetoric more appropriate to a celebrity profile than a books piece:

> *When I first began reading about Susan Sontag I thought: My God, she is Marilyn Monroe, beautiful, successful, doomed, needing (it is Arthur Miller's best phrase) a blessing. We have heard there are no second acts in American*

*lives. Death kit indeed. And the reviewers will look for
Miss Sontag in her new novel. (But she isn't there. It isn't
her book anymore, except in the sense that it's my book,
your book. She knows it's no longer the sort of book she
would like to read.)*

At the height of her fame Sontag agreed to be profiled by an
Esquire writer, to whom she remarked: "A legend is like a tail . . . it
follows you around mercilessly, awkward, useless, essentially unre-
lated to the self." There is always a bit of self-dramatizing in modesty
of course, and the only sort of person who can easily reject a legend
is one who knows she already has one to give away. But you can see
pretty easily that she was right: the persona of Susan Sontag, by the
late 1960s, had less to do with her work than could possibly have
been comfortable for her.

Nonetheless, Sontag's celebrity had its uses. Many of the male
intellectuals of the time became intimidated by Sontag's image in
the press. In early 1969, for example, out of the blue, she received
a letter from Philip Roth, the author of a new novel called *Portnoy's
Complaint.* He had just been profiled by *New York* magazine. In the
opening pages of the article, he'd referred to Sontag as "Sue. Suzy Q.
Suzy Q. Sontag." Apparently upon seeing his words in print, Roth
was seized with remorse and dashed off a letter:

> *Since, as you may or may not know, I've always been
> touched by your personal charm, and admiring of the integ-
> rity of your work, I'm appalled at the reporter's complete
> misunderstanding and misreporting of what I remember
> saying, and the spirit in which it was said.*

It was a gracious apology for what could only have been considered a very lightly insulting, erroneously reported, mention. But it
gave a sense of how large a figure Sontag had begun to cut, despite the

middling critical reviews of her actual work. She commanded enormous respect as a thinker and as a public intellectual. She could cow Philip Roth, who was not exactly known to apologize for himself on a regular basis.

As her star rose, Sontag was determined to move away from criticism and essay writing. She started a third novel instead. She took up film, after receiving an offer from Sweden to make art films on a minuscule budget there. And she dropped abstract criticism in favor of writing directly about current events. In 1967, the *Partisan Review* hosted the written symposium "What's Happening in America." Sontag's response to the questionnaire was a screed against the state of the country she'd never quite felt she belonged to, anyway; in insulting it she drew on metaphors straight from her California childhood:

> *Today's America, with Ronald Reagan the new daddy of California and John Wayne chewing spareribs in the White House, is pretty much the same Yahooland that Mencken was describing.*

Never one for rote recitations of patriotic values, Sontag went on to point out that if indeed America was the "culmination of Western white civilization . . . Then there must be something wrong with Western white civilization." The white race, she writes, is "the cancer of human history."

Once again, an essay in a little magazine was suddenly news. William F. Buckley, the conservative writer and founder of the *National Review*, lifted these and other phrases from Sontag's piece for a thunderous editorial. Sontag, a "sweet young thing," he wrote sarcastically, was simply pro-Communist. A horrified sociology professor at the University of Toronto could not even bring himself to print the name of the "Alienated Intellectual" who had written such a phrase out of her "self-destructive" impulses. The "cancer of human history" remark would follow her for almost the rest of her life.

But her work was then already beginning to travel beyond the pages of small magazines. In late 1968 Sontag traveled to Vietnam to have a look around on assignment for *Esquire*, which was then under the editorship of Harold Hayes. Hayes was eager to elevate the magazine from a men's fashion magazine to a literary force, and Sontag could help with that.

It was not precisely an independent trip. Sontag was the guest of the North Vietnamese, who were then in the habit of inviting prominent antiwar writers and activists to come see what was happening as a kind of propaganda effort. While Sontag disclosed that she had not really been able to see the country independently of her North Vietnamese guides, she did not meditate on the ethical quandary this might cause for her reporting. That said, she was careful to present the article not as an authoritative account of the current situation of Vietnam, but rather as a personal experience. For once, there was open confession of her direct experience of something:

> *Made miserable and angry for four years by knowledge of the excruciating suffering of the Vietnamese people at the hands of my government, now that I was actually there and being plied with gifts and flowers and rhetoric and tea and seemingly exaggerated kindness, I didn't feel any more than I already had ten thousand miles away.*

As this suggests, the resulting piece of writing—at the rough length of a novella, it was later published as a stand-alone book—was not so much about the Vietnamese as it was about how Sontag apprehended and reacted to them. Reviewing the book for the *New York Review of Books*, the journalist Frances FitzGerald likened the approach to being a patient in psychoanalysis. Sontag wasn't hoping to better understand the country so much as she was hoping to better understand the empire in which she already lived. She found herself, even amid what she found to be the goodness of the Vietnamese people, longing for the "astonishing array of intellectual and aesthetic pleasures" that her "unethical" home country possessed. "In the end, of course," she finished, "an American has no way of incorporating Vietnam into his consciousness."

Sontag was not, by far, the only American journalist to make such a trip and find herself stymied. In fact, just two years before Sontag landed in Hanoi, Mary McCarthy had done it and published the results in the *New York Review of Books*. Her analysis of the situation was somewhat more direct than Sontag's, the resulting book a less reflective document altogether:

> *I confess that when I went to Vietnam early last February I was looking for material damaging to the American interest and that I found it, though often by accident or in the process of being briefed by an official.*

McCarthy's directness worked against her, because in being so direct she was seen to be credulous regarding the claims of the North Vietnamese. McCarthy was also thought to have slipped up factually: FitzGerald, in her *New York Review* essay, delicately referred to McCarthy's failure to "do the work of a careful ethnologist, by keeping close watch over her evidence." Neither book was considered a triumph at the time. Sontag later seemed embarrassed by her book, saying, "I was really dumb in those days."

Still, McCarthy wrote to Sontag when her book was published, eager somehow to highlight the parallels in their thinking. "Interesting that you too were driven to an examination of conscience," McCarthy wrote, "Possibly feminine egotism . . ."

> *You will certainly be censured for writing about Susan Sontag, rather than about schools, hospitals, etc. But you are right, and more right, I think, than I in that you carried it further, made no bones about saying "This book is about me."*

The elder writer really did put her finger on something about Sontag's evolving style. In a notebook, ten years before, a younger Sontag had reproached herself. "My 'I' is puny, cautious, too sane. Good writers are roaring egotists, even to the point of fatuity." The Hanoi essay was an experiment for a writer who'd barely ever used the first person before. There was a new type of confidence in it. Even the critics who didn't like her—one *New York Times* writer, Herbert Mitgang, called her "last year's literary pin-up" in opening his review—had to admit she'd delivered a thoughtful piece of work.

McCarthy, for her part, seemed to recognize it. She added an uncharacteristically sheepish postscript to her three-page letter: "I'm assuming you've read mine. In case you haven't, the last chapter is where the stock-taking goes on." It wasn't an unfriendly letter but there was some air of light incredulity to it, an unspoken question: how is it that we keep meeting, in prose, like this?

In the meantime, Sontag was growing frustrated with her public reputation as an essayist. "I don't write essays anymore," Sontag told an interviewer in October 1970.

> *That's something in the past for me. For two years I have been making movies. And it's somewhat of a burden to be thought of primarily as an essayist. I'm sure that Norman Mailer didn't like being known for 20 years as the author of* The Naked and the Dead *when he had done a lot of other things. It's like referring to Frank Sinatra in terms of the "Frankie" of 1943.*

But Sontag couldn't get away from her "Frankie," either. The films she was making were savaged by critics. They were abstract, boring. What was more, they impoverished Sontag, who worked with small budgets overseas and rarely made any money doing them. Instead she went into debt, and within a few short years, she had to get back out again. Her self-confidence had taken a battering, she wrote in her notebooks, from the terrible reception of her movies. As a matter of making money she proposed books to Farrar, Straus and Giroux that she never finished: one on China, for example, that she told people would read like a cross between Hannah Arendt and Donald Barthelme.

She also began to speak more freely, suddenly, of feminism and the women's movement. Sontag's career had only just begun when the second-wave feminist movement began to get under way in the late 1960s. As an organized movement, feminism had been dormant nearly forty years. The energy of the suffragette had gotten squelched under the heel of the flapper, as historians came to see it—once the women's vote was secured, younger women in particular had difficulty relating to the struggles of their forebears. This meant that a woman writer wasn't asked, as she would be almost routinely nowadays, whether or not she was a "feminist." Parker and West had each declared sympathies with the suffragette movement, but feminists made few demands on them. For McCarthy and Arendt, there had been little question of involving themselves, as writers, in any kind of organized feminist movement. It simply didn't exist, for much of their careers.

But by the early 1970s, when Sontag was ascendant as America's most visible woman intellectual, the women's movement was in full, fervent swing, with marches and rallies and women's collectives springing up everywhere, especially in New York City. New York Radical Women, a collective formed by among others the critic and journalist Ellen Willis, was coming into prominence in New York itself. Consciousness-raising circles were the rage. And gradually, as those debates came to dominate the media, Sontag was expected to declare some kind of fealty.

In large part the New York intellectuals looked on the teeming, chaotic energy of the movement with disgust. They could not understand it. They mostly seemed to find it vulgar. And here Sontag began to show a streak of contrarianism not unlike that of the writer who was "never important to her," Mary McCarthy. She embraced it more fully and freely than almost any other member of the *Partisan Review* and *New York Review of Books* set.

The first time Sontag spoke openly as a feminist fellow traveler was in 1971. She appeared at a Town Hall feminist panel set to confront Norman Mailer over a disdainful essay he'd published in *Harper's* about the women's movement, titled "The Prisoner of Sex." Like a schoolboy, the forty-eight-year-old Mailer was still intent on attracting feminine attention by lobbing insults at women. The essay took Mailer on a tour of many of the major figures of the feminist movement, whose level of attractiveness he never failed to measure as he insulted and dismissed their ideas. During his travels he called Kate Millett, a prominent feminist critic and the author of the polemic *Sexual Politics*, a "dull cow." Bella Abzug, a lawyer and eventual congresswoman, was a "battle-ax."

Sontag was not on the panel but in the audience that night. She rose with a question for Mailer. "Norman, it is true that women find that, with the best of will, the way you talk to them [is] patronizing," she said in a calm, almost bemused tone of clear authority. "One of the things is your use of the word 'lady,'" she continued. "I don't like being called a 'lady writer,' Norman. I know it seems like gallantry to you, but it doesn't feel right to us. It's a little better to be called a woman writer. I don't know why, but you know words count, we're writers who know that."

Later, too, Sontag gave a long interview to *Vogue* in which she insisted she had herself felt the effects of discrimination in her life as a writer. The interviewer tried to say she had been under the impression, until that night, that Sontag "shared Mailer's contempt for women as intellectuals."

Where did you get that idea? At least half of the intelligent people I've known have been women. I couldn't be more sympathetic to women's problems or more angry

*about women's condition. But the anger is so old that in
the day-to-day sense I don't feel it. It seems to me the old-
est story in the world.*

As though to drive the point home, Sontag promptly published
an essay in the *Partisan Review*, originally meant for then fledgling
Ms. magazine. But Gloria Steinem's new venture found Sontag's
essay too didactic, so it went to the "boys" instead. They titled it "The
Third World of Women." Among the recommendations in the essay
was that women should engage in outright revolt against patriarchy: "They should whistle at men in the streets, raid beauty parlors,
picket toy manufacturers who produce sexist toys, convert in sizable
numbers to militant lesbianism, provide feminist divorce counseling,
establish make-up withdrawal centers, adopt their mothers' family
names." But she seemed to blow out her steam in that one essay; it
would be the only full, direct address of feminism she'd make in her
intellectual writing.

The essay project that stuck instead was something Sontag
dreamed up over lunch with Barbara Epstein in 1972. She'd just
been to see an exhibit of Diane Arbus photographs at the Museum
of Modern Art. She found herself ranting about them, and Epstein
suggested she write a piece about the show for the *New York Review
of Books*. Over the course of the next five years, Sontag would write
six of them, the essays that would eventually be collected into *On
Photography*.

One critic suggested that *On Photography* should have been
called *Against Photography*, because at times Sontag seemed to be
questioning the very practice of photography itself. "They are a grammar and, even more importantly, an ethics of seeing," she wrote of
photographs. And often Sontag did not see much to recommend in
those ethics. Photographs often presented themselves as reality, she
remarked, but there were always motives hidden in the way they
were framed. The widespread popularity of taking photographs, too,

came under fire: "A way of certifying experience, taking photographs is also a way of refusing it—by limiting experience to a search for the photogenic, by converting experience into an image, a souvenir."

To keep money coming in she also began to write regularly for *Vogue*, essays she would never include in her later collections. One piece, coauthored with then twenty-three-year-old David Rieff, counseled readers on "how to be an optimist" in 1975. Amid the advice: "Assume that we are born to die, that we suffer uselessly, and that somewhere, we are always afraid." A piece titled "A Woman's Beauty: Put-Down or Power Source?" urged readers of America's most popular fashion magazine to consider that "the way women are taught to be involved with beauty encourages narcissism, reinforces dependence and immaturity." She continues:

> *What is accepted by most women as a flattering idealization of their sex is a way of making women feel inferior to what they actually are—or normally grow to be. For the ideal of beauty is administered as a form of self-oppression.*

Whenever her feminist principles were challenged, Sontag had a habit of firing back tenfold at the person who dared challenge them. One such person was the poet Adrienne Rich, who had become deeply involved in the women's movement by the time she sat down to read Sontag's essay on Leni Riefenstahl, "Fascinating Fascism," in a February 1975 issue of the *New York Review of Books*. Rich noticed in the essay Sontag's claim that Riefenstahl was included in so many film festivals because "feminists would feel a pang at having to sacrifice the one woman who made films that everybody acknowledges to be first-rate." She wrote in to question why feminists were being blamed.

Sontag, taking clear offense, responded in the pages of the *New York Review* with nearly two thousand words about Rich's "flattering, censorious letter." She pointed out that her essay was not in fact about feminism, but about Fascist aesthetics, and Rich's willingness to point out only the part that bothered her was emblematic of the kind of blunt thinking in the women's movement that she abhorred. "Like all capital moral truths, feminism is a bit simple-minded," Sontag argued.

The two would make up later, by letter, agreeing they had some common ground worth exploring. "Your mind has interested mine for a number of years—though we often come from very different places," Rich wrote to Sontag. But Sontag would find herself defending the words of her exchange with Rich in later interviews. Most seemed to see in it proof positive that Sontag was against feminism, a belief that persisted despite what she had written about gender politics and feminism. At some point, she simply began snapping at interviewers. "Since I'm a feminist too, the situation can hardly be described as a difficulty between me and 'them,'" she told one.

But everything came to a halt when, in the fall of 1975, Sontag was diagnosed with breast cancer. Her doctors told David Rieff that she was not expected to live. It was a stage 4 tumor, and though Sontag was not directly told she was dying, she seemed to know the risks. She opted for a radical form of mastectomy in the hope that by removing more tissue than was required she might survive. It worked. Her cancer went into remission. The experience, however, changed her profoundly. The treatment, she wrote, left her feeling shell-shocked and worn, as if she'd been through the Vietnam War all by herself.

My body is invasive, colonizing. They're using chemical weapons on me. I have to cheer.

She felt, at the time, "flattened," noted that she'd become "opaque to myself." She worried, too, that in fact some of her repression—of her anger at her mother, of her lesbianism, of her feelings of artistic despair—had caused the cancer. She plainly knew such thoughts were irrational. But she emerged from the illness feeling the only thing to do was to purge herself of them totally.

The purging process was the writing of *Illness as Metaphor*. This long essay, published in book form in 1975, is not technically a memoir. Sontag discussed the way humanity had aestheticized tuberculosis and cancer entirely in the abstract, making no specific reference to her own treatments or to any personal experiences of sentimentality or cruelty from her doctors. But if asked, she would be quite clear that she thought of the text as a cri de coeur:

> *I wasn't in the slightest detached. It was a book written in the heat of rage, fear, anguish, terror, indignation—at a time when I was very ill and my progress was poor . . . But I didn't become an idiot just because I had cancer.*

Illness as Metaphor became the vehicle of complaint. Chiefly, Sontag's problem with the metaphors novelists and writers had attached to disease was that they tended to blame the victim, as she had, briefly, in her sickbed. She directed anger at "cancerphobes" like Norman Mailer, who recently explained that had he not stabbed his wife (and acted out "a murderous nest of feeling") he would have gotten cancer and "been dead in a few years himself." She writes of Alice James, younger sister of the novelist Henry James, dying in bed of breast cancer, some hundred years before. In those moments, though it does not employ the first person at all, the text is clearly personal, the anger palpable.

Many reviewers, the eventual *New York Times* book critic John Leonard among them, took Sontag to task for having used a cancer metaphor in the essay about the state of America. (Remember: the white race was "the cancer of human history" for Sontag back in 1967.) But they all saw the anger animating the writing, and even if they had reservations about the execution of the book, were compelled by it. In the *New York Times*, the Irish critic Denis Donoghue remarked:

> *I have found* Illness as Metaphor *a disturbing book. I have read it three times, and I still find her accusations unproved. But the book has some extraordinarily perceptive things about our attitudes: how we view insanity, for instance, or heart disease.*

Donoghue goes on to say that he finds Sontag's style blunt, that to her "writing is combat." This is meant, one thinks, as a criticism. But in terms of where Sontag started out, with her cerebral style and detached sensibility, it was an improvement. She still wasn't, for the most part, able to write in the first person. But she got mad. And people heard, behind all the layers of intellection, all the references to works of art and philosophers with which they might not have been familiar until she introduced them, the record of a very frightening and threatening human experience.

The serious style of *Illness as Metaphor* was in line with how Sontag always wanted to see herself: as a serious thinker. But always, always, it was "Notes on 'Camp'" that would follow her around, "Notes on 'Camp'" that married her name to popular culture. She didn't like that. Sontag's friend Terry Castle told a story of being with Sontag at a party in the late 1990s when a guest had the misfortune to tell Sontag he loved that essay.

> *Nostrils flaring, Sontag instantly fixes him with a basilisk stare. How can he say such a dumb thing? She has no interest in discussing that essay and never will. He should never have brought it up. He is behind the times, intellectually dead. Hasn't he ever read any of her other works? Doesn't he keep up? As she slips down a dark tunnel of*

rage—one to become all-too familiar to us over the next two weeks—the rest of us watch, horrified and transfixed.

The frustration with the way "Notes" dogged her was partly about wanting to get away from her youthful work. But she was also, evidently, genuinely disturbed by the way it had been read. In the eighties and nineties, she would witness a surge in intellectual interest in pop culture while high art began to struggle. She felt some responsibility, but of course it wasn't all hers. She had had fellow travelers in the advocacy of pop culture, not the least of them a film critic named Pauline Kael.

9

Kael

Pauline Kael had been waiting a long time for a break when Robert Silvers, the editor of the *New York Review of Books*, reached out to her in August 1963. It was a last-minute request, but would she mind reviewing a novel for the paper? The novel in question was Mary McCarthy's *The Group*.

Kael, only seven years younger than McCarthy, had long been a fan. She was just twenty-three when *The Company She Keeps* appeared—the perfect age to appreciate its sexual frankness. And by the time the enormous success of *The Group* rolled around, Kael had long been working as a McCarthy-like, gimlet-eyed movie critic, without the mainstream success or recognition. She was also, by then, forty-four, and clearly beginning to wonder if any ship from the East Coast intellectuals would ever come in. Nothing seemed to come easily to her, by then.

So when Silvers telephoned to assign the piece in August 1963, she immediately accepted. He wanted only fifteen hundred words, and he wanted it fast, but Kael felt she could do it. The only problem was that she did not particularly like *The Group*. The intelligence that had so attracted her to *The Company She Keeps* was entirely gone. As she put it in her draft:

> *As a group, the girls are as cold and calculating, and as irrational and defenseless and inept, as if drawn by an anti-feminist male writer. Those who want to believe that*

the use of the mind is really bad for a woman, unfits her for "life," miscellanies her, or makes her turn sour or nasty or bitter (as in the past, Mary McCarthy was so often said to be) can now find confirmation of their view in Mary McCarthy's own writing.

Kael knew something, by then, about what "the use of the mind" might do for a woman. She was often accused of being "sour or nasty or bitter." In fact, just at New Year's in 1963, she'd read a listener complaint on her radio show on KPFA, a Berkeley radio station. "Miss Kael," it began, "I assume you aren't married. One loses that nasty, sharp bite in one's voice when one learns to care about others." Kael reads this passage with the relish of a predator in perfect attack position. She unleashes a torrential reply:

I wonder, Mrs. John Doe, in your reassuring, protected marital state, if you have considered that perhaps caring about others may bring a bite to the voice? And I wonder if you have considered how difficult it is for a woman in this Freudianized age, which turns out to be a new Victorian age in its attitude to women who do anything, to show any intelligence without being accused of unnatural aggressivity, hateful vindictiveness, or lesbianism. The latter accusation is generally made by men who have had a rough time in an argument; they like to console themselves with the notion that the woman is semi-masculine.

The palpable frustration here was the result of experience, not political conviction per se. Kael was not, like Sontag, a prodigy immediately recognized as such by everyone who read her. She was a person who had to fight for the things she had. Her belligerent spirit was not always well received by onlookers, and even when this angered her, she didn't wish to adjust herself to meet their expectations of "caring about others" or anything else. It's plain she was hoping the brilliance of her work would be enough, as it would be for a man in her position.

For the first half of her life, it wasn't. Kael had the kind of intel-ligencence that seemed to alienate her from all but close friends, a quality she shared with Arendt. She wasn't good at cultivating relation-ships and struggled to get a foothold as a writer. As it happened, she had needed the younger Sontag's help to finally, after many years of trying, get the attention of the New York intellectuals who populated the pages of the *New York Review*. Sontag and Kael had met some months before *The Group* came out, in some forgotten place. The younger woman was evidently impressed by the elder. And so it was Sontag who brought Kael's name up to Hardwick and Silvers when they were looking for someone for *The Group*. Kael must have felt very grateful, at first, when that phone call came in: reviewing Mary McCarthy on her home turf, should the piece be accepted, presented a good opportunity for Kael to finally arrive in the place where she felt she deserved to be.

Kael had made it a long way from home. She was born in 1919 on a poultry farm in Petaluma, California. Her parents were New York Jews who'd moved to the area in search of a kind of progressive agricultural commune. They already had four children to raise by the time Kael came along. She spoke of her early years on that farm as an idyll, or as much of an idyll as could be had by farmers' children who had constant chores and parents whose marriage was troubled by financial instability and infidelity. The Kaels managed to remain in Petaluma only until 1927, when Isaac Kael lost all his money in a stock market crash and the family went to San Francisco, where he tried, and mostly failed, to come up with more steady work.

In high school, Kael's talents began to surface. She was a good student, played violin in the school orchestra, served on the debate team. Like Sontag, she went on to study philosophy at the University of California at Berkeley. But unlike Sontag, Kael did not

immediately leave California. She loved California. In a review of
Hud, she rhapsodized about the unself-conscious egalitarianism of
her childhood home. "It was not out of guilty condescension that
mealtimes were communal affairs with the Mexican and Indian
ranch hands joining the family, it was the way Westerners lived,"
she wrote. And San Francisco was cosmopolitan enough to satisfy her artistic leanings; it had so many movie theaters, so many
artists, so many jazz clubs. After college, she kicked around the
bohemian ends of the city, dreaming and working with a friend, the
poet Robert Horan, on various projects. Horan was gay and Kael
knew this, and even though the two were onetime lovers, according
to her biographer Brian Kellow, she simply wasn't bothered by his
attraction to men.

In November 1941, Horan and Kael moved to New York together
in the time-honored manner of aspiring artists: penniless hitchhikers
hoping they would figure out some way to support themselves on
arrival. Instead, they starved, sheltering themselves at Grand Central
Terminal. Horan went looking for work and was promptly taken in
by a gay couple he charmed on the street. Kael was not part of the
arrangement, and was suddenly left to fend for herself, Horan quickly
turning all his attention to his new benefactors. Perhaps it was no
surprise after that that Kael had trouble believing New York would
ever accept her.

In those first years, she had to work as a governess and a clerk in
a publishing house because her efforts to publish her own work were
all stymied. She watched the New York intellectuals at close range,
and held in particularly high esteem a journal started by Dwight
Macdonald, that friend of McCarthy's and Arendt's, called *Politics*.
But she could not break through. She blamed New York; she blamed
the scene. "The place is cluttered up with 'promising' young poets
who are now thirty-five or forty writing just as they did fifteen years
ago or much worse," she wrote to a friend. By 1945 she gave it up
and returned to San Francisco.

Back among the bohemian oddities of her hometown, Kael met a poet/experimental filmmaker names James Broughton. A man who spent his life, as he often explained, getting over an overbearing mother, he was prone to short love affairs rather than long commitments. He made tiny experimental films, like *Mother's Day* (1948), which saw a naked blond child wandering around as a woman's voice alternately praises and scolds him. Kael moved in with Broughton for a short time. When she became pregnant, he kicked her out and disavowed the child. Gina James was born in September 1948. Kael didn't put Broughton's name on the birth certificate.

The child changed things for her, as children always do. It meant Kael desperately needed a steady living, but she was soon forced into freelance work because if she were to leave home there wouldn't be anyone else to care for the child. She reviewed books. She tried her hand at playwriting. She wrote a treatment for a screenplay but it was rejected. The only thing that ended up working for her was meeting a man in a café who wanted a review of *Limelight* for his new little cinema magazine called *City Lights*. (This man, Lawrence Ferlinghetti, would go on to found City Lights Bookstore in San Francisco.) Released in October 1952, the film was a vehicle for an aged and doubled Charlie Chaplin, whose work Kael had never particularly cared for.

She wrote the review anyway, having something to say about the man himself. "The Chaplin of *Limelight* is no irreverent little clown; his reverence for his own ideas would be astonishing even if the ideas were worth consideration," she wrote. "They are not—and the context of the film exposes them at every turn." She called Chaplin a "Sunday thinker" who fit neatly into one of Socrates's observations about artists: "Upon the strength of their poetry they believed themselves to be the wisest men in other things in which they were not wise."

This, the first movie review Pauline Kael ever published, appearing in the Winter 1953 issue of *City Lights*, revealed several things about her. One was that she looked at a film in something larger than an aesthetic sense. Despite becoming known later in her life as a defender of popular taste in movies, a defender of visceral reactions, she had larger questions about them: about the quality of the ideas they represented, about the way they fitted into the larger puzzle of both cultural and intellectual life in America. Another was the exuberant energy that would eventually become the Kael trademark. She was not a critic who wrote too much in the first person. A tidbit here and there of her "I" comes through. But mostly her personality is in the vigor with which she analyzes something, turning it over, looking for clues. Another was that, interested in the mass audience as she was, she would never be afraid of kicking a popular phenomenon in the teeth. Chaplin may have been at the tail end of his career, wizened and grizzled, but he was still Charlie Chaplin, America's Little Tramp. But Kael's role as a critic, she believed, was to run roughshod over the politics of reputation. This did not make her popular.

On her first trip to New York, she was initially impressed by the way people dressed and their serious demeanor. "When I was a kid I thought there were a lot of brilliant people who wrote dull stuff because they were corrupt," she told an interviewer. "And it took me a long time to realize that most of them just couldn't write that much better." But after the *Limelight* review appeared, the doors in New York that had always been closed to Kael opened, just a crack. Suddenly she was getting enthusiastic responses from *Partisan Review* editor Philip Rahv, though he still felt some of her pieces were too long. And in Berkeley, she inherited the movie critic post at KPFA from a friend, the poet Weldon Kees, who first invited her on as a guest. "Pauline, let's start positively," he would sometimes say as they began the broadcast. But in 1955, he committed suicide, and the radio station offered Kael the spot. It paid nothing. But she took it and developed a following. She was always contrarian and always systemic. She, like West and McCarthy before her, sometimes liked to take direct aim at the preoccupations of other critics:

I would like to talk about the collapse of film criticism in this country, so that there are no intelligent guides, either for audiences or filmmakers, and about why our young filmmakers make spitballs instead of movies.

One of her listeners was a man named Edward Landberg, who ran a small movie house in Berkeley called Cinema Guild. A slightly eccentric man with a healthy dose of self-esteem and a stubborn devotion to his own tastes, he had built a small audience for his repertory house in a storefront on Telegraph Avenue, which played only films he personally liked. He called to say he liked the show. They began to date, and they married soon after, in December 1955. It is unclear how much it was a love match. What it was, clearly, was an alliance of two people deeply devoted to movies.

Even before they wed, Kael was basically running the Cinema Guild alongside Landberg. She became closely involved in the programming, but her big innovation was to add criticism to the circular flyers the theater would hand out on the street, hoping to attract patrons. Despite those flyers being marketing material, she was never afraid of taking shots at the big shots there, either. "Welles not only teases the film medium with a let's-try-everything-once over lightly, he teases his subject matter once over heavily" is how she'd describe *Citizen Kane*. This punchy style of summarizing films worked to sell them even as it mocked them. Through Kael's efforts, the Cinema Guild became popular enough that it could open a second screen.

But the union wasn't destined to last. Landberg resented his wife's stubbornness. No doubt she felt the same way about him. What put them on the path to divorce, Landberg told a documentarian, was that she had put a copyright in her own name on the circulars. By October 1960, he had fired her from the only successful job she'd ever had. Kael responded in rough kind. First, she took seven thousand names from the Cinema Guild's regular mailing list from the circular and put a resignation letter in her edition:

> For 5½ years I have written these programs, made up the displays and talked with thousands of you over the telephone. I think the Cinema Guild and Studio has been the only theatre in the country for which the taste and judgment of one person—the writer—has been the major determinant of selecting films. It is with deep regret that I must announce that irreconcilable differences with the owners have made my position untenable: this is the last program I will prepare.

When he sent out the full edition of the circular, Landberg blacked out this resignation letter. Kael then sued Landberg for fifty-nine thousand dollars in back wages and profits. She did not win the lawsuit, and Landberg retained ownership of the Cinema Guild, leaving Kael without an income yet again.

But by then she was at least beginning to have an easier time publishing her criticism. After her marriage to Landberg, Kael drafted the first of her great pieces, an essay called "Fantasies of the Art-House Audience," for *Sight and Sound*. It was the first articulation of what would come to be Kael's deepest insight as a critic. In brief, she believed that those who insisted on watching foreign films, who believed themselves to thus be watching a higher and better sort of art when they eschewed the popular movie houses, were full of it. And she was not afraid of attacking their darlings, among them *Hiroshima Mon Amour*, a film Susan Sontag had much admired.

Much of Kael's objection had to do with the script, by Marguerite Duras, which she found repetitive and finally too much about the female character's feelings:

It began to seem like True Confession at the higher levels of spiritual and sexual communion; and I decided the great lesson for us all was to shut up. This woman (beautifully as Emmanuelle Riva interpreted her) was exposing one of the worst faults of intelligent modern woman: she was talking all her emotions out—as if bed were the place to demonstrate sensibility. It's unfortunate that what people believe to be the most important things about themselves, their innermost truths and secrets—the real you or me—that we dish up when somebody looks sympathetic, is very likely to be the driveling nonsense that we generally have enough brains to forget about. The real you or me that we conceal because we think people won't accept it is slop—and why should anybody want it?

This is an unintentionally revealing argument. The exposure of feelings in art was and is a point much debated, because just as Kael points out here, the question tends to be gendered. Among women writers this is a familiar sort of war. There have always been those who insist that full-on confession of every flaw and feeling is the only honest way to write, and then those, like Kael, who would argue that it reinforced terrible stereotypes about women and gave voice to their worst qualities as intelligent human beings. But the savagery of the last line—the insistence that the inner self was slop that nobody sensible could possibly want to know about—could not simply be Kael talking about art or *Hiroshima* or Marguerite Duras. It had to be the statement of someone who believed this about herself.

The thrust of all her criticism makes it clear that Kael did not consider herself to be particularly sentimental. She would not have liked being posthumously sweetened by armchair psychoanalysis. She hated pathos. And yet, the odd sense of self-savagery is sometimes there in her frustration with opponents. She wants them to be linear thinkers, to be clear and direct; people who didn't think this way drove her crazy. She seemed to seek out writers who needed a healthy dose of common sense.

In what might have seemed like a paradox Kael also despised grand-scale theorists, people who provided not so much clear-sighted lines of analysis as myopic ones. In the 1962 piece "Is There a Cure for Film Criticism?" in *Sight and Sound*, for example, she dismantled Siegfried Kracauer, a German theorist who had written a long, turgid treatise on the nature of film. This she could not abide, nor the respect for it that seemed to her to contaminate movie writing in general:

> There is, in any art, a tendency to turn one's own prefer-
> ences into a monomaniac theory; in film criticism, the more
> confused and single-minded and dedicated (to untenable
> propositions) the theorist is, the more likely he is to be
> regarded as serious and important and "deep"—in contrast
> to relaxed men of good sense whose pluralistic approaches
> can be disregarded as not fundamental enough.

She likened Kracauer to boring suitors, the kind whose love doesn't appeal to their beloveds. If Kracauer was right about "cinema," she wrote, she was going to dump him. And this was just a warm-up to the blow she would deliver to a newish critic named Andrew Sarris, who had published an article in the Winter 1962–1963 issue of *Film Culture* called "Notes on the Auteur Theory." Kael found the thing so preposterous she promptly wrote the blistering reply "Circles and Squares."

One of the ironies of this famous exchange is that Sarris didn't invent the idea behind his modest essay. The auteurist theory came from the French, who had more or less invented film criticism. In brief, it holds that a film director has a detectable style that can be identified and analyzed even in the context of a commercial Hollywood production. In its simplest form, this idea is so unobjectionable that even Kael did not completely disagree with it. She, too, was prone to talk about a director as having a very high degree of control over the film eventually produced, a presumption she attached to the work of everyone from Charlie Chaplin to Brian De Palma. But what she found silly and pompous was the way Sarris had built it into a system for evaluating art, a kind of plodding, overly determined approach that she abhorred.

Sarris had largely opened the door for her by trying to identify clear premises of auteur analysis, which stated abstractly did sound rather dim: "The second premise of the *auteur* theory is the distinguishable personality of the director as a criterion of value." Kael pounced on the obvious weakness with a no-nonsense attitude: "The smell of a skunk is more distinguishable than the perfume of a rose; does that make it better?" This would become a favorite technique of hers, always presenting herself as more sensible than the pretentious critics she detested, never letting an idea balloon into a paragraph when a pointed sentence would do.

Kael was also not afraid to turn the latent sexism of writers against them. Sarris's essay had mumbled something in passing about an "essentially feminine narrative device," apropos of very little. "Circles and Squares" ends with a rhetorical bang turning the idea of "feminine" and "masculine" techniques back on him:

> *The auteur critics are so enthralled with their narcissistic male fantasies . . . that they seem unable to relinquish their schoolboy notions of human experience. (If there are any female practitioners of auteur criticism, I have not yet discovered them.) Can we conclude that, in England and the United States, the auteur theory is an attempt by adult males to justify staying inside the small range of experience of their boyhood and adolescence—that period when masculinity looked so great and important but art was something talked about by poseurs and phonies and*

sensitive-feminine types? And is it perhaps also their way
of making a comment on our civilization by the suggestion
that trash is the true film art? I ask; I do not know.

Sarris reacted like a scolded child: he complained of the injustice of these comments for the rest of his life. "Pauline acted as if I
were a great menace of American criticism," he told her biographer,
but his own feeling at the time was that he was little read, and even
less remunerated, and he had been attacked out of all proportion to
his actual influence. (His critic's post at the *Village Voice* would not
come until a little later.) What further confused him was that for all
"Circles and Squares" had laid waste to Sarris's ideas, Kael was not
personally angry with him. In later years, she'd often remark that she
found some of his other writings insightful. In fact, when Kael arrived
in New York the year after "Circles and Squares" was published, she
called Sarris and asked him out to dinner.

Sarris would tell a few different versions of this story—which he
wrote about more than once—but suffice it to say he was surprised
to get the call. He complained that Kael presumed he was gay (Sarris
would go on to marry Molly Haskell). At first, living in the farther
reaches of Queens, he hemmed and hawed about going into Manhattan. She said, "What's the matter? Won't your lover let you go?"
He also made it clear he found her abrasive and aggressive, and that
she talked too much about sex for his taste. They never seem to have
repeated the encounter.

The funny thing about this small feud is that while it is now
reputed to have held the attention of the film world for months
after, in fact there wasn't much of a kerfuffle at the time. Certainly
the mainstream press did not pick up the argument, and even the
chatter in film journals does not seem to have been particularly wide-
ranging. Other men had clearly felt targeted by that last paragraph—
mostly the editors of the British film magazine *Movie*, whom Kael
had ridiculed for being devotees of bad films. They complained that

she had implicitly tarred them as homosexuals in her last punch of a paragraph: "Were we to infer (with almost as little justification) from Miss Kael's fanatical feminism that she is a lesbian, that would be equally irrelevant to her capacity as a critic," they sniffed. But according to these editors, gender was relevant to one's capacity as a critic. "When Miss Kael says that there are no female auteur critics, she is right," the *Movie* editors wrote. "She could have gone further: there are, alas, no female critics."

This was a bad tactical move. Kael went in for the kill in her reply. She named a number of female critics, and asked, "And why that offensive, hypocritical, 'alas'—as if the editors of *Movie* regretted that women were not intellectually strong enough to support the rigors of their kind of criticism."

Heated letter exchanges in the pages of small journals would never have been enough to make this debate the eternal standoff it became. What kept it alive was Sarris, who over the years reheated the argument, dutifully panning each of Kael's later books, mentioning repeatedly his feud with her, which culminated in a ripping piece in 1980. She never responded. In 1991, she told an interviewer: "I've always been a little surprised he took it so personally." Brian Kellow, Kael's sole biographer to date, charges her with careerism for writing "Circles and Squares," a complaint that seems baffling in light of Sarris's profession of his own obscurity at the time. She couldn't have been trying to leapfrog Sarris, because by his own account he had no status as a film critic worth leaping over.

But it is true that the publication of "Circles and Squares" occurred on the cusp of a career change for Kael. The same year it appeared, 1963, she got a Guggenheim fellowship. She'd been recommended for it by, among others, Dwight Macdonald, who noted wryly in response to the request: "Despite your implacable harassment of me in print, I have, as a good Christian atheist, turned the other cheek and written a fulsome recommendation of your project to the Guggenheim people." This project was the compilation of the book *I Lost It at the Movies,* assembled from Kael's various essays for *Film Quarterly,* the *Atlantic,* and *Sight and Sound.*

But 1963 was also the year Bob Silvers commissioned the review of *The Group,* the piece that was supposed to mark her proper acceptance into the New York intellectual set. Kael finished a draft very quickly and submitted it. She hoped it would be an entry into the intellectual milieu she had wanted to belong to since her twenties. But Hardwick rejected Kael's piece by letter, simply saying she thought it irrelevant to criticize McCarthy about her treatment of women. Perhaps it was simply that Mailer had, by then, agreed to write a review for the book himself. But perhaps Hardwick was being sincere.

Kael was injured. She got word of the rejection back to Sontag— who did not keep her side of this correspondence—and sent her a copy of the draft review. Sontag wrote back that she had hated Mailer's take on McCarthy. "Too hard on her personally, and too easy, in a perverse way, on the book." But she thought there was room for improvement in Kael's piece, too, she said. She didn't think the arguments about feminism were the best attack on the book. "To me, what you say about the novel and the way character is developed, and the relation between fact and fiction is more interesting, and original, than your indignation—though I share it entirely—at McCarthy's slander on women," Sontag added.

Perhaps owing to this tidbit of encouragement, Kael saved the draft of the review. But it is also at this point that Kael stopped commenting on the relations between the sexes in her work. It just stops coming up the way it had in her previous criticism. People began to say and believe that Kael had no relationship to feminism because of that silence. One feminist critic who met Kael in the 1970s told her biographer: "I thought Pauline was deaf to feminism. Not hostile. It just wasn't something she could hear." This was probably true, as far as it referred to the formal second-wave feminist movement of the 1970s. But it's just as possible that having been told by someone she respected that these comments on gender were unserious, Kael simply accepted the premise and decided to go about the rest of her critical life with less of an eye to defending women as women. She could not let go of her desire to be taken seriously.

She did not quite let go of *The Group*, though. When she heard there was a film to be made of the novel, she promptly got herself an assignment from *Life* magazine to cover it. She incorporated her observations about McCarthy's book—chiefly the bit that accused the book of slandering women of intelligence—into her questions to both the film's director and its producer, Sidney Lumet and Sidney Buchman. She wrote that they didn't care much for the themes of the novel, though, and became alarmed when Buchman gave her his summary of its themes: "Higher education does not fit women for life."

> *Not being used to the role of an observer (I never did get used to it), I shot back, "What does? Does higher education fit men for life?"*

It would be some time before the producer got back to Kael with a straight answer. Evidently he felt education corrupted everyone, but added, "You know, Pauline, I don't know what the damn thing's about." She remained courteous about what she saw as the director's shortcomings, apparently, until a party held after the movie wrapped. According to the director, Sidney Lumet, in the midst of a heated discussion about the role of a critic, Kael burst out with: "My job is to show him [Lumet] which way to go." The piece displayed the frustrations its writer felt while writing it. It was so long and opinionated that *Life* refused to print it, and Kael had to put it in one of her books, instead.

When Kael's *I Lost It at the Movies* was eventually published in 1965, no one expected a collection of movie criticism to be a hit. But somehow it became a bestseller. The *Atlantic* published the introduction to the book, under the title "Are the Movies Going to Pieces?"

in December 1964. In it Kael was a town crier, complaining that the vitality was going out of movies. In part she blamed studio executives. And as usual she blamed critics who had become so abstruse and against meaning that they were defending films that made a fetish of technique without carrying any meaning. Kael singled out one writer for criticism:

> In the Nation of April 13, 1964, Susan Sontag published an extraordinary essay on Jack Smith's Flaming Creatures called "A Feast for Open Eyes" in which she enunciates a new critical principle: "Thus Smith's crude technique serves, beautifully, the sensibility embodied in Flaming Creatures—a sensibility based on indiscriminateness, without ideas, beyond negation." I think in treating indiscriminateness as a value, she had become a real swinger.

By then, the two women knew each other, so this was all very curious. To be fair, Sontag was not Kael's kind of critic. She did not write colloquially. And while not exactly a proponent of grand theories, Sontag was from every other available angle Kael's idea of a snob: interested chiefly in "cinema," in foreign films, in form and style over content. (It's worth keeping in mind that Sontag had not yet published "Notes on 'Camp'"—in which she betrayed at least some affection for popular culture.) And here, in print, more than a year after the strange transaction with the *New York Review of Books*, Kael kept shaking Sontag like a dog with a bone: "Miss Sontag is on to something and if she stays and rides it like Slim Pickens, it's the end of criticism, at the very least." As the critic Craig Seligman later noticed, Kael may have gotten to Sontag with that: The version of Sontag's essay that appears in *Against Interpretation* has a change in wording. Instead of praising "indiscriminateness," it praises a sensibility that "disclaims ideas." The slight tweak does move Sontag's argument out from under Kael's knife.

At any rate, Kael's argument caught the attention of the newspapers and when the full book appeared, the critics loved it. In the *New York Times*, a movie magazine editor raved that it proved "she is the sanest, saltiest, most resourceful and least attitudinizing movie critic currently in practice in the United States." He admired especially the way she summed up her approach in "Circles and Squares":

I believe that we respond most and best to work in any art form . . . if we are pluralistic, flexible, relative in our judgements, if we are eclectic. Eclecticism is not the same as lack of scruple; eclecticism is the selection of the best standards and principles from various systems. It requires more care, more orderliness to be a pluralist than to apply a single theory.

This was more or less how Pauline Kael would continue to write for the rest of her life, consistently inconsistent, tending to passionate riffs, insisting that the only principle worth defending was pleasure. Some people, naturally, found this "exasperating," as did a critic in her old haunt *Sight and Sound*, who complained about "the destructive emotionality of her polemical pieces." Nonetheless, the book was by any measure a success. Kael moved back to New York on the money it made.

For the first time in her life, at forty-six, she could make her living by writing. Her daughter came with her; the two lived on the Upper East Side. Kael threw herself into work, apparently sure the only thing that followed success was more of it. She had nabbed what looked to be a regular gig: a position at *McCall's* (where Dorothy Parker had written some forty years earlier), reviewing films for a circulation of 15 million subscribers. The editor hired her because he knew the audience of the magazine was changing, and he was hoping Kael's vivaciousness might attract a younger demographic. He signed her up for a six-month contract.

This man had perhaps not read enough of Kael's work previously to understand her project. Perhaps he expected that because she had once defended trash, she'd find some redemption in every trashy film. In any event, he would report himself horrified later, when he saw she had criticized one of Lana Turner's lesser films—*Madame X*—for casting the fifty-year-old Turner in a role she was far too young for. She would recommend something like Godard's *Masculin Féminin*, and then pan *Doctor Zhivago*. The final straw, widely reported in the media, was a review, ostensibly of *The Singing Nun*, which Kael took as an opportunity to trash *The Sound of Music*. She mentioned that most in the business now referred to this sort of musical as *The Sound of Money*, then continued:

> *Whom could it offend? Only those of us who, despite the fact that we may respond, loathe being manipulated in this way and are aware of how self-indulgent and cheap and ready-made are the responses we are made to feel. And we may become even more aware of the way we have been used and turned into emotional and aesthetic imbeciles when we hear ourselves humming those sickly, good-goody songs.*

This piece, coming at the three-month mark of the contract, was enough for the editor. When he fired her, the press leaped on it and claimed she'd been dismissed because of pressure from the studios. This would mark the first time, though not the last, that she would appear under the headline "The Perils of Pauline." Her editor made a kind of apology tour to the trade newspapers, primly telling *Variety* that "Miss Kael became more and more critical about the motives of the people who were making films, rather than sticking to the films themselves."

Kael recovered quickly, landing at the *New Republic* as a replacement for the rather more gentlemanly film critic Stanley Kauffmann, who had been hired away by the *New York Times* as a drama critic. At first it seemed a better match as the *New Republic* catered to an audience with a higher tolerance for intellectual disagreement than *McCall's*. But it paid far less, and within one or two pieces she was back having disagreements with her editors, who often cut at will from her work. The break came when a long essay she'd written on a new film called *Bonnie and Clyde* was rejected entirely by the magazine. She resigned and for just a moment it seemed she would be back to freelancing, making income piecemeal, all while she was nearing fifty. But then she was put in touch with William Shawn at the *New Yorker*.

By the 1960s, the *New Yorker* was no longer the simple humor magazine it had been under Harold Ross. When William Shawn took over as editor in 1952, the tone changed considerably. Shawn was a retiring man with idiosyncratic tastes, but when he really liked a writer, he *really* liked a writer. He would give such writers a spot at the magazine and simply let them have at it. Many would hold on to their *New Yorker* jobs for life, defining themselves against the regular run of magazine journalists. Writers that "Mr. Shawn" liked had a sort of tenure, a spot they could always come home to.

Kael had already caught Shawn's eye. A few months earlier she'd published her first piece at the *New Yorker*, called "Movies and Television," a long articulation of her complaint that television's flat style was infecting the movies. Shawn had liked it, and now, receiving the seven-thousand-word essay on *Bonnie and Clyde*, he liked that too. He published it in October 1967, even though the film was by then old news, having come out in August. While it had done respectably at the box office, as a matter of prestige it was a sinking ship, with reviewers taking it to task for glamorizing violence. Kael hauled it ashore. "How do you make a good movie in this country without being jumped on?" she wrote. The negative reaction had only proved to her that most people were hostile to art. "Audiences at *Bonnie and Clyde* are not given a simple, secure basis for identification," she argued.

"They are made to feel but not told *how* to feel." People might not have liked that *Bonnie and Clyde* made violence fun, but that didn't make the picture bad. It was a judgment on the audience, not the art. Kael still thought morality had a role to play, though. The film's "whole point," Kael said, was "to rub our nose in it, to make us pay our dues for laughing."

By now Kael had mastered her idiosyncratic form of film criticism. She kept one eye on what other critics had written, on the flaws and pieties of their logic; one eye on the audience and its reaction to what was being presented onscreen, because Kael believed that the experience of going to the movies was as important as the movie itself; and finally, a third eye was on the *fun* of it all. Fun might be a subjective quality, but Kael was sure it was the movies' highest value in a way the more high-minded critics—Sontag among them—were not. It subjected her all her life to accusations of crassness, of lack of caring, and of simplemindedness. But in her avowedly "eclectic" style, fun was the one thing Kael was consistently devoted to. She made it a credo.

Shawn, not normally remembered as a man inclined to *fun*, nonetheless liked her style in the *Bonnie and Clyde* review so much he asked her to become one of two regular movie reviewers for the *New Yorker*, a post she would occupy until her retirement. Having blundered her way out of several contracts recently, Kael asked for a condition on her employment: she wanted an agreement that her copy would not be substantially changed without her permission. Shawn gave it, but once Kael arrived at the *New Yorker*, he went back on his word and did what he did with every other writer at the magazine, going over her drafts with a fine-tooth comb. Kael fought with him about it. Among other things, her stubbornness prevented her from being very popular at the *New Yorker* offices. Shawn had set a tone of bourgeois propriety, and her fondness for swearing and "deliberately crude" prose—her characterization—was a perennial subject for discussion between them. They seemed to find a kind of truce in argument, as between the two of them. But others did not share it:

I remember getting a letter from an eminent New Yorker *writer suggesting that I was trampling through the pages of the magazine with cowboy boots covered with dung and that I should move out with my cowboy boots.*

Shawn stuck by her, although he would sometimes call in the night about comma placement. Kael was finally secure, and she continued to publish books that collected her reviews. Her second, *Kiss Kiss Bang Bang*, did almost as well as *I Lost It at the Movies*. It contained the piece she'd written about *The Group* for *Life*. But by then, having become a regular reviewer of movies, she had developed a reputation not just for exuberance but for cutting remarks. From her niche at the *New Yorker* she was busting up consensus right and left, and she tended to do so with a flair for drama. From the beginning of that gig it was clear she would be a force to be reckoned with.

Some people had more flattering ways of describing her approach than others. Kael sent a copy of *Kiss Kiss Bang Bang*, for example, to the silent film star Louise Brooks, with whom she'd long corresponded. Brooks replied, "Your picture on the dust cover made me think of Dorothy Parker when she was young in a moment of happiness." Waspish but happy seemed something like what Kael was going for with her persona in print. But Kael's enemies, a growing list, pegged her as too brash for the entire business. A headline in the December 13, 1967, issue of *Variety* read:

Pauline Kael: Zest but No Manners; She Tramples Down Polite Males

This was perhaps overstating it. William Shawn was definitely a "polite male." But he had a will of steel, and he didn't really want general essays on the state of the movie art or movie criticism and ran enough interference with Kael to prevent them from appearing in his genteel magazine. Kael, too, felt early on that she needed to settle into being a more ordinary sort of reviewer. In the 1960s she published just one more long essay, which ended up in the February 1969 issue of *Harper's*, titled "Trash, Art, and the Movies."

Just as Sontag's "Notes on 'Camp'" has sometimes been mischaracterized as a wholesale defense of camp, "Trash, Art, and the Movies" is sometimes wrongly described as a defense of trash as art. But Kael spends most of her time explaining that there are key differences between the two. She wanted to explain why, on a certain level, questions of technique are irrelevant:

> *The critic shouldn't need to tear a work apart to demonstrate that he knows how it was put together. The important thing is to convey what is new and beautiful in the work, not how it was made.*

This argument is not very far from some of the claims Sontag persistently made about the interaction of form and content. In fact, one way to quickly summarize "Trash, Art, and the Movies" is in terms borrowed from Sontag's "Against Interpretation." In "Trash, Art, and the Movies," Kael argues at length for erotics in the place of hermeneutics. As ever, she is interested in reaction, not aesthetics. Audiences respond most to the movies that please them, she says, even when they are trash and not art. But she also argues that art, in the movies:

> *is what we have always found good in movies only more so. It's the subversive gesture carried further, the moments of excitement sustained longer and extended into new meanings.*

The problem with the interplay of trash and art, Kael worried, is that increasingly it meant that people were willing to call trash art when there was no need. Probably few disagreed with her that this sort of sophomoric pretentiousness was damaging. Where Kael again began to run afoul of quite a few critics, most of them male, was when she classified the work of Hitchcock as trash, but then got angry with those who insisted that trash needed some kind of justification. "But why should pleasure need justification?" she asked. It was not that Kael couldn't see trash corrupting, on some level, the entire tone of the culture: "It certainly cramps and limits opportunities for artists." But she thought of it as a kind of gateway drug, in the famous formulation of her final line: "Trash has given us an appetite for art."

The analogy with Sontag's ideas about camp and interpretation is not one-to-one. Sontag had written that there was a kind of pleasure in analysis, in the taking apart and putting back together of things, something that Kael could never abide. Sontag believed in a less popularized version of pleasure and could not have cared less about how the average moviegoer encountered the higher values; an admission of pure enjoyment of trash—unmediated by the ironies of camp—would have been totally beyond her. But strangely, despite their shared interest in the question of what made art, well, art, Sontag and Kael never crossed swords again. Neither wrote a word about the other except that one brief exchange in 1964. Kael seemed to lose interest in these grand pronouncements. Her reviews, while still sterling and brilliant, settled into relatively conventional review form. In fact, for the rest of her life she never again wrote anything like "Trash, Art and the Movies," eschewing these kinds of broader essays for the most part.

There was a reason for that. The one major project Kael was able to persuade William Shawn to publish at the *New Yorker* was a long essay about Orson Welles's *Citizen Kane*. Originally, Kael had meant to write an introduction to an edition of the screenplay, but it ballooned, in her hands, to a fifty-thousand-word treatise on the relationship of a writer to the whole process of making movies. The *New Yorker* published it in two parts in October 1971, no doubt thinking it would showcase the crown jewel Kael had become as one of the most famous film reviewers in the country, a figure of cultish popularity. Instead, it was a career disaster.

Kane is set aside almost immediately. Kael declares it valuable as a "shallow masterpiece," which according to her personal scale of value did not make the film a bad one. She had her sights set on a different question: she wanted to know who, exactly, was responsible for what brilliance could be found in *Kane*. She attributes much of the film's genius not to the much-laureled Welles, but rather to the relatively forgotten screenplay writer, Herman Mankiewicz. Mankiewicz had been a hanger-on around the Round Table, and like Dorothy Parker he had been offered Hollywood work and taken it for the money. In explaining his career, Kael rapidly turned up the dial to rhapsodize about the achievements of 1920s and 1930s screenwriters:

> *And though, apparently, they one and all experienced it as prostitution of their talents—joyous prostitution in some cases—and though more than one fell in love with movies and thus suffered not only from personal frustration but from the corruption of the great, still new art, they nonetheless as a group were responsible for that sustained feat of careless magic we call "thirties comedy."* Citizen Kane *was, I think, its culmination.*

Kael explicitly included Dorothy Parker in that crowd. And while she acknowledged that in Hollywood these writers had mostly become drunks, she also concedes that they managed to pound out a few good films, forcing their writing to become "cruder and tougher, less tidy, less stylistically elegant, and more iconoclastic." This was her basis, it seemed, for having so much faith in Mankiewicz, in making him into a kind of tragic figure eclipsed by the giant ego of the star Orson Welles. Though Kael didn't overstate Welles's role as a villain, he nevertheless came off as one, using his big profile to deliberately throw the screenwriter into the shadows of the project.

At first, people loved Kael's novel approach to *Kane*. In the *New York Times*, the Canadian novelist Mordecai Richler praised her account of the making of the film, especially loving Kael's claim that *Citizen Kane* was a "shallow work, a shallow masterpiece." But he thought she'd overstated the talents of the Algonquin Round Table, quoting back at Kael Parker's sour assessment that they had been "just a lot of people telling jokes and telling each other how good they were."

But then, disgruntled critics—many of whom loved *Kane* and idolized Welles as an unquestionable auteur—started checking facts. Kael was not a reporter or researcher by trade. She didn't have the kind of systematic mind it required. So there were holes. Orson Welles was still alive, but Kael had not interviewed him. She later explained that she thought she already knew what he'd say about who had written the script, that obviously he would vigorously defend himself. Instead, she had gotten much of her sense of Mankiewicz's involvement from talking to John Houseman, a producer who'd worked with Welles; and from a UCLA academic named Howard Suber, whom she paid for his research. These two were both convinced that Welles had not had any hand in the script; Pauline repeated their take without testing it against claims from the other side.

This inflamed her enemies. Once again, she was accused of careerism. Opponents claimed that the true goal of her essay was to cut Welles down to size, and as Welles was widely agreed to be a great man, critics rushed into the breach to protect him. Andrew Sarris, for his part, thought this was a concealed broadside on him and his auteurist ideas once again. He sniffed back, now at the *Village Voice*:

Orson Welles is not significantly diminished as the auteur of Citizen Kane *by Miss Kael's breathless revelations about*

Herman J. Mankiewicz any more than he is diminished
as the auteur of The Magnificent Ambersons *by the fact*
that all the best lines and scenes were written by Booth
Tarkington.

Sarris was not the only person to see Kael as mounting a proxy attack on the very notion of an "auteur," doubling down on what she'd already said in "Circles and Squares." Bellicose metaphors abounded even in the higher-minded reviews. The sympathetic Kenneth Tynan, in the *Observer* in London, saw Kael as conducting a crusade: "I support her war, but on occasion feel she has picked the wrong battlefield."

Orson Welles, after reportedly crying in his lawyers' office about it and considering a lawsuit against Kael (he ultimately demurred), wrote to the *Times* of London insisting that the screenplay had been a collaborative effort. Then, it is widely believed, he enlisted a proxy to defend him in *Esquire*—the then magazine writer, now film director Peter Bogdanovich. Titled "The Kane Mutiny," Bogdanovich's article is barely about *Citizen Kane* at all: it is about dismantling Kael's essay piece by piece, apparently with a great deal of help from Welles. Bogdanovich landed the attack that truly stuck it to Kael: he excoriated her for not crediting the work of the UCLA academic Suber, whose research she paid for. To make matters worse, Suber was evidently angry with Kael. He told Bogdanovich he wasn't even sure he agreed with Kael that Mankiewicz had written the script alone.

Bogdanovich's article had a second purpose: it was also advance marketing for a book he was writing on Welles. He quoted from interviews he'd been conducting with the director since 1969, in which Welles was relatively generous about acknowledging Mankiewicz's contributions to the script. (Bogdanovich would not publish the book until 1992.) Bogdanovich quotes Welles as saying, "Mankiewicz's contribution . . . was enormous . . . I loved *him*. People did. He was much admired you know." From there, Bogdanovich proceeds to dismantle nearly every other sentence of Kael's essay with refutation from Welles—though he quotes few other sources himself. Bogdanovich also ended on a note that emphasized how hurt Welles was by this speculation, quoting from the man himself:

> *I hate to think what my grandchildren, if I ever get any, and if they should ever bother to look into either of those books, are going to think of their ancestor: something rather special in the line of megalomaniac lice ... Cleaning up after Miss Kael is going to take a lot of scrubbing.*

It didn't matter that, in her reviews of his work, Kael had hailed Welles as a visionary who had done marvelous things. In fact, nearly everything she'd ever written that touched on his work had been superlatively praiseworthy. These were all swept aside, no longer relevant because of the *Kane* essay. There was, certainly, some fault to be laid at Kael's doorstep. She'd posed an almost impossible task of firmly determining the authorship of a collaborative work. She wavered. Even before Sarris and Bogdanovich went on the hunt, she was already telling an interviewer at the *Saturday Review* that she did not mean to diminish his role; Welles had been the key figure in the film, she admitted.

> *Marvelous as Mankiewicz's script was, the picture might have been an ordinary picture with some other director ... and certainly, with some other actor as Kane.*

This qualification achieved little, in part because early in the controversy it no longer mattered what Kael had actually thought about the matter. Her mistakes had exposed a vulnerability in her good reputation, and the people who disliked everything she stood for would not pass on the opportunity to take her down. She liked to fight in print and hardly seemed to fault others for doing the same.

As a rule, Kael advanced her arguments like forward companies in an army, marching without pause. Throughout her professional life, she knew that to write with authority entailed projecting extreme, even superhuman confidence.

This was, however, still only a projection. Kael was brash, but she was also precise. Her capacity for self-editing was legendary. As her friend and sometime protégé James Wolcott put it, she was "as fanatical a tinkerer as any fussbudget from the E. B. White elf academy." Could she have been sloppy with the facts, even given that insane attention to detail? Undoubtedly the answer is yes. Curiously enough, in a career filled with ripostes and ongoing arguments in letters pages, this proved one instance in which Kael chose not to press her argument further. According to Kellow, she had dinner with Woody Allen shortly after reading Bogdanovich's essay and asked him if she should answer. "Don't answer," Allen apparently said. Kael was evidently wounded, but she seemed to learn a lesson from this, that she ought not anymore engage in reporting. She also stopped engaging people who didn't like her work in print.

But it stuck to her. A few years after the whole debacle, Kael found herself at an Oscars party with a screenwriter named John Gregory Dunne. When he wrote about it he immediately placed the renowned film critic in the context of what he clearly thought her great disgrace. When *Raising Kane* eventually came out in book form, he said, he'd declined the opportunity to review it. It was, in his view, "an arrogantly silly book that made me giggle and hoot as much as any I had ever read about Hollywood." But he'd been afraid of falling afoul of someone who could pan the movies he worked on. So he kept his own counsel and allowed it to color his view of the book's writer. At the party where they met, he wrote, Kael had arrived wearing a "Pucci knockdown and orthopedic shoes." When he introduced himself, she knew his name. And she promptly asked to meet his wife, Joan Didion.

10

Didion

Didion and Kael would often find themselves lumped with Sontag, because they all came from California, and in New York intellectual circles that was considered a remarkable coincidence. Often they didn't like the way their names were linked. Certainly, Didion and Kael never felt they were kindred spirits. John Gregory Dunne wrote that when Kael asked to meet Didion, all he could think about was the way she hated one of Didion's novels, and the film based on that novel too, "a princess fantasy" in Kael's view. "I know I have a lower tolerance for this sort of thing than many people; but should it be tolerated? I found the Joan Didion novel ridiculously swank, and I read it between bouts of disbelieving giggles." He introduced them anyway, seeing commonality in them, even if they couldn't find it themselves: "Two tough little numbers, each with the instincts of a mongoose and an amiable contempt for the other's work, putting on a good old girl number."

"Tough" is not always a word associated with Didion. "Elegant" and "glamorous" are more common descriptors, and those words aren't always used as compliments—she has been subject to recurrent complaints of the kind Kael made about her "ridiculously swank" style. But, as Didion well knew, surfaces could be deceiving. Although her style was neither as colloquial nor as directly combative as Kael's, Didion was just as much a master of shattering others' self-illusions. She prefers an elegant attack to blunt combat.

Didion was born to a middle-class Sacramento family in 1931. Her father, Frank, was no idealistic poultry farmer like Kael's, nor a dreamer like McCarthy's or West's or Sontag's. He was a practical, steady man who, until World War II, sold insurance. He then joined the National Guard in 1939. The family moved around with him to bases in Durham, North Carolina; and Colorado Springs. It was, from most perspectives, a very normal and placid sort of American childhood. But later, Didion would say it was the constant moving that first induced her sense of herself as an outsider. She was a naturally shy child, too, which didn't help. Even in her shyness, though, she dreamed of a life lived in public. Her first dream was to become an actress, not a writer. (This she shared with McCarthy.) She told Hilton Als: "I didn't realize then that it's the same impulse. It's make-believe. It's performance."

But there were certain things about Frank Didion she never wrote about. Didion made her name as a personal essayist, so many concluded she was relentlessly self-exposing. Yet until she was nearly seventy, she did not publish a single word on the other disconcerting event of her early life: in her first year at Berkeley as an English student, her father was committed to a mental hospital in San Francisco.

Her mother was a less melancholy soul, more aligned with the kind of tough California pioneer spirit Didion has spent much of her life articulating and defending. But Eduene Didion was not without an inner life or dream, either. Didion says it was she who had pointed out the item in *Vogue* that advertised a prize for the best essay: a trip to Paris. She told her daughter she thought she could win it. When her daughter did win, in 1956, she drove home from Berkeley to show her parents and her mother said, "Really?"

This was actually the second prize Didion won in her early twenties. She'd already spent the summer of 1955 in the guest editor program at *Mademoiselle* in Manhattan. (The same program had most famously hosted the poet Sylvia Plath a couple of years before, and was described and lampooned in her autobiographical novel *The Bell Jar*.) For that issue of the magazine, she'd written a tidy profile of the novelist Jean Stafford, then not so long out of a marriage with the poet Robert Lowell. She wrote up Stafford's musings on the marketability of novels versus short stories quite dutifully, with the control and poise of a very good student. There was no hint of the voice people would come to hear.

Didion never went to Paris. Instead, still a senior at Berkeley, she asked *Vogue* to give her a job in Manhattan. The magazine found her a place in the copy department and she moved out in the fall of 1956. These two entrances into New York are elided, somewhat, in the opening of Didion's famous essay about eventually leaving the city again, "Goodbye to All That." She first saw New York she says, when she was twenty—the *Mademoiselle* trip. But much of what she discusses in the essay is the experience that followed her second arrival—from the employers who told her to go outfit herself at Hattie Carnegie to being so poor she had to charge things at the Bloomingdale's gourmet shop, indulging even when broke as the young do.

To be clear, this is no real deception. The elision of the two arrivals is subtle, and in any event most people who have ever come to New York to work can testify that the feeling she describes—"nothing was irrevocable; everything was within reach"—is a renewable resource, something one can dip back into again and again. But there is something of Didion's method to be learned here: the fact that she was, often consciously, fashioning something from her experiences that was more than bald self-revelation.

At *Vogue*, Didion was at first shuffled into the advertising department, then later took up the role once occupied by Dorothy Parker: she drafted captions. By then the prim regime of Parker's editor Edna Woolman Chase was over. *Vogue* was somewhat more ambitious, especially when it came to the clothing showcased in its pages. Still, the intellectual tone in the *Vogue* offices hadn't changed much. The magazine was still populated by people who were unquestionably richer than Didion, but they were neither particularly literary nor intellectual. But they chased trends, and sometimes those trends led them to very good writers.

As Didion always told it, the first of her signed pieces for *Vogue* came about as an accident. Other copy required for the issue did not arrive, and she wrote to a word count. The item she came up with, a short meditation on the nature of jealousy, does not have the force of its convictions. The rote thesis is that jealousy has some force in life:

> *Talk to anyone whose work involves an investment of self: to a writer, to an architect. You hear how good a writer X was before the* New Yorker *ruined him, how Y's second novel, no matter what Diana Trilling said, could have been only a disappointment to those of us who realized Y's real potential.*

If this sounds like a writer fortifying herself for a brilliant future career, it is important to remember that at the time Didion was not writing for a magazine that garnered much literary and intellectual respect. The subjects of her essays, which *Vogue* permitted her to do more of in 1961 and 1962, sometimes seemed to reflect Didion's inner frustrations. They were about self-respect, the ability to take no for an answer, emotional blackmail.

Vogue was not the only magazine Didion was writing for at the time. She also had arrangements with *Holiday* and *Mademoiselle*. "I was writing pieces that I just sent out," she told interviewers. "I really didn't have any control over them." And the pieces do read somewhat as tryouts for a writer developing a craft. She didn't include them in later collections of essays, evidently not feeling them her best work.

Didion also contributed occasionally to the conservative *National Review*, writing mostly books or culture columns. There she was given the space to elaborate more fully on subjects less susceptible to accusations that they were mere magazine fluff, self-help written in literary diction. Instead she got to do things like review J. D. Salinger's *Franny and Zooey*, which she panned high-handedly. At a party, she recalled in her review:

> There was, as well, a stunningly predictable Sarah Lawrence girl who tried to engage me in a discussion of J. D. Salinger's relationship to Zen. When I seemed unresponsive, she lapsed into language she thought I might comprehend: Salinger was, she declared, the single person in the world capable of understanding her.

This statement now evokes considerable dramatic irony, given what Didion would become to the next few generations of young women, who likewise insisted she had articulated their innermost thoughts in her essays. But when Didion set out originally to write, she wasn't aiming to be popular in that way. In fact, in Salinger she saw an opportunity to take down a large man: *Franny and Zooey* she said was "finally spurious." She saw a man who flattered his readers by giving them the sense they were part of some elite who knew how to live better than other people, when in fact he did nothing but focus on the trivial. He confirmed others in their obsession with minor, superficial things, and in that way, could offer them only something like self-help.

One person who agreed with her on this was Mary McCarthy, writing in *Harper's*. Still a year out from the all-consuming reception of *The Group*, she laid her finest set of knives to work on the book. She also complained that Salinger lingered too long on trivialities: drinking from a glass, lighting cigarettes. The Salingerian worldview, though, was what McCarthy especially hated: the idea that only the people inside his circle of trust were real, that everyone else was lying. She could not abide the ambiguity of the suicide of Seymour Glass that haunts the pages of *Franny and Zooey*. She wanted to know why he'd killed himself, whether it was because he had married badly or because he was too happy. She ended with an unforgettable line:

> Or because he had been lying, his author had been lying, and it was all terrible, and he was a fake?

Salinger was then at the height of his popularity and just about to go into hiding. But something is revealed in McCarthy's and Didion's shared irritation with him: there was something about Salinger that suggested only surfaces. Funnily enough, both of these women would in time be tarred with the same brush, praised as impeccable stylists whose ideas and observations never quite lived up to the beauty of their prose.

When Kael went after Didion's "swank" image, for example, she was arguing in that vein. But Kael also knew that Didion had skill, admitting even as she trashed her that there were flashes of genius: "The smoke of creation rises from those dry-ice sentences." Kael just wanted Didion to be less injured, less melancholy, less—overall—of a victim. And yet, that really seems only a disagreement as to personal style: Kael spent her life running away from any admission of fault or weakness, particularly in her prose.

And though it's now rarely remembered this way, the pair once had grounds for professional rivalry, too. Didion was *Vogue's* film critic for a short time in the 1960s, and she had taken up those duties around the same time Kael arrived at the *New Yorker*. Didion had much less space than Kael, and was clearly not as interested in the internal battles of film criticism, per se. But she had, like Kael, a skeptical attitude toward popular taboos, and a distrust of certain sentimental licenses taken by movie directors. At least once, on a specific film, Kael echoed Didion, too. In 1979, the *New York Review of Books* asked Didion to take a look at Woody Allen's *Manhattan*, and something not unlike Kael's breakthrough, biting *Limelight* review had come back. "Self-absorption is general," Didion began, "as is self-doubt":

"When it comes to relationships with women I'm the winner of the August Strindberg Award," the Woody Allen character tells us in Manhattan; later, in a frequently quoted and admired line, he says, to Diane Keaton, "I've never had a relationship with a woman that lasted longer than the one between Hitler and Eva Braun." These lines are meaningless, and not funny: they are simply "references," the way Harvey and Jack and Anjelica and Sentimental Education are references, smart talk meant to convey the message that the speaker knows his way around Lit and History, not to mention Show Biz.

Ironically, for all her complaints, and although she had often been a booster of Woody Allen's, Kael shared Didion's exasperation with *Manhattan*, and had the same concern that all its deep talk was masking a fundamental superficiality. "What man in his forties but Woody Allen could pass off a predilection for teenagers as a quest for true values?" she asked a year later, as she sideswiped *Manhattan* in her review of *Stardust Memories*.

Obviously Didion never had any problem using the "I" when she was writing nonfiction. But by 1964, just three years after she started writing those searching essays for *Vogue*, she was plainly itching to write about something other than herself. Her life was also changing. She had published a slim novel, *Run River*, whose journey to the bookstore had been a grand disappointment. The title had been chosen by the publisher, and the editor had altered the form of the novel entirely, changing its experimental structure into something quite conventional. She had also married John Gregory Dunne, a sometime friend, after he'd supported her through the end of a long love affair. The pair decided to quit their magazine jobs and move to California, where they had a vague plan to make careers in television.

Vogue, apparently unwilling to cut apron strings altogether, asked Didion to begin reviewing films for it. In her opening column for 1964, written just a month before she married, Didion declared her critical approach would be somewhat democratic:

> *Let me lay it on the line: I like movies, and approach them with a tolerance so fond that it will possibly strike you as simple-minded. To engage my glazed attention a movie need be no classic of its kind, need be neither L'Avventura or Red River, neither Casablanca nor Citizen Kane; I ask only that it have its moments.*

She went on to cast positive votes for *The Philadelphia Story*, *The Spirit of St. Louis*, and *Charade*. Kael had not yet quite broken through to mainstream movie reviewing and *I Lost It at the Movies* hadn't yet been published, but we can see in Didion's words a relatively similar approach. She too would spend her career insisting there were moments of brilliance even in what was unquestionably trash.

Didion alternated her assignment on the movies with another writer, which seems to have prevented her from reviewing memorable films. She was trying to write with flair, though, in short spaces, and most of the reviews are sprightly, wisecracking things that seem more like Parker than Didion. She hated *The Pink Panther*: "possibly the only seduction ever screened (David Niven vs. The Princess) with all the banality of the real thing." She liked *The Unsinkable Molly Brown*, but commented that Debbie Reynolds "tends to play these things as if the West was won by jumping up and down and shouting at it." She confessed a weakness for teenage surfing movies, "an enthusiasm I should try to pass off as sociological." Like Kael, she too hated *The Sound of Music*, calling it:

> *More embarrassing than most, if only because of its suggestion that history need not happen to people like Julie*

*Andrews and Christopher Plummer. Just whistle a happy
tune, and leave the Anschluss behind.*

Gradually, though, Didion got bored with film reviews. Her
review of *The Sound of Music* was so caustic that *Vogue* fired her,
as she tells it. (This was another connection to Kael, who had been
fired for panning the same movie at *McCall's*.) In any event, she was
moving on to other subjects in a column that she and Dunne soon
set up at the *Saturday Evening Post*.

At the *Post*, Didion's writing would undergo a major shift in
tone, too. There are hints of the elegiac, distinctive earlier Didion
voice in "On Self-Respect," and in another essay she wrote for *Vogue*
on American summers. But, given the *Post*'s willingness to send
her into the field, she found a groove. It helped that California of the
1960s was fertile ground for twisting stories that provided Didion with
the opportunity to follow a disturbing note longer than a column or
two. She started off writing for the *Post* about Helen Gurley Brown
(whom she found silly) and John Wayne (whom she did not), but it
was the first of the crime pieces that hit a chord with the magazine's
readers—and also reads as the first true Didion piece.

It was titled "How Can I Tell Them There's Nothing Left?" But
the title Didion would give it in her own collection, "Some Dreamers of the Golden Dream," was the one that would stick. Nominally
chronicling a local murder, in which a wife was accused of burning
her husband to death in the family car, Didion immediately pulled
back to a wide-angle view of everything that was plaguing California,
not to mention most of the rest of America:

*This is the California where it is easy to Dial-a-Devotion,
but hard to buy a book. This is the country in which a
belief in the literal interpretation of Genesis has slipped
imperceptibly into a belief in the literal interpretation of
Double Indemnity, the country of the teased hair and the*

*Capris and the girls for whom all life's promise comes
down to a waltz-length white wedding dress and the birth
of a Kimberly or a Sherry or a Debbi and a Tijuana divorce
and a return to hairdresser's school.*

The woman was eventually convicted of murdering her husband, but naturally the residents of the San Bernardino valley—the part of California Didion was describing in that long, unwinding opening paragraph—did not take kindly to being characterized this way. "I am worried about Joan Didion," wrote one Howard B. Weeks, who also listed his profession: vice president for public relations and development at Loma Linda University. "We recognize these feelings as symptoms commonly observed in young New York writers who venture into the Great Unknown beyond the Hudson." This letter illustrates that Didion hadn't quite yet broken through to the mainstream; Howard B. Weeks did not know he was lecturing the woman who would become the signature American writer from California on the subject of her own home.

Didion did not slide into her groove immediately. The next piece she wrote seemed almost a step away from anything that could possibly annoy anyone. It was entitled "The Big Rock Candy Figgy Pudding Pitfall." Despite her having savaged Helen Gurley Brown and J. D. Salinger for being essentially trivial persons, one guesses this was the kind of piece Didion wrote for money. It details an effort to cook twenty figgy puddings and make twenty hard-candy trees. But it seemed to reflect a state of distress about how her domestic arrangements were working out:

*I am frail, lazy and unsuited to doing anything except
what I am paid to do, which is sit by myself and type
with one finger. I like to imagine myself a "can-do" kind
of woman, capable of patching the corral fence, pickling
enough peaches to feed the hands all winter, and then*

*winning a trip to Minneapolis in the Pillsbury Bake-Off.
In fact, the day I stop believing that if put to it I could win
the Pillsbury Bake-Off will signal the death of something.*

Dunne appears in this article as a benevolent, comic figure, who upon confrontation with the supplies asks, "Exactly what kind of therapy are we up to this week?" But nowhere in this article does Didion mention that earlier that year, she and Dunne had adopted a child they named Quintana Roo Dunne. The anxiety, though, about being some kind of domestic goddess—"the kind of woman who made hard-candy topiary trees and figgy puddings"—smells of what the women's magazines all call nesting.

For one of the first issues of the new year, she wrote an essay the magazine entitled "Farewell to the Enchanted City." (Later generations of readers would come to know it better by the title "Goodbye to All That.") This was when the first hint of her career-long obsession with the stories we tell ourselves would begin to explicitly emerge. Didion suggests that the New York of her imagination had dominated the real one the whole time she actually lived there:

*Some instinct, programmed by all the movies I had ever
seen and all the songs I had ever heard about New York,
informed me that it would never be quite the same again.
In fact it never was. Some time later there was a song
in the jukeboxes on the Upper East Side that went "but
where is the schoolgirl who used to be me," and if it was
late enough at night I used to wonder that. I know now
that almost everyone wonders something like that, sooner
or later and no matter what he or she is doing, but one of
the mixed blessings of being twenty and twenty-one and
even twenty-three is the conviction that nothing like this,
all evidence to the contrary notwithstanding, has ever
happened to anyone before.*

This essay is so famous it is said to have spawned its own mini genre of essays about leaving New York. Like the song on the jukebox, it expresses the feelings everyone has about a common experience. The brilliance of the essay is that even in the act of writing it Didion reenacts an emotional cliché, the narrator telling a past self how silly and stupid she was to fall for a story that everyone falls for. This self-conscious style, a personal matter conveyed at a distance, would become Didion's signature. Even when she wrote about something as personal as her divorce, she did it at a remove, turning it over in her hand, polishing it to a shine that concealed certain roughnesses in the center.

Dunne and Didion soon had a regular column in the *Saturday Evening Post*, sharing a byline. It looks odd to contemporary eyes, especially because of the illustration the magazine used at the top of each column, drawings of them both. If Dunne had written the column, the illustration would show his face in front of Didion's; if she had written it, her face would move in front of his.

Her columns were generally the more interesting explorations of the pair, her knack for inspiring a reaction was top-notch. Her essay on migraines would appear in that space, as would her reporting of a decommissioned Alcatraz and a devastating sketch of Nancy Reagan, then the first lady of California:

> She has told me that the governor never wore makeup even in motion pictures and that politics is rougher than the picture business because you do not have the studio to protect you . . . "Having a pretty place to work is impor-tant to a man," she has advised me. She has shown me the apothecary jar of hard candies she keeps filled on the governor's desk.

Almost a month later, Nancy Reagan was still smarting from the sting, telling the *Fresno Bee*, "I thought we were getting along fine together. Maybe it would have been better if I snarled a bit."

This technique—appearing to let the subject simply carry on without interruption from Didion's evaluations or thoughts making themselves absurd—became her standard mode of operation. It would be the way she would spend large swaths of her famous explorations in Haight-Ashbury. She would begin the essay with a long incantation about how the "center was not holding," then trek into the widening abyss to find people who would reveal themselves in a line or two. Meeting two young Deadheads, for example:

> *I ask a couple of girls what they do.*
> *"I just kind of come out here a lot," one of them says.*
> *"I just sort of know the Dead," the other says.*

The flatness of these answers spoke for the emptiness of those who spoke them. Most of the readers of the *Saturday Evening Post* agreed with Didion on this point, the letters unusually full of praise for her insight into the barbarians of the hippie cult, as it was popular to call them at the time. There were some objectors, like Sunnie "The Daisy" Brentwood, who continued to insist that "the majority of the flower children are good kids who are trying to improve the world and make it a better place to live."

Didion's view won out in the end, not least because this essay would become the title piece of her stand-alone 1968 collection *Slouching Towards Bethlehem*, the book that established Didion's reputation. Reviewing it for the *New York Times*, Didion's friend Dan Wakefield argued that Didion was "one of the least celebrated and most talented writers of my own generation." He pointed out that Didion was easier to interpret, for example, than another trendy young woman writer of the moment named Susan Sontag. Wakefield's thorough celebration of the book was echoed by just about every reviewer. Some of them stumbled over the pairing of Didion's brilliance with her gender: Melvin Maddocks of the *Christian Science Monitor* cryptically remarked, in what appeared to be a compliment:

> *Journalism by women is the price the man's world pays for having disappointed them. Here at their best are the unforgiving eye, the unforgetting ear, the concealed hat-pin style.*

That is one way of looking at it; though the reference to hat pins is clearly trivializing, the notion that the opinions were a "price" rather than a gift is somewhat revealing. Didion had cultivated a persona in her writing that was just as disappointed with women— Gurley Brown, the Deadheads, Nancy Reagan, the figgy pudding domestics—as it was with the "man's world," wherever that was. It wasn't feminine so much as just perceptive, sharp. Certain doors of perception are more open to women, but it doesn't mean that men can't see what women are pointing out, if only they'd settle down, listen, and look.

After *Slouching Towards Bethlehem*, the literary profilers came out of the woodwork. In droves, they began to interview her, attaching the beautiful photographs of her slight frame to headlines like "Joan Didion: Writer with Razor's Edge," and "Slouching Towards Joan Didion." It was by then the 1970s. Alfred Kazin, that old friend of Hannah Arendt's, promptly got himself assigned to fly out to California. He met the Didion-Dunnes in high spirits at the house they then occupied in Malibu, together writing a screenplay based on *Play It as It Lays*, her 1970 novel about a dissatisfied actress named Maria Wyeth that had gotten her rave reviews. Kazin noted the difference between the way Didion often spoke of herself in print: as fragile, ill, on the verge of divorce in a famous *Life* column in 1969, and the way she was in person, more a creature of sensible steel than frivolous silk:

> *Joan Didion is a creature of many advantages, as is clear from her own belief that she had the sense to get born and to grow up in Sacramento before so many discomfiting things began to happen to the Golden State.*

Kazin continued to catalog discrepancies. Didion's voice was "so much stronger than her own little girl's voice!" Though the address in Malibu would seem to connote relaxation, he finds the sound of the waves below deafening: "People who live in a beach house don't know how wary it makes them." He called her a moralist, pointed out that she had an obsession with seriousness. He notes that always she was writing as a cultural critic, even in fiction, wanting to diagnose the ills of whatever subject she had—a propensity she shared with Mary McCarthy, though their fiction voices are far apart. He even connected her with Arendt, who had once told him that Americans seemed to despair far more than she had ever seen people do in Europe.

By the time Kazin's profile was published, Didion was, quite simply, a star. But the *Saturday Evening Post*, the place that had let her write lyrically about migraines, about going home to Sacramento, or that flew her to Hawaii for a piece, had folded. She looked for other homes. *Life* magazine offered her a contract to write a column. But the relationship soured immediately; Didion asked to go to Saigon, because many writers—including Sontag and McCarthy—had already been there. Her editor demurred, telling her that "some of the guys are going out." Her anger at this blithe dismissal turned into the now-famous column she wrote about visiting Hawaii during the prediction of a huge tidal wave:

> *My husband switches off the television set and stares out the window. I avoid his eyes, and brush the baby's hair. In the absence of a natural disaster we are left again to our own uneasy devices. We are here on this island in the middle of the Pacific in lieu of filing for divorce.*

This essay poses as self-revelation, but here the frame of marital trouble dissolves. Didion begins telling you instead how disconnected she had felt from everything, how difficult it was to feel. She confesses that she has become, as that old boyfriend predicted, someone who feels nothing. The piece is so relentlessly dark and despairing it is no wonder the *Life* editors were apparently startled by it. They gave it a title that reflected their bewilderment: "A Problem of Making Connections." Subsequent deeply personal columns were not to their taste either, and Didion would end up relinquishing the contract before it was up because the editors would not run her column. She would get back at the editor for his nonchalant remark many years later, when she'd report it in *The Year of Magical Thinking*.

This hints at something important about Didion's work: even when she is reporting unendurable despair, feeling that her life is falling apart alongside the country's, another engine is at work there. No person as depressed and lost as Didion purports to be could possibly draft prose this precise, words that cut so directly to the heart of her subject. In the case of the confession of her potential divorce, the engine behind it was anger, anger at having been prevented from using the full measure of her powers by an editor who considered Joan Didion less daring a writer than the "guys" going out to Saigon. It was a mistake that belongs in the museum of poor editorial decisions.

Didion returned to novel writing. She occasionally contributed to *Esquire*, but had trouble fitting in there too. She was one of the boys, clearly, in the sense that men had noticed her writing and wanted to publish her. But she also couldn't quite fit into their regime.

Still, turning to the women's magazines would have been intolerable for her, just when the women's liberation movement was at its height. Like Sontag, she was no doubt being asked about her loyalty to the consciousness-raising circles that were suddenly everywhere. But she does not seem to have directly commented until finally, in 1972, she published an essay called "The Women's Movement" in the pages of the *New York Times*. She listed sixteen books as inspiration. But she had clearly been moved to frustration by the "special issue on women" that *Time* had published some months before.

Didion was not willing to grant much ground or sense to the nascent second wave of feminism. She leveled some of the most direct insults of her career at it. "It seemed very New England, this febrile and cerebral passion," she said of the radical feminist writings of Shulamith Firestone. She referred to some of the movement's methods as Stalinist, singling out the British writer Juliet Mitchell's relation of Maoist practice to the consciousness-raising session. She also defended Mary McCarthy from those feminist theorists who would deconstruct her heroines in *The Company She Keeps* and *The Group* into an unrecognizable, overly politicized caricature: "enslaved because she persists in looking for her identity in a man."

Yet there was something less than a total rejection of the notion of feminism going on in Didion's article. She presented herself as merely worried that what she sweepingly saw as one unified movement had become mired in arguments over trivial issues, like the division of domestic duties such as washing the dishes.

> *Of course this litany of trivia was crucial to the movement in the beginning, a key technique in the politicizing of women who perhaps had been conditioned to obscure their resentments even from themselves . . . But such discoveries could be of no use at all if one refused to perceive the larger point, failed to make that inductive leap from the personal to the political.*

Didion also thought that in their books the feminists had constructed a kind of self-delusion, one she called Everywoman, "persecuted even by her gynecologist," "raped on every date." Didion did not deny that women were victims of condescension and sex-role stereotyping. Indeed, it's hard to imagine how she could, given the way she was written about in the period, given her inability to fit tidily into the male-dominated magazine world. But she found the expressed wishes of the main movement writers to be childish in the extreme. "These are converts who want not a revolution but 'romance,'" she concluded.

Didion had addressed the condition of women several times before, often in the context of writing about Doris Lessing. She wrote about her twice: once for *Vogue* and once for the *New York Times Book Review*. In *Vogue*, she'd had only enough space to say she did not share Lessing's view that there was some "injustice" involved in being a woman. By the time Didion was enlisted to review the science fiction novel *Briefing for a Descent into Hell*, she had softened her view of Lessing, in part because Lessing had softened her view of feminist politics by then. *Briefing*, which as Lessing termed it, was an "inner space fiction," was more about madness and alienation than about a critique of modern social structures. And while Didion didn't particularly like it, she went out of her way to congratulate Lessing on what she saw as Lessing's disenchantment with all blunt forms of political thought and action, as Didion saw feminism to be:

> *The impulse to find solutions has been not only her dilemma but the guiding delusion of her time. It is not an impulse I hold high, but there is something finally very moving about Mrs. Lessing's tenacity.*

There's a little daylight between Didion and her rejection of feminism, here. It seemed, in a cloaked way, that she had some sympathy for the aims and hopes of those feminists whose tactics and writing she still detested. It was not much, but it was something.

This is something that could not really be said for the other side. Several feminist activists wrote to the *Times* to complain, among them Susan Brownmiller, whose *Against Our Will* had been listed as one of the books examined in the essay. Pointing out that Didion had never exactly positioned herself as a leftist, and had written for the *National Review*, Brownmiller cryptically continued:

> *Isn't it interesting that the real toughies are always on the other side? I'll take boots and blue jeans over manicured, Mandarin fingernails any day of the week.*

The piece would cut Didion forever out of the women's movement. In fact, it inaugurated a common complaint about her: that she was, in her own way, acting out a certain kind of stereotypical femininity. And for all her defense of complexity, she was afraid to recognize that there were any number of interior ideological fights going on in the movement she was describing: the novelist Alix Kates Shulman was on one side of the fence, and the tract-writer Shulamith Firestone on another. But in Didion's view they were all the same, all the Everywoman, all capable of making different choices from the ones they had made.

For the rest of the 1970s, Didion mostly threw herself into filmmaking and fiction. She and Dunne would work on a film version of *Play It as It Lays*, as well as an update of *A Star Is Born*. She published *A Book of Common Prayer*. She had the occasional article in *Esquire*, but her energy seemed subdued. The Didion-Dunnes, who had avoided divorce more than once in the intervening years, were great party givers, and that took up time too. It wouldn't be until the end of the decade that she'd publish a second collection of nonfiction called *The White Album*.

The title essay, "The White Album," which begins with the famous incantation, "We tell ourselves stories in order to live," is a fragmentary bit of work. Though that first line is often quoted as a kind of self-help mantra, in the essay proper Didion goes on to list delusional fantasies, finally concluding that writers especially are guilty of imposing a kind of narrative order on existence that simply "freeze[s] the shifting phantasmagoria of our experience."

Some of the elements of the essay included projects that Didion had tried to take up, and which had failed, over the years. Specifically, she mentions an acquaintance with Linda Kasabian, the twenty-three-year-old member of the Manson family who had driven the car when a group of them murdered Sharon Tate and her houseguests in August 1969.

On the outside, the Kasabian story had looked like a perfect Didion subject. Here was a person who had gotten caught up in the promises of love and grooviness that were the allure of the hippie movement—the promises that, as Didion had written, at length, were bogus. Kasabian had gone so far that she got caught up in the most notorious murders in America, murders so savage they stood out in a country that treated crime as nighttime entertainment. But Didion never got the project under way. Instead the Manson murders, and Linda Kasabian, became another dreamlike element in the political and social morass of the late 1960s, years when Didion would write that she barely knew her own mind:

> *I remember all the day's misinformation very clearly, and I also remember this, and wish I did not. I remember that no one was surprised.*

In *The White Album*, Didion never says what shook her out of her misery at the morally and philosophically empty conditions of the 1960s, not exactly. It could have been the films she was making, or that she was finally being recognized as a proper novelist. *A Book of Common Prayer* was very well received. It could be that without the violence and anomie of the 1960s, she found herself enjoying life suddenly. Quintana was growing up, her marriage got past its rough point, and she was making good money.

It was in the 1970s that she got very lucky. She met an editor who, like her old ones at the *Saturday Evening Post*, was prepared to let her talent work for itself in nonfiction articles. Bob Silvers, who was now one of the two lead editors of the *New York Review of Books*, was happy to let Didion roam over the pages of the magazine. Her first piece was nominally a review of Stanley Kauffmann's film criticism in the *New Republic*, though Didion had other targets in mind:

> *I used to wonder how Pauline Kael, say, could slip in and out of such airy subordinate clauses as "now that the studios are collapsing," or how she could so misread the*

*labyrinthine propriety of Industry evenings as to charac-
terize "Hollywood wives" as women "whose jaws get a
hard set from the nights when they sit soberly at parties
waiting to take their sloshed geniuses home."*

Didion proceeded to mock those, like Kael and Kauffmann, who
wrote about film without having any idea how a film was produced and
made. She said the most they could hope for was to bring a specific
brand of intelligence to film, but that it was "a kind of *petit-point*-on-
Kleenex effect which rarely stands much scrutiny."

Kauffmann, upon reading the review, discovered that in fact he
was little-mentioned in it, and that four of the quotes Didion used
had come from an entirely different book he had written. He wrote
in to the *New York Review* to state his objection, and added:

*A possible reason: In the December 9, 1972, issue of the
New Republic, I reviewed Miss Didion's film Play It as It
Lays, referred to her novel of that name, and stated my
utter loathing of both. (On much the same grounds that
she substantiates in her article: the film pretended to deal
with serious subjects but was patently an industry product.) Perhaps Miss Didion would dislike my writing just as
much if I had praised her work. I hope so. But your readers
might care to know about a possible tit for tat.*

Didion was typically cutting in reply. Had he reviewed her work
positively, she insisted, she would still dislike his work, and "I would
also have some doubts about my own."

"Self-absorption is general, as is self-doubt," she'd memora-
bly begin that Woody Allen piece. Her complaints about Allen were
pretty much the same ones she'd voiced eighteen years before about
J. D. Salinger. Allen's characters were "clever children," who spoke
in smart remarks that no serious adult could sustain as easily. They

were obsessed with trivialities when they listed among their reasons to live Willie Mays and Louis Armstrong:

> *This list of Woody Allen's is the ultimate consumer report, and the extent to which it has been quoted approvingly suggests a new class in America, a sub world of people rigid with apprehension that they will die wearing the wrong sneaker, naming the wrong symphony, preferring Madame Bovary.*

She called out the one character in *Manhattan* who is in high school. That was Mariel Hemingway's Tracy, a character drawn in what Didion terms "another adolescent fantasy." She found Tracy too utterly perfect, and with no real family to hold her back from dating Allen's forty-year-old neurotic. A man wrote in to object, at length, to the way Didion had disrespected what was obviously his favorite filmmaker. Her reply? "Oh, wow."

Kael and Didion never gave up the grudge and became friends. James Wolcott reported in a memoir that Kael loved to snicker, especially, at a quote Didion had given Alfred Kazin: "I am haunted by the Donner Party." This was a shame. The pair could have commiserated on more subjects than just the matter of Woody Allen, for around this time Didion too started to be subjected to the kind of bizarrely personal attacks that follow success.

One such attack was from the writer Barbara Grizzuti Harrison, a sometime reviewer for the *Nation*, who wrote a piece called "Only Disconnect." While Harrison made some good points about the unrelenting misery Didion could sometimes project, she rather undermined her own project by making fun of Quintana's name right out of the gate.

The other attack came somewhat later, and from a more familiar quarter: Mary McCarthy. Didion was something of a fan; she frequently quoted McCarthy in her essays on women, explicitly mentioning McCarthy's fiction in her attacks on Helen Gurley Brown and on the women's movement. But when McCarthy finally addressed Didion, reviewing her 1984 novel *Democracy*, she found only disappointment, "deathlessness":

> *Perhaps all the elements in the puzzle are out of movies. Perhaps Joan Didion is just wishing that she were an old-time screenwriter rather than a novelist. If that is it, I am irritated. To be portentous, one ought to be deeper than that.*

Silvers, at this point, seems to have decided that Didion's fine intelligence needed better targets, subjects she could spend hours of exploratory surgery on. She and Dunne had been talking for months about going to Latin America, and she told an interviewer that in fact it was her idea to go.

By 1982, when Didion arrived in El Salvador, there was little question the Communist government of the country was a regime of terrifying violence. An archbishop was shot in the pulpit; massacres were being documented by photojournalists. Alma Guillermoprieto was tracking all of it in the *Washington Post*. Tom Brokaw told the Didion-Dunnes it was the only country in which he'd never felt safe. And so, like Sontag and Mary McCarthy before her, Didion decided to wander into a heart of darkness and see what she could find there.

Unlike Sontag and McCarthy in Vietnam, Didion found little reason in El Salvador to examine her conscience. There was too much lying around in wait of dreadful cataloging.

> *There is a special kind of practical information that the visitor to El Salvador acquires immediately, the way visitors to other places acquire information about the currency rates, the hours for the museums. In El Salvador one learns that vultures go first for the soft tissue, for the eyes,*

the exposed genitalia, the open mouth. One learns that
an open mouth can be used to make a specific point, can
be stuffed with something emblematic; stuffed, say, with
a penis, or, if the point has to do with land title, stuffed
with some of the dirt in question.

It was in El Salvador that Didion began to question her tech-niques. In a shopping mall that "embodied the future for which El Salvador was presumably being saved," she began to wonder if it was really a good idea to be cataloging all the consumer items being sold there, so incongruous with the murder and horror outside. The irony with which she could present them in her work no longer seemed funny, or trenchant. She would write about this explicitly in the essay she produced, feeling that she was witnessing not so much a "story" as a "noche obscura."

This focus on the simplicity of narrative was a point, obviously, that Didion had already made in her essay "The White Album." To tell a story was to boil an event down to its supposed essentials, but sometimes the essentials were not a proper representation of the whole. This was a point she had first learned in writing about her own life. She would write what looked, to readers, like confessional essays about divorce, about her practice of keeping a notebook, about self-respect. But she knew what she was selecting, and what she was holding back; she knew certain elements of her story were being concealed. The public's willingness to accept the image she projected had clearly taught her something.

She'd go on to write extensively about politics throughout the 1980s. America had by then stabilized from the hallucinogenic, dreamlike 1960s, and had taken its conservative turn into the Reagan years. It was telling itself about "Morning in America," and the mass media machine that was only beginning to shape the presidential elections of the 1960s and 1970s had become more sophisticated. Didion began writing about politics after the idea was put to her by

Bob Silvers at the *New York Review of Books*; he seemed to understand that narrative was Didion's best subject, and nowhere were the narratives more bizarre than in national politics—a point that would surface repeatedly.

It was almost as if American politics had not learned some of the lessons of her earlier work. The fact that "we tell ourselves stories in order to live," Didion had written in "The White Album," was not exactly laudatory. It inflicted some kind of damage. The stories were, after all, self-deceptions. We used them to conceal an element of the truth from ourselves, because the whole truth was somehow unbearable, or else, especially in the case of politics, unmanageable.

So the reporters on the failed 1988 Michael Dukakis presidential campaign were, in her view, too credulous, too willing to take the story the campaign fed them and send it back out to the public without much independent scrutiny. In that story, Dukakis was said to be "becoming presidential," but the elements of that transformation were kept vague, with political writers apparently expecting readers to accept the narrative they were being given, no questions asked. "The narrative is made up of many such understandings, tacit agreements, small and large, to overlook the observable in the interests of obtaining a dramatic story line," Didion wrote. This critique of access journalism was something that was rarely seen at the time, because it could be done only by someone of Didion's standing. Didion's observations could not stop the collusion between reporters and the public relations people on political campaigns, but she did help make society more aware of this problem.

While Didion's critique of the servitude of political reporters was clearly brilliant, there was perhaps something more animating it too, a bit of personal perspective on the lives of political journalists. Long ago, at a party, she had met and befriended a young writer named Nora Ephron. Ephron had gone on to marry Carl Bernstein, one of the two reporters who had effectively impeached Nixon with their accounts of the Watergate scandal. Their courtship had not been a happy thing, but the marriage, was, at first, very solid. Bernstein was, as the muckraking of Watergate suggested, not the kind of obeisant servant of the White House party line that Didion abhorred. The two became friends; when, in the late 1980s, Bernstein would write a memoir of his Communist parents, Didion would be among the first he'd show it to.

But things with Ephron and Bernstein would not go very well in the end.

11

Ephron

The only novel Nora Ephron ever published was about Carl Bernstein and the way he'd ruined her life. The pair met in swinging 1970s New York, perhaps hitting it off because they both had somewhat combative spirits. Bernstein still had the laurels of his role in Watergate; Ephron was a bestselling feminist writer and a staple on television, already established as a kind of public wit. In tabloid terms, it was kismet, two brilliant people hitting it off. They quickly became a kind of It Couple, marrying in 1976. They were both on top of the world—until he cheated, and then they weren't.

This, at least, is the situation *Heartburn* drops you into: the blood-and-guts end of what could have been a perfectly good marriage. "The first day I did not think it was funny," Ephron's narrator Rachel Samstat writes. "I didn't think it was funny the third day either, but I managed to make a little joke about it." Or not so little, because *Heartburn* is one long joke, interrupted by recipes, about the despair inherent in having to leave one's philandering husband while handling two toddlers. The narrator lacerates herself for not having noticed the affair sooner, but it is true that she is much harder on her husband. "The man is capable of having sex with a Venetian blind," Ephron wrote. The book is even self-conscious about the way it skewers the husband:

Everyone always asks, was he mad at you for writing the book? And I have to say, Yes, yes, he was. He still is. It is

*one of the most fascinating things to me about the whole
episode: he cheated on me, and then got to behave as if
he was the one who had been wronged because I wrote
about it!*

Heartburn was the epitome of the line Ephron always used to
describe her own mission: "Everything is copy." She'd taken a horrible
experience and turned it into something everyone loved. Though it
attracted a few skeptical press notices, *Heartburn* was a bestseller. It
made Ephron temporarily rich; it got her away from Bernstein. So
it served many of the purposes it was meant to serve, except one: it
meant she'd always be defined by this experience. And Nora Ephron,
by all accounts, did not like to dwell on anything uncomfortable.
"Above all, be the heroine of your life, not the victim," she told a
crowd of graduates at Wellesley, late in her life.

If that line sometimes sounded both glib and inspirational,
Ephron knew a little something about victims. Of all the people in
this book, she was the only one with a direct connection to Dorothy
Parker. Her screenwriter parents had befriended Parker in Hollywood.
Ephron's own memories of her were hazy, though Parker was in and
out of the house throughout Nora's childhood: "She was frail and
tiny and twinkly." Still the young Ephron came to idolize Parker, or at
least the figure she cut. Ephron was enchanted by the idea that Parker
had been "the only woman at the table," the wit and the genius who
was the life of every well-spoken party in Manhattan. She wanted to
do that too. She called it her Dorothy Parker problem. Of course, a
biography of Parker would later disabuse her of those illusions about
Parker's life, would fill her in on the alcoholism and the "victim."
Ephron claimed to have then abandoned the dream, albeit reluctantly.
"Before one looked too hard at it, it was a lovely myth, and I have
trouble giving it up."

The bursting of that bubble came closer to home than Ephron
admitted. Born in 1941, Nora was Phoebe and Henry Ephron's eldest

daughter of four. And by an alchemy of disposition and natural talent, the family generated plenty of text on themselves. All four sisters would eventually become writers. Three of them wrote memoirs. Henry Ephron wrote one too. The art of self-presentation began, by all accounts, at the Ephron dinner table. Nightly, there was a contest to be the funniest person in the family. In the family annals, and particularly those that Nora left behind, these were largely portrayed as jocular occasions. They taught her the liberating power of humor, she said.

Funniest of all was her mother, Phoebe. Like Rebecca West's mother, she was a woman of many talents. Also like Rebecca West's mother, she had possibly married the wrong man.

Phoebe Ephron grew up in the Bronx. She worked as a shop clerk. When she met Henry, then just an aspiring playwright, at a party, it was he who pursued her. Before she'd agree to marry him, she insisted that she get to read his work, to see if it was good enough. This was a cherished family story. She was always an authority in her own right, always holding the attention of a room. She told her daughters there were no values in life higher than independence. "If I haven't raised you to make your own decisions, it won't do any good to tell you what I think," Nora recorded her mother saying to her children from the time they were very young. She lived her life as a kind of exception, too. Phoebe Ephron was, along with Parker, one of the few female screenwriters in Hollywood, and she insisted on doing things that only men did:

> She was not doctrinaire or dogmatic about it; although she named me after the heroine of The Doll's House, she could not bear being called a feminist. She merely was, and simply by her example, we all grew up with blind faith in our own abilities and destinies.

That all sounds adorably plucky, a perfect feminist story about someone who hated the word "feminist." (There is also a beautiful coincidence here in both Ephron and West owing Ibsen their names.) But Ephron would reveal, later, that when she was fifteen her mother began to drink heavily. "One day she wasn't an alcoholic," she wrote. "And the next day she was a complete lush." With the drinking came a good amount of screaming and fighting. (Henry also drank, and was a serial philanderer to boot.) Ephron confessed that in Phoebe's later years, she even became frightened of her mother. Once, when Phoebe visited Wellesley, where Ephron attended college, Ephron found herself continually waiting for the other shoe to drop. To Ephron's classmates Phoebe was something of a glamorous figure then; Ephron's parents had written a play that was a great success on Broadway at the time. Ephron spent the night terrified her mother would start on one of her screaming jags. The alcoholism would continue for fifteen years, more or less uninterrupted, until Phoebe Ephron died at the age of fifty-seven from cirrhosis of the liver.

The eulogy Nora Ephron gave for her would not mention all of this, because it took a very long time for Ephron to process it. Phoebe Ephron was the person who'd coined the phrase "Everything is copy." But not everything was copy, at first. It would take until Ephron's seventies for her to admit in print that she had wished her mother dead for a long time. Before that the story was cleaner, more idyllic, the simple passing of the talent for wisecracking from one generation to the next. Ephron often retold a certain deathbed story:

> She knew, I think, that she was dying, and she turned to me. "You're a reporter, Nora," she said. "Take notes." That makes her sound tougher than she really was. She was tough—and that was good—but she was also soft, somewhat mystical, and intensely proud.

The "Take notes" quote was something Ephron would repeat again and again, but the bit about softness—about her mother's contradictions—mostly disappeared until Ephron wrote about her mother's alcoholism in one of her last essay collections in 2011. So Phoebe Ephron, tough and funny as she was, taught her daughter a little something about humanity, too.

From the time Ephron was very small, she had to build a kind of persona. Her parents took "Everything is copy" seriously, to a fault. When she was a baby, her parents wrote a play about their experiences living in the Bronx with Phoebe's parents called *Three Is a Family*. It was just a light farce, meant as an evening's entertainment, but it provoked bad reactions. When the play was made into a film, Bosley Crowther, the imperious *Times* movie reviewer Pauline Kael so hated, called it "strictly infantile." Then, when Ephron was at Wellesley, her letters home inspired another play, in fact her parents' last real hit: *Take Her, She's Mine*. Evidently proud of their daughter's wit, they couldn't resist directly quoting her in the play:

> *P.S. I'm the only one in my class still wearing a retainer on her teeth. It's not the kind of thing I care to be individual about. Please ask Dr. Schick if it's essential. If he says yes, I shall probably lose it.*

It debuted on Broadway while Ephron was still a college student at Wellesley in Massachusetts. The critics immediately loved it. *Women's Wear Daily* called it a "Tempest of Mirth." *Variety* approved of it, saying it was "told interestingly and there are knowing chuckles and substantial guffaws which pepper the dialog." It ran for nearly a year, from 1961 to 1962. On campus, everyone knew about it.

Ephron would report all of this with the nonchalance that was her trademark. But at a very young age, she had already had the opportunity to learn the frustration that came with being fodder for someone else's work, having her life mined for plays and screenplays. As Joan Didion famously put it, "Writers are always selling somebody out." Ephron knew that rule at an earlier age than most people. She never spoke of it bothering her, but it informed everything she did.

She clearly wasn't fond of looking back, anyway. When Ephron left Wellesley to go to New York in 1962, she always said she felt she was coming home. The bulk of her childhood was spent in Beverly Hills, but she insisted she had never liked it there. She did not write much about high school, and photographs of her as a teenager make her look awkward, not at all a snappy dresser. She did not seem to have any particular professional ambitions; she was not, like Sontag, spending her teenage years pining for an imaginary Europe. When she arrived in New York she simply went to an employment agency and announced that she wished to be a journalist. The employment agency had some openings at *Newsweek*, but the agent told her women were not writers there.

> *It would never have crossed my mind to object or to say,*
> *"You're going to turn out to be wrong about me." It was*
> *a given in those days that if you were a woman and you*
> *wanted to do certain things, you were going to have to*
> *be the exception to the rule.*

She lived together with a friend on Sullivan Street, in what was then known as a southern part of Greenwich Village, and moved in in the middle of a neighborhood celebration of the Feast of St. Anthony.

The *Newsweek* job was not as a reporter, merely as a researcher. So it was a bit of a bust, writingwise; the closest Ephron came to bylines was seeing them on the desk of the editor in chief for whom she worked. Like so many others in this book, she got her break not from the editor of an established magazine, but rather from the editor of a smaller one, in this case a humor magazine called *Monocle*. The editor was Victor Navasky, who would later go on to become the editor of the *Nation*. Ephron met him at one of the many parties the magazine held. He found her funny. And when the newspaper strike hit in late 1962, he asked her to write a parody of what was then a famous gossip column, called the Lyons' Den, written by Leonard Lyons. This got the attention of the editors of the *New York Post*, who promptly offered her a job as a reporter.

It was the publisher of the *Post*, a society matron named Dorothy Schiff, who'd been impressed and suggested they grab up the talent. Schiff embodied a kind of moneyed female independence that she shared with Katharine Graham, the later publisher of the *Washington Post*. Ephron would later write a scathing assessment of Schiff, one so mean that she felt compelled to preface it with: "I feel bad about what I'm going to do here." But without Schiff, there never would have been the Nora Ephron that America came to know. Being a reporter first and a writer second was an important part of Ephron's persona in those years. She alternated the people she'd say inspired her to become a journalist. Sometimes she'd say it was Hildy Johnson in the 1930s comedy *His Girl Friday*. Ephron liked jokes and she liked comedy. She viewed them as essential survival skills. And that meant early on that Ephron knew she wanted to be an observer rather than a participant in public affairs:

> People who are drawn to journalism are usually people who, because of their cynicism or emotional detachment or reserve or whatever, are incapable of being anything but witnesses to events. Something prevents them from becoming involved, committed, and allows them to remain separate. What separates me from what I write about is, I suspect, a sense of the absurd that makes it difficult for me to take many things terribly seriously.

There was absurdity aplenty, apparently, at the *New York Post*. Although she would always credit the place with having taught her how to report and how to write quickly, she did not like the facilities. The entire office was filthy; reporters did not have assigned desks and had to fight for their spots anew each day. But Ephron had an innate toughness, perhaps inherited from or even cultivated by her mother. She seemed to flourish under the challenge. She reported on every-thing: a great deal of crime, quite a few profiles of local politicians, even one of a hot new young writer named Susan Sontag. (The article is pedestrian; they talked about life in the spotlight, about Sontag's stepfather and how he told her she'd never marry if she read too much.)

But the work was not always good. Schiff, who was not particu-larly serious about either her paper's reputation or her own, was a recurring source of oddity and anxiety. She was cheap and did not like to be generous to her employees. Schiff was the only woman publisher in New York at the time, but she was no feminist. She disliked Betty Friedan because she worried that reading the *Feminine Mystique* had encouraged her daughter to leave her husband and get into politics. Once, Dorothy Schiff tried to get Ephron to investigate whether the director Otto Preminger, who lived next door to Schiff, had installed a sauna in his apartment. As evidence of this possibil-ity, Schiff said she could hear running water at all hours of the day. Ephron patiently sent her a memorandum explaining that saunas did not employ running water. Schiff assigned the story to another investigative reporter. He couldn't find anything either.

It bears mentioning that we know so many stories about the absur-dity of Dorothy Schiff—an absurdity that might otherwise have sunk from the historical record—because Nora Ephron herself recorded them. Long after she left the *Post*, Ephron listed not only all Schiff's bad qualities but also the shortcomings of the newspaper, in a media column she was writing for a magazine. In the column she said that although she had recently patched things up with Schiff after telling the Preminger story on the radio, she was going to attack Schiff again. Mostly because the *Post* was a "bad newspaper," and because Schiff was the Marie Antoinette who helmed it: "As in let them read schlock."

The very quality of detachment that had made Ephron a good reporter also made her quite willing to attack her employers. Over the years, her willingness to anger the people she knew, to attack them the same way Kael or West or any of her predecessors had, would become a professional asset. The ferocity of her remarks about, say, Julie Nixon Eisenhower—"I think she's a spider"—is what got her on television and made her reputation as a social critic. This was all long before she became known as the warmer, more forgiving writer of 1980s romantic comedies, but on some level detachment was a habit that never left her. "I think she was more devoted to language than to people," the actress Meg Ryan once said.

Ephron went freelance after she left the *Post*. Sensing a good reviewer in the making, the first place that really began to make use of her talents was the *New York Times Book Review*. It was there that she published a parody of Ayn Rand's Hemingway-with-a-traumatic-brain-injury prose style:

> *Twenty-five years ago, Howard Roark laughed. Standing naked at the edge of a cliff, his face painted, his hair the color of a bright orange rind, his body a composition of straight, clean lines and angles, each curve breaking into smooth, clean, planes, Howard Roark laughed.*

Every subject the *Times* gave her, she tore into with great appetite. Dick Cavett, the host of a talk show where writers argued about concepts that were over his carefully coiffed head, got an early Nora Ephron profile. His manager called Cavett Mr. Television, which at first seemed to embarrass Cavett. But his repudiation of the title, and his self-criticism, took up four long, trivia-laden paragraphs, which Ephron quoted without interruption to give a sense of Cavett's self-absorption:

> *I also got letters asking me why I always wore the same tie. I don't. I have two ties.*

She wrote an appreciation of Rex Reed, the journalist who would later become a film critic, by calling him "a saucy, snoopy, bitchy man who sees with sharp eyes and succeeds in making voyeurs of us all." These, she made clear, were all qualities that pleased her in a writer.

Nonetheless, Ephron did not collect a lot of these early pieces, and reading them against her other work one suspects the problem, usually, was that the editor assigned her a banal subject. In 1969, she wrote the piece "Where Bookmen Meet to Eat" for the *New York Times* chronicling the easy-to-parody subject of the long publishing lunches to which agents, book editors, and writers are prone. The piece goes over the subject with a delicate hand, even though at the end Ephron manages to convince one agent to admit that "lunch is two hours out there in the world that could be spent returning telephone calls."

Of course, she had to be careful to preserve her own ability to make a living. In interviews from and after that period she describes herself as having just enough to live on, no more than ten thousand dollars a year before 1974. Ephron, like Sontag before her, wrote for women's magazines for money, especially *Cosmopolitan*. These pieces were not always enjoyable to write, because, as she put it, they could not be done at the "intellectual level that is most satisfying to me as a writer." There is some reason to suspect they were also the pieces that drove her toward the women's movement, out of sheer frustration with the work she was getting, especially from Helen Gurley Brown. The opportunities there were what you'd expect: articles about makeovers, travel, sex, Copacabana showgirls.

But Gurley Brown did let Ephron do one thing that broke out of *Cosmopolitan*'s usual peppy mold. Perhaps feeling hurt by how the fashion tabloid *Women's Wear Daily* had frequently written about her—it often chronicled Gurley Brown's career as a magazine editor in less than flattering terms—she allowed Ephron to write about it. Ephron laid waste to its editorial pretensions. It was a gossip rag, she wrote, targeting a narrow audience called "The Ladies," whose pampered lives she mercilessly pilloried: "There was something a little embarrassing about just doing nothing and having lunch in between." She said the magazine was a "surrogate bitch," a kind of excuse to make fun of the appearance of the famous while calling it journalism.

Ephron was taking down the magazine in its own style: its habit of adopting a confiding, giggling persona to cover up the undermining remarks it made about professional women, about the way they looked and the way they dated and the way they managed their professional affairs. *Women's Wear Daily*, not noticing the ironic resemblance in tone and style, threatened to sue, Ephron wrote later.

But—and perhaps Helen Gurley Brown should have seen this coming—in writing for *Cosmopolitan* she was also gathering material on the magazine itself, and more specifically its editor. Ephron's writings had caught the eye of the editors at *Esquire*. The first Ephron piece they ever published was a profile of Gurley Brown, one that sought to highlight her worst personality traits. In the profile, Ephron takes the view that Gurley Brown's problem was not her bad habit of crying when confronted with criticism, nor was it the potential corruption of morals her critics often identified when she advised young women, for example, to date married men. Instead, she went after her former editor for something that perhaps only a former writer for the magazine could see so clearly: the way Gurley Brown insulted the intelligence of women, generally:

> She is demonstrating, rather forcefully, that there are well over a million women who are willing to spend sixty cents to read not about politics, not about the female liberation movement, not about the war in Vietnam, but merely about how to get a man.

This argument bears some resemblance to Didion's view of Helen Gurley Brown. Didion complained in her article about the vulgarity of a popular magazine editor who wants to be "the little princess, the woman who has fulfilled the whispered promise of her own books and of all the advertisements, the girl to whom things happen." But Ephron didn't write from the standpoint of a superior, disdainful mind; she understood, in a way Didion did not, the appeal of this frivolity. She therefore came at Gurley Brown from a more democratic place. She admitted she was among *Cosmopolitan*'s readers and writers. "How can you be angry at someone who's got your number?" Ephron asked. The sympathy was initially lost on Gurley Brown. She hated the article and especially the picture printed with it, but within a few days forgave Ephron.

The next targets of Ephron's ire were Erich Segal, the Yale classics professor who had written the bestselling novel *Love Story*, and the poet Rod McKuen. Ephron professed herself a lover of trash, and particularly the novels of Jacqueline Susann. "I have never believed that kitsch killed," she averred. But she could not abide Segal's and McKuen's sentimentality. She also could not abide their public personas, especially Segal's. Philip Roth's *Portnoy's Complaint* was competing with Segal for a space on the bestseller lists at the time, and Segal made a habit of giving speeches condemning Roth's graphic depictions of sex. (Perhaps unusually for a trashy book, *Love Story* has no sex scenes at all.) Ephron looked on in disbelief:

> *Everyone loves Erich's speech. Everyone, that is, but Pauline Kael, the film critic, who heard an earlier version of Erich's speech at a book-and-author luncheon in Richmond, Virginia, and told him afterward that he was knocking freedom of speech and sucking up to his audience. To which Erich replied, "We're here to sell books, aren't we?"*

This ability to speak from inside a wide phenomenon, to know how it catered to and tricked the basest aspects of one's personality, and then to be able to criticize it from the perspective of an insider would make Ephron a better chronicler of the 1970s—and especially the women's movement—than just about anyone else. She was inside and outside at once, a detached person who was always in the middle of it all. She had a perceptive gift, and it was best put to use in those years. Of course, Ephron's fame as a filmmaker would eclipse almost all her work as a writer. But it was her writing that left the indelible mark of her actual personality, her capacity to size people up and, when they really needed it, cut them down with aplomb. It made her the kind of friend people were proud to have, eager to please, and mildly afraid of. And it made this early work of hers all very brilliant.

For most of her career, Ephron wrote in the first person and all her life, because of her early training as a reporter, she felt a little dirty doing it. Originally, she needed to be prodded by her editors, having been trained at the *Post* not to make herself the story. But when she came to collect her early pieces in a book called *Wallflower at the Orgy*, in 1970, she confessed she had chafed somewhat at the restriction.

> *There are times when I am seized with an almost uncontrollable desire to blurt out, in the middle of interviews, "Me! Me! Me! Enough about you. What about me?"*

Years later, after she had been interviewed six ways from Sunday as a truly famous person, this bit of youthful vanity would embarrass her. But no piece offered so complete a sense of Ephron herself, of her voice and her perspective, as the article she would write in 1972 for *Esquire*, "A Few Words About Breasts."

The subject demands an observation: Ephron was unusually flat chested. Apparently it ran in the family; she records her caustic mother, upon being asked by her daughters to purchase a first bra, saying: "Why not use a Band-Aid instead?"

Women engaged in a continuous game of "competitive remarks made about breast size," Ephron wrote. She confessed to having obsessed over the subject, an obsession that extended to purchasing the kind of snake-oil bust enhancement systems that were everywhere in the seventies and eighties. A college boyfriend's mother implied to her, in conversation, that she would never be able to satisfy sexually because of this disability. Ephron ended on a note that would become her signature move: a consideration of all the alternative arguments against her experience, the people who insisted that smaller breasts actually made clothes fit better, occasioned less teasing. This was a gesture at the objectivity of journalism, something Ephron said she never believed in, even before she was afraid to write completely from the "I." And then she punctured it all:

> *I have thought about their remarks, tried to put myself in their place, considered their point of view. I think they are full of shit.*

It may mean something that this article, published in the May 1972 *Esquire*, was the first thing Ephron published after her mother's death. It brought in mail to the magazine.

After the piece about her breasts, *Esquire* offered Ephron a column. Over the years, conflicting things were said about whether it was Ephron's idea or the magazine editors' that the column should focus on women. Whoever can take the full credit, it was an excellent match.

Ephron had already been into the women's movement for some time when she began writing, which meant she had already gathered a fair number of observations. Her first column explored a question that haunts the writings of nearly every feminist, though few at the time were willing to say it out loud: would the feminist revolution spark a change in the way men and women sexually fantasized about each other? Ephron still had enough dignity, she thought, to avoid saying precisely what her own fantasies were, but they involved domination, and she knew already that feminists were not meant to want to be dominated in sex with men. She left the column open-ended, not having any real answer, but offered a self-conscious final paragraph:

Writing a column on women in Esquire *is, I realize, a little like telling a Jewish joke to a bunch of Irish Catholics. The criticisms I may make of the movement will seem doubly disloyal; the humor I hope to bring to the subject will seem flippant in this context.*

Ephron was indeed wading into enemy territory, at least to a degree. The *Esquire* of the time was less celebrity-driven than it is now, and considered itself more of a literary magazine than a fashion one. But Ephron's columns were unique. She was not, like Sontag and Didion, viewing the movement from a distance, criticizing it in the abstract. Neither was she plunging headlong into it, in the sense that she did not so much see her columns as an effort to endorse any platforms.

The first hit she landed was on another writer, Alix Kates Shulman, author of the popular novel *Memoirs of an Ex–Prom Queen*. The book was a bestseller in its time, opening with the main character's account of being raped by her first husband. It turns from there to its real subject: the perils of beauty in a male-dominated culture: "If I could know for sure I was still beautiful, I thought, it would be easy to leave." Shulman went on to claim that in fact beautiful people had just as many problems as ugly people, only different ones. She used, among others, Marilyn Monroe as an example of beautiful suffering.

Ephron, having never been considered much of a beauty, found this line of argument hard to take. "There isn't an ugly girl in America who wouldn't exchange her problems for the problems of being beautiful," she insisted, including herself:

"They say it's worse to be ugly," Alix Shulman writes. Yes, they do say that. And they're right. It's also worse to be poor, worse to be orphaned, worse to be fat. Not just different from rich, familied and thin—actually worse.

This piece thus punctured a line that had been quite popular within the women's movement itself, where Shulman was an established figure who had published in *Ms.* magazine the marriage contract she'd made with her husband, in which every domestic task imaginable was enumerated and allocated to each party in the marriage. No one else took her to task in quite this way, though Didion had offered Shulman's marriage contract as evidence of the growing obsession with trivial matters in the women's movement. But Ephron was not using Shulman as a reason to reject the whole; in fact, she tried to end this ripper of a piece on a slightly more sympathetic note. She was being unfair to Shulman, she said, and even to the movement. "I'm working on it," she said. "Like all things about liberation, sisterhood is difficult."

Sisterhood Is Difficult could have been an alternative title for the collection of these columns. (Ephron went instead with *Crazy Salad* when she published it in 1975.) The fact was that most of the essays see Ephron struggling to describe the movement—not the principles underlying feminism, but the way they were being articulated by actual women out in the world—in happy terms. One column was spent reporting from the 1972 Miami Democratic Convention, where Gloria Steinem and Betty Friedan were butting heads. The goal of feminist activists at the convention was to get some concessions on the Democratic party platform, but instead, as Ephron watched, they managed to get very little done beyond infighting. What was happening wasn't pretty, and Ephron had to describe it, especially Friedan's anger at the way a younger generation was sidelining her:

> *It's her baby, damn it. Her movement. Is she supposed to sit still and let a beautiful thin lady run off with it?*

Gloria Steinem, then at the height of her media visibility as an actual feminist leader, did not come off much better when seen through Ephron's lens. Though she was more high-handed than Friedan, she had friends who did the dirty work for her. And when

Steinem was left behind by George McGovern, who had made her certain promises about the Democratic party platform, she cried about it. Ephron is not so much critical of Steinem's crying—as she was of Helen Gurley Brown's—as she is mystified by the occasion for it. "I have never cried over anything remotely political in my life, and I honestly have no idea what to say."

Ephron told an interviewer that this bit of reporting—her simple mention of Steinem's tears—got her friends "yelling and screaming at me." Some of them were angry for years.

Yet for most, Ephron's sympathetic but skeptical tone worked well. We have a habit, now, of assuming that people had only one kind of reaction to the women's movement: either they were all in, or they were all out. But the second wave was not, as its critics like Didion sometimes framed it, a united front. Its internal politics were fractious, with arguments about the way age and race and any number of other intrafeminine fault lines inflected this business of "being a woman." Any real person, looking at all that, had to have a conflicted take on it all. It was possible to feel extreme, uncontrollable surges of hope *and* disappointment.

All those conflicted feelings are perhaps what made Ephron such a resonant spokesperson about all of it: she could be cutting about the movement's absurdities and ugliness, but she was doing so from the position of an insider. And though she was gentle, occasionally she would offer corrections to the elisions of the critics. In one column, she distinguished herself from Didion's insistence that life as a woman would involve "blood, birth and death," a definition she called "extraordinary and puzzling." Didion and Ephron had, by then, become friendly, as they ran in all the same circles. Perhaps Ephron was a good influence. Asked about her position on the women's movement in the 1990s, Didion seemed to retract her earlier critique.

I think that piece was about a specific moment in time.
I thought the women's movement was becoming mired

*in the trivial, that it was going in a direction that wasn't
the ideal direction, that it had hit a wall and kept talking
about small things. Trivialization wore itself out, though,
and the movement managed to survive, not so much as a
movement anymore, but as a changed way of life.*

Ephron obviously had had no problem talking about women's
bodies; there was, after all, the article about breasts. She had also written, in early 1973, a long investigative piece called "Dealing with the
uh, Problem," which had gamely explored the manufacturing, use,
and marketing of the feminine odor spray—i.e., "a deodorant for the
external genital area (or, more exactly, the external perineal area)."
Her detachment suited her well here, for with very little editorializing
she managed to make the whole business seem so ridiculous.

It was easy to write about the ridiculous things men said and did
to women, harder to write about the ridiculous things women did to
themselves. She found herself arguing one day with Susan Brownmiller about wearing makeup. The divisions in the movement were
terribly apparent by that point, and she had worked the experience
into the Shulman piece, without attaching a name:

> *Once I tried to explain to a fellow feminist why I liked
> wearing makeup; she replied by explaining why she does
> not. Neither of us understood a word the other said.*

One column wrestled directly with this alternating enthusiasm
for and ambivalence about the movement. She found it difficult to
be at once committed to it and to be a writer. One of the "recurring
ironies of this movement is that there is no way to tell the truth
about it without, in some small way, seeming to hurt it." She found
it difficult she said, to review books by women about the second-
wave feminist movement because although she agreed with their
passions, she didn't really like the way those women wrote. She

knew she was supposed to count their good intentions into the final critical calculus, of course:

> *This is what's known in the women's movement as sister-*
> *hood, and it is good politics, I suppose, but it is not good*
> *criticism. Or honesty. Or the truth. (Furthermore, it is every*
> *bit as condescending as the sort of criticism men apply*
> *to books about women these days—that unconsciously*
> *patronizing tone that treats books by and about women as*
> *some sort of sub-genre of literature, outside the mainstream,*
> *not quite relevant, interesting really, how-these-women-do-*
> *go-on-and-we-really-must-try-to-understand-what-they-*
> *are-getting-at-whatever-it-is.)*

There was, of course, something of self-criticism in this, for there was something ultimately sort of patronizing about *Esquire* sectioning off its analysis of women from the rest of the magazine, too, not to mention that the magazine targeted men as its readers and did not have nearly as wide a circulation among women. And something was ultimately wasteful about keeping Ephron writing only about that. Later she'd say it was her decision to quit writing the columns, that she'd grown tired of it, said what she needed to say.

But the subject continued to provide her with copy for some time after that. She was poached by *New York* magazine. There she was to keep writing pieces about women. In the first of those, she attacked a friend, the writer Sally Quinn, for saying she had always used flirting as a reporting technique. And in analyzing her anger over Quinn's remark, Ephron mentioned what a recent interviewee, and growing friend, had to say about the matter of women and professional competition:

> *"Dashiell Hammett used to say I had the meanest jealousy*
> *of all," Miss [Lillian] Hellman said. "I had no jealousy of*
> *work, no jealousy of money. I was just jealous of women*

*who took advantage of men, because I didn't know how
to do it."*

For *New York* Ephron began to return to an older form for her:
the simple takedown of prominent media figures. Bob Guccione,
the publisher of *Penthouse*, decided to launch a magazine for women
called *Viva* in 1973, with the tagline: "Brought to you by men who
unashamedly enjoy women." In the column you can practically see
Ephron's excitement as she gets to lay bare the particular contours of
Guccione's ignorance, quoting him at length and without comment
just as she had done to Dick Cavett and Helen Gurley Brown:

*As near as possible, everything considered, I hate to say
it but I think it's true, I know women better than women
know themselves.*

Viva would last seven years after this, but it would not become
the kind of emblematic publication that women cited to each other,
contrary to Guccione's dreams and hopes.

The next person Ephron went after was Julie Nixon Eisenhower,
who Ephron found to be a phony. In the aftermath of Watergate,
attractive Julie tended to be the person the Nixons put in front of
the press. The Washington press corps, as Ephron chronicles, was
practically in love with her.

*As one journalist put it, this is not to say that anyone
believes what she is saying but simply that people believe
she believes what she is saying. They will tell you she is
approachable, which is true, and that she is open, which is
not . . . It is almost as if she is the only woman in America
over the age of twenty who still thinks her father is exactly
what she thought he was when she was six.*

This statement may have some personal bite in it, because once Phoebe Ephron was dead, Henry Ephron had become the burden of his daughters. He began to write a memoir he called *We Thought We Could Do Anything*, a title he took directly from the eulogy his daughter had given for her mother. Ephron later insisted the memoir was full of nonsense. Moreover, it seemed like a naked attempt to capitalize on the growing fame of his eldest daughter, which must have bothered her.

Nora Ephron was by now famous. She was appearing in the society gossip rag she'd excoriated years before, *Women's Wear Daily*, quite frequently—more frequently even than Helen Gurley Brown had. She was on television often. On one show, the host brought up the way she often cut people to the quick.

> Host: *You can be malevolent, can't you?*
> Ephron: *Oh, sure.*
> Host: *It's kind of fun to be malevolent, isn't it?*
> Ephron: *No, you're—*
> Host: *I'll tell you something you were malevolent in.*
> *Your piece on Julie Nixon.*
> Ephron: *You have a soft spot for Julie Nixon.*
> Host: *I like Julie, yes.*
> Ephron: *Well, I don't. I think she's a chocolate-covered spider.*

This was the frame that almost all Ephron's subsequent pieces would take. At some point she'd return to *Esquire*, where instead of women her targets became the media, and many individuals she knew in the media: *People* magazine, Theodore White, the pretensions of certain *New Yorker* writers. (She didn't mention Kael in that piece.) At one point, caught up in a dispute *Esquire* had with the writer Richard Goodwin, she even hit back at *Esquire*. She wrote a column criticizing its decision to settle with Goodwin over a profile of him she had edited for the magazine.

This aspect of Ephron's life—what some have called her meanness—seems not to have been totally apparent to readers at the time. It was sometimes not even apparent to Ephron herself. Interviewed by the Associated Press when *Crazy Salad* was published in 1975, Ephron said:

> *You can write the most wonderful piece in the world about someone and the only word they'll see is "plump" . . . You learn very early that you're not in this business to be friends with the people you write about. If you are, you start pulling punches.*

The dilemma she articulated here was one she felt acutely in her own writing. By the time Ephron was a household name, the men occasionally appeared to be sniping back at her in columns, calling her brainy and cute instead of brilliant, opining on how much they'd like to sleep with her. She saw that this affected what she was asked to write and what she was asked to think about in her career as an essayist. She told an interviewer in 1974 that "there are certain magazines that will not assign pieces to women or even think of women in connection with certain subjects such as economics or politics."

"Being single is a distraction," a freshly divorced Nora Ephron also said to that interviewer in 1974. (She was briefly married to another humor writer, Dan Greenburg, in the early 1970s.) "I mean one of the things about marriage that is good for both men and women is that it frees you from all that energy that you use to put into dating. You can put it into work. You don't have to worry about who is going to take you to the dinner party tomorrow. It takes time to be single, it seems to me." Bernstein ended that.

For whatever reason, Ephron's connection with Bernstein happened at the same time as a sudden decline in her interest in writing for magazines. In fact, her writing dropped off almost entirely in the latter half of the 1970s, as she turned her attention to screenplays. She began collaborating with Alice Arlen on *Silkwood*, and after what was apparently a somewhat rocky courtship, she married Carl Bernstein. "We decided to get married on Sunday, we got married on Wednesday, and the perfect part was that we made the decision to get married while we were on the Eastern shuttle," she said to an interviewer. But she also told him that "the test of whether a marriage works is not necessarily whether it lasts forever."

As we know from *Heartburn*, it didn't last forever. "I'm terrible about making stuff up," she'd say when interviewers asked if she had any intentions of writing fiction. But she also said that from the moment she left her second husband she kind of knew she would write about the experience. The husband of the woman Bernstein had been cheating with—his name was Peter—asked her to lunch:

> We meet outside a Chinese restaurant on Connecticut Avenue and fall into each other's arms, weeping. "Oh, Peter," I say to him, "isn't it awful?"
>
> "It's awful," he says. "What's happening to this country?"
>
> I'm crying hysterically, but I'm thinking, someday this will be a funny story.

Ephron said she eventually realized that the thing her mother had repeated throughout her life, "Everything is copy," was a matter of control:

> When you slip on a banana peel, people laugh at you; but when you tell people you slipped on a banana peel, it's your laugh. So you become the hero rather than the victim of the joke.
>
> I think that's what she meant.

Heartburn became a giant bestseller, making Ephron rich. She wrote the screenplay for the film version, to be directed by her friend Mike Nichols. Bernstein was, by all accounts, furious. He made it a condition of their divorce that the film not portray him as anything other than a loving father. Some of her friends apparently thought the move in bad taste too; in a gossipy *New York* magazine article that came out just before the novel appeared, her first husband, Dan Greenburg, told the reporter: "Nora is a much classier person and a much better writer than is evident in this book."

The book has become a kind of legend now, notwithstanding the fact the movie never quite lived up to the cleverness of the novel, perhaps because Bernstein imposed conditions on the adaptation for the sake of the couple's two children, and perhaps because a movie cannot easily replicate the consciousness of one funny narrator the way a novel can. Too much was dependent on the Rachel character sounding just like Nora, having the same gimlet-eyed way of looking at the world and at her situation, and that interiority was too hard for even Meryl Streep to pull off on-screen. But it was one of the great pop acts of feminist revenge, one that not all the treacly films Ephron would make in her late career could quite gloss over.

12

Arendt & McCarthy
& Hellman

For the last few years of her life, Hannah Arendt was teaching and
publishing at the enviable pace that is possible only for someone
who has reached a place of profound comfort in her life. But that
changed in October 1970. "HEINRICH DIED SUNDAY OF A HEART ATTACK,"
Arendt told McCarthy in a telegram. McCarthy was then living in
Paris with her last husband, Jim West, a diplomat. She flew to New
York immediately for the funeral.

Arendt and Blücher had, by then, been together for more than
thirty years. She was bereft without him. "I am now sitting in Heinrich's room and using his typewriter," she wrote to McCarthy not
long after his death. "Gives me something to hold on to." And in
fact, she would not last very long without him. On December 4,
1975, Arendt died of a heart attack herself as she was having dinner with friends.

McCarthy was named Arendt's literary executor, and she also put
herself in charge of the funeral arrangements, negotiating with the
family. In another sort of friendship, this might have been unusually
intimate, but this was the kind where the best friend was the natural
mourner in chief. In New York, McCarthy gave a eulogy in which
she talked of Arendt sometimes in the mode of a lover, praising her
looks, the way she'd lie on a sofa and think. She even talked about
Arendt's legs and ankles in a way that would get her mocked. But it

fitted if you considered McCarthy described her friend as someone who embodied thought:

> The first time I heard her speak in public—nearly thirty years ago, during a debate—I was reminded of what Bernhardt must have been or Proust's Berma, a magnificent stage five, which implies a goddess. Perhaps a chthonic goddess, or a fiery one, rather than the airy kind. Unlike other good speakers, she was not at all an orator. She appeared, rather, as a mime, a thespian, enacting a drama of mind, that dialogue of me-and-myself she so often summons up in her writings.

McCarthy then gave up over two years of her own writing time to work on compiling and editing Arendt's last project. It was to be a three-volume treatise called *The Life of the Mind*. The first volume would consider the act of thinking, the second the act of willing, and the third the act of judging. Arendt had substantially completed drafts of only the first two parts, and left, for the third, just two epigraphs on a sheet of paper still in her typewriter when she died. Though McCarthy's German was not good and fundamentally she was no theorist, she considered it a matter of honor to finish the book. And she did, though the publisher paid her only a quarter of the advance and royalties to do so, the rest going to Arendt's extended family.

It was an act of extraordinary generosity. Time is the one thing artists covet most; as Sontag once remarked, it's the main thing they use money to buy. But in the last twenty years of her life, McCarthy was not producing as much work as she once did. She finished one novel, *Cannibals and Missionaries*, which was to be her last. Arendt's death, and later Robert Lowell's, depressed her. She was still a figure of considerable influence—though *Cannibals and Missionaries* is not her best work, it got favorable reviews—but she was floundering a bit in search of a real role.

Perhaps this explained what then happened with Lillian Hellman.

Hellman was, to say the least, a complicated person. Her first great success as a writer was a play called *The Children's Hour*, in which children accuse two teachers at a boarding school of lesbianism. The success of the play, and the contracts she could subsequently command in Hollywood because of it, made Hellman rich. Her wealth and fame were, however, an odd match for her politics. Like Parker, whom she befriended in Hollywood, Hellman was a leftist activist in her youth. Unlike Parker, Hellman tended to lie about that. Hellman was widely believed to have lied to the House Un-American Activities Committee in the 1950s when she testified that she had no current link to the Communist Party, or indeed "any political group." Her testimony rescued her from the jail time served by more honest witnesses, like Hellman's partner, Dashiell Hammett. The whole affair made her very unpopular with left intellectual types like McCarthy and her friends.

As to any personal animus, McCarthy had met Hellman only twice. The first time was at a lunch at Sarah Lawrence College, where McCarthy taught for a while in 1948. There, she overheard Hellman bashing John Dos Passos to a group of students, saying he'd abandoned the anti-Fascists during the Spanish Civil War because he hated Spanish food. McCarthy, never one to let an opportunity for correction pass her by, pointed out that in fact Dos Passos had said in his writings that he had become disenchanted because of the murder of a friend. McCarthy saw Hellman's anger at the time, she wrote to a friend in 1980:

> *I remember that on her bare shriveled arms she had a great many bracelets, gold and silver, and that they began to tremble—in her fury and surprise, I assumed, at being caught red-handed in a brain-washing job.*

It seems neither Hellman nor McCarthy ever forgot the incident. Then suddenly, while doing publicity rounds for *Cannibals and*

Missionaries, McCarthy decided to bring it up. First she told a French interviewer about it. Then, invited on *The Dick Cavett Show*, she was fatefully asked which writers she considered "overpraised":

> McCarthy: *The only one I can think of is a holdover like Lillian Hellman, who I think is tremendously overrated, a bad writer, and dishonest writer, but she really belongs to the past, to the Steinbeck past, not that she is a writer like Steinbeck.*
> Cavett: *What is dishonest about her?*
> McCarthy: *Everything. But I said once in some interview that every word she writes is a lie, including "and" and "the."*

Many people later told McCarthy's biographers they had found this "reckless," her delivering such a pointed insult "with that smile of hers." Apparently Hellman had been watching too: she called Dick Cavett in an absolute fury, as he later told the story:

> *"I guess I never thought of you as defenseless, Lillian," I managed.*
> *"That's bullshit. I'm suing the whole damn bunch of you." In that, at least, she proved a woman of her word.*

McCarthy thought she had simply been saying something everyone knew. Instead, she found herself staring at a lawsuit she could not really afford to defend herself against. The lawsuit asserted that McCarthy had known her statement was false and that she had made the accusation that Hellman was a liar with malice. Hellman named McCarthy, *The Dick Cavett Show*, and the PBS station on which it appeared as defendants and demanded 2.25 million dollars in damages. The *New York Times* called Hellman for comment on the suit, and she speculated about McCarthy's reasons:

I haven't seen her in 10 years, and I never wrote anything about her. We have several mutual friends, but that would not serve as a cause for her remarks. I think she has always disliked me. It could go back to the Spanish Civil War days, in November or December of 1937, after I had returned from Spain.

For her part, McCarthy told the *Times*:

I barely knew her . . . My views are based on her books, especially Scoundrel Time, *which I refused to buy, but borrowed. I did not like the role she had given herself in that book.*

Never one to avoid an opportunity for publicity, Norman Mailer took it upon himself to try to referee the dispute. "They are both splendid writers," he offered. "They are, however, so different in their talents that it is natural for them to detest each other. Writers bear this much comparison to animals." He called McCarthy's remark "stupid" and "best left unsaid." Coming from a man who considered pugilism an essential virtue, this was a remarkable position. No one listened to him.

Martha Gellhorn, the pioneering female journalist and former wife of Ernest Hemingway, also came out of retirement to lob sixteen pages of attacks at Lillian Hellman in the *Paris Review*, pointing out that nearly every date in Hellman's *An Unfinished Woman* had to be wrong. Gellhorn was particularly knowledgeable about Hemingway's activities during the Spanish Civil War and more or less destroyed Hellman's claims about them. "In my unspecialized study of apocryphism," she concluded, "Miss Hellman ranks as sublime."

Privately, McCarthy was worried. Not so much about whether she would ultimately prevail in the suit, for she was quietly gathering materials that would show Hellman's lies. She did learn of one concrete example, not then widely known, in Hellman's memoir *Pentimento*, one section of which had been made into the Hollywood film *Julia* starring Jane Fonda. This "Julia," according to Hellman, was a childhood friend who been a kind of Zelig of the early twentieth century, analyzed by Freud, heroically at the front in the Spanish Civil War, and then died during World War II.

It did turn out that Julia was fiction, drawn in part from the life of a woman named Muriel Gardiner, who had written to Hellman of the similarities between her life and Julia's and received no response. But none of this was public knowledge at the time McCarthy went on the Cavett show. Everyone had suspicions; in particular, Martha Gellhorn thought most of Hellman's assertions complete lies.

Proof or no proof, the legal costs were worrisome. McCarthy had not had a bestseller since *The Group*, back in 1963. Meanwhile, Hellman was unqualifiedly rich, and far more determined to see the thing through to the end. She even won the first couple of skirmishes, getting a judge to rule against McCarthy's initial motion to dismiss the case.

It was sheer luck that before she could see her vendetta through to its end Hellman died, in late June 1984. A dead person can't be slandered or libeled, so the damages became largely academic. By August the suit was gone entirely. But the spectacle had become legendary; today it is often the only thing the public remembers about Mary McCarthy at all. Late in her life, still obsessed with the subject, Nora Ephron wrote an entire play about the enmity, which she titled *Imaginary Friends*. She had been, for a while, befriended by Hellman:

> *It was quite a while before I began to suspect that the fabulous stories she entertained her friends with were, to be polite about it, stories. When she sued McCarthy years afterward, I wasn't surprised. She was sick by then, and legally blind. And her anger—the anger that was her favorite accessory—had turned wearisome, even to those who were loyal to her.*

Ephron's play went up on Broadway in 2002. It was not success-ful, running for only seventy-six performances over three months. But for Ephron, at the time living in what she called movie jail after a string of flops, it was a passion project, a kind of relief, a return to form. "I could write about a subject that has interested me since my days as a magazine journalist: women and what they do to each other." But she didn't quite manage to pass her passion along; the play was totally forgotten by the time she died in 2012.

13

Adler

Nineteen eighty was a year of fighting, as it happened, because Renata Adler, already in her forties, saw a ripe target in an elder. Pauline Kael had only just returned to the *New Yorker* after a brief stint in Hollywood as a producer with Warren Beatty, a stint that had barely lasted a year. It had gone badly, the job responsibilities disintegrating almost immediately upon her arrival in Los Angeles. She'd gone to LA to work on a particular film, James Toback's *Love and Money*, and when that didn't work out, she ended up working in a studio proper as a production executive.

Suffice it to say it was not a good fit. She'd later say that Hollywood executives thought she was a spy. And when she went back to the *New Yorker*, William Shawn had to be talked into taking her back. As another editor told *Vanity Fair*, "Mr. Shawn felt Pauline had sullied herself." But he took her back anyway.

In the summer of that year, a new collection of Kael's criticism, *When the Lights Go Down*, was published to mostly glowing reviews. The arguments over the *Citizen Kane* debacle were by then ten years old. So, failed Hollywood experience notwithstanding, Kael was still very much considered at the top of her craft. She had fans.

Renata Adler, on the other hand, numbered herself among the dissenters. In the *New York Review of Books*, she tore into Kael's book with a ferocity unusual even among celebrated critics:

Now, When the Lights Go Down, *a collection of her reviews over the past five years, is out; and it is, to my surprise and without Kael- or [John] Simon-like exaggeration, not simply, jarringly, piece by piece, line by line, and without interruption, worthless.*

This judgment appears halfway through the review, after a long discussion of the pieces of Kael's writing Adler preferred. Adler attributed the decline in Kael's style not so much to personal faults of Kael's—in fact very little about Kael as a person is said in this work—but rather to the repetitiveness of a staff critic's job, which requires churning out so many pieces and seeing so many movies that their reviews naturally suffer from exhaustion and repetition. But it didn't matter how many qualifications Adler laid out ahead of that savage statement. She had clearly declared war on Kael. And she made a decent case.

Adler's surgical work was mostly directed at Kael's prose style rather than her critical acumen. The thing that bothered her about Kael's work was the way it was written, which she felt was almost pure bombast, devoid of ideas:

She has an underlying vocabulary of about nine favorite words, which occur several hundred times, and often several times per page, in this book of nearly six hundred pages: "whore" (and its derivatives "whorey," "whorish," "whoriness"), applied in many contexts, but almost never to actual prostitution; "myth," "emblem" (also "mythic," "emblematic"), used with apparent intellectual intent, but without ascertainable meaning; "pop," "comicstrip," "trash" ("trashy"), "pulp" ("pulpy"), all used judgmentally (usually approvingly) but otherwise apparently interchangeable with "mythic"; "urban poetic," meaning marginally more violent than "pulpy"; "soft" (pejorative);

"tension," meaning, apparently, any desirable state; "rhythm," used often as a verb, but meaning harmony or speed; "visceral"; and "level."

Adler would come back to this technique again and again in her career, counting the number of words and turning them back on a subject to make them look foolish. Against Kael, who had so much copy available to analyze—all of it written in the structure of movie reviews—it was devastating. It was so devastating, in fact, that many felt moved to stick up for Kael. The *New York Review of Books* letter pages filled with, among others, a defense from thirteen-year-old Matthew Wilder, who called Adler's essay a "depressing, vengeful, ceaseless tirade." The *New York Times*' John Leonard chided her too: "To be sure, the staff critics I know are as hard on themselves as Miss Adler is on Miss Kael. They worry about their adjectives. They speak of their '800-word minds.'" Kael's other friends, including James Wolcott, also stepped up to defend her in print. But the damage was done. Adler's words about Kael's work would appear in every obituary when Kael died in 2001.

A younger Kael, the Kael of the "Circles and Squares" era, might have offered a withering response. But she wrote nothing and gave no interviews about the incident, other than telling a reporter: "I'm sorry that Ms. Adler doesn't respond to my writing. What else can I say?" William Shawn, contacted by the papers, simply said it was how Adler always wrote. He should know. Adler had, by that time, been writing for the *New Yorker* on and off for seventeen years. She had spent many of those years on the attack. Adler is a relentlessly analytical writer, who can be a bit like a dog with a bone when she senses logical fallacy. Anyone who'd read about her prior career knew two things: that she was, mostly, smarter than those who surrounded her, and that she liked to show it off in print.

For someone who often argues in black-and-white, Adler's biography is full of strange contradictions. A *New York* profile once called her "as assertively and publicly 'private' as Woody Allen," a comparison that now seems odd given how much we know about Allen. But it is true that Adler has lived a life both very visible and very invisible. Of her childhood we know little, except that she is the daughter of German refugees, and was born in Milan in 1937. Her parents arrived in Connecticut sometime during World War II, with her in tow.

From the time she was a child, anxiety dominated her life. At first, she had trouble learning English, she told a magazine interviewer. But when her parents tried to put her in boarding school to help, it only made her more nervous. Her anxieties followed her to Bryn Mawr, a women's college in Pennsylvania, where she became the sort of person who reported *herself* for honor code violations like smoking. It got so bad she claimed that she'd had to consult psychiatrists, and have her brother write papers for her. She thought of going to law school when she graduated, but eventually she ended up in graduate school at Harvard instead, studying philosophy like Sontag before her. Also like Sontag, she never finished that degree, though she spent a year in Paris on a Fulbright, studying with the famous anthropologist Claude Lévi-Strauss.

Adler didn't want to stay in academia, though she claims to have fallen out of the academic track almost by accident. At Harvard, she met the now-forgotten *New Yorker* writer S. N. Behrman and translated one of his plays. He was the one who suggested she interview for the *New Yorker*, and it was almost by accident that she came to be employed there. Writing still did not come very easily to Adler. Later she would say that her first pieces were written, primarily, to impress her fiancé, Reuel Wilson, the now-grown-up son of Edmund Wilson and Mary McCarthy.

When McCarthy met Adler in Italy one summer, she described her as though she were a character in a novel: Reuel's "thin, rather Biblical-looking Jewish girl friend . . . who is either quite homely, or a beauty, according to taste." If there was any hostility between them, any rivalry of strong intellects as there had been between McCarthy and Sontag, it went wholly unrecorded. Adler later said she hadn't read McCarthy before she met her. "I was shy in those days, and she was extraordinarily kind to me," she said. "Later, when I read her writing and recognized that critical intelligence to be feared, I was surprised." That sort of disconnect would come to define Adler. Few who met Adler as she was in person—anxious and soft-spoken—would relate that image to the ferocious way she could grab the page.

Yet her ability to offer an opinion with godlike certainty was her gift from the start. The first piece of writing Adler published under her own name (one early effort was hidden under a pseudonym after an editor ripped it apart) was a review of a book by a *New Yorker* writer: the reporter John Hersey. Hersey, most famous as the author of the long study *Hiroshima*, had collected his magazine pieces under the somewhat self-important title *Here to Stay: Studies in Human Tenacity*. It's safe to say that Adler did not like Hersey's writing:

> *His book begins with the statement: "The great themes are love and death; their synthesis is the will to live, and that is what this book is about"—which perfectly illustrates the kind of folksy, meaningless rhetoric that characterizes the entire book.*

By then, Adler was also a full-time staffer at the *New Yorker* proper. She was mostly restricted to writing unsigned "Talk of the Town"s. But her primary subject, even there, was books and the world of publishing, which she found unspeakably silly. In one unsigned piece, she went after the bestseller lists, which she noted had recently:

> *included a coloring book for adults, a journal kept by a child, a pamphlet of newspaper photographs with humorous captions, the autobiography of a baseball manager,*

the reminiscences of a lawyer who had appeared for the defense in a sensational Hollywood trial, a discussion of dieting, and a study of the sexual activities of unmarried women.

Plainly, under these conditions, Adler would go on to say, there was no reason to rely on a bestseller list. It was merely "a helpful guide to the anxious semi-literate." She suggested the *Times* stop publishing it altogether. Eventually, these commentaries on the literary scene allowed Adler to write a few proper books columns of her own for the *New Yorker*. In 1964, at age twenty-seven, she took up the perennial subject of the weakness of book reviews. Like her foremothers, Adler couldn't stand the bad reasoning skills of contemporary book reviewers. But she also didn't exactly love the "New Reviewing," which had appeared to replace them, a genre she felt was overly determined by polemic:

In literary criticism, polemic is short-lived, and no other essay becomes as quickly obsolete as the unfavorable review. If the work under attack is valuable, it survives adverse comment. If it is not, the polemic dies with its target.

It was the first Adler polemic against polemic, something that would become a theme of her writing. Despite the fact that she would often be accused of a hyperbolic style, an excessive harshness of argument, this approach was something Adler continually criticized in others. (Her quarrel with Kael's late-career reviews, too, was that they were overly polemical.) She also was never much for staying in the traditional confines of a review. In this piece, Adler was in theory reviewing books by Irving Howe and Norman Podhoretz, but gradually her critique of them came to expand and cover most of the young intellectuals who had started up the *Partisan Review*. Adler argued that the whole movement of small magazines was now experiencing growing pains: "After the Second World War, old issues began to cloud, old protégés made good, and expository writers with a low tolerance for complexities were at a loss." There was no place for an Irving Howe—a relic of that earlier age—anymore. And even with someone younger, like Norman Podhoretz, Hannah Arendt's great foe, Adler had little patience.

Arendt would become Adler's mentor. When *Eichmann* came out and the opinion pages were in a furor, Adler even tried to convince William Shawn to run a response. She had been an Arendt acolyte for a while, after reading the Rahel Varnhagen biography. At first, Shawn did not want Adler to write anything at all, because typically the *New Yorker* ignored any controversy that might attach to one of its articles. But Adler insisted, and when the *New York Times* ran that very damaging review of *Eichmann* by Michael Musmanno, he relented. They had hoped the letters page of the *New York Times* would print Adler's response, but it was rejected. The *New Yorker* ran the piece itself, which took a high-handed tone:

> *To Miss Arendt's quiet, moral, rational document [Musmanno] opposed such rhetorical exclamations as "Himmler!", "Hitler!", as though these were enlightening statements in the philosophy of history . . . The refusal to listen, the frightening breakdown of communication, is nothing new; we have grown accustomed to it in life and in the headlines. But the very essence of literature is communication, and to find such a breakdown in the literary section of a major newspaper is profoundly disappointing.*

This piece led Arendt to invite Adler to tea. "If anyone was, in Lillian Ross's phrase, sitting adoringly at her feet," Adler wrote later, "it was I." Adler also fell in love with Heinrich Blücher. The couple spoke German with her; they took her on as a kind of protégé, with Adler terming Arendt a "strict parent"; they were always encouraging her to go back to school and finish her doctorate, perhaps thinking about how difficult it had been for Blücher to support himself teaching without one.

She got the spot, in other words, that Susan Sontag had seemed to want. Arendt, Adler insisted, "did not care for Ms. Sontag." Asked why, once, she said, "It's not that Hannah Arendt hated Sontag. It's just that she wasn't all that interested in Sontag's work—which I think is a tenable position." It was, but Adler and Sontag were also perhaps in unknowing competition. She won the same *Mademoiselle* merit award Sontag did, three years after her younger peer. With her secure position at the *New Yorker*, she was more financially stable than Sontag. But she was not a media star, not an It Girl, certainly not in the explosive way Sontag was.

So when Adler fell upon Podhoretz in 1964, she had in her sights someone who had profoundly disagreed with *Eichmann*. There was a relish in her tone as Adler sliced and diced his book. Her manner of attack was precise and unrelenting. Podhoretz tended to repeat certain phrases, and the phrases he chose were those of a buffoon. This was the same technique she'd later deploy against Kael, one that allowed her to reveal tics and hypocrisies in devastating succession. As to Podhoretz's essay against the *New York Review of Books*, titled "Book Reviewing and Everyone I Know," Adler eviscerated Podhoretz with a single observation:

First, "everyone I know" occurs fourteen times (aside from its appearance in the title) and "someone I know," "no one I know, "someone I don't know," and "everyone they know" make one appearance each. Although it must be admitted that repetition is a rhetorical device of which, in any case, Mr. Podhoretz has always been inordinately fond ("what really happened in the thirties" occurs nine times in another essay, and "tells us nothing about the nature of totalitarianism" several times in a row), it seems quite safe to say that

"Book Reviewing and Everyone I Know" is pervaded by a sense of comradeship and solidarity; Mr. Podhoretz clearly does not consider himself a speaker in isolation.

She could do more with this than accuse him of infelicitous word repetition, too. Adler argued that the result of such pomposity was that the new reviewers were simply a small club, all talking to and complimenting and insulting each other, at the expense of intellectualism generally. They were turning themselves into celebrities without regard for the books they were analyzing. This, of course, laid Adler open to charges that she was doing the same—just as Kael was accused of careerism when she wrote "Circles and Squares." The conservative writer Irving Kristol, writing in the *New Leader* during a Socialist phase before his conversion to Republicanism, remarked:

Though I may have read things by Miss Adler before, I have no recollection of them. It is her review—written faithfully according to Podhoretz's prescription—that has made her, for me, a "literary personality."

Kristol was certainly right that this essay was the first to crystallize the Renata Adler the world would come to know in print. The piece bears several hallmarks of the Adler style, already fully present at the outset of her career. The voice talking to us in the essay is never ingratiating, jokey, or otherwise distracted by personality. It's pure analysis, pure reason, all business. There is often an "I" but it is never personal; it is more analytical, like Sontag's. Adler writes like a laser beam, but she is less interested in dazzling the reader with beauty than piercing a mind with an idea. She rarely tells any kind of story, but amasses evidence for a thesis and bears down on the subject with bull terrier determination. Adler often feels more like a prosecutor than a storyteller.

The Podhoretz essay, among others, made William Shawn think Adler could do more. She, too, wanted to do what he called fact pieces: the long, ambitious articles that had become the *New Yorker*'s stock-in-trade in the 1960s. For the first of these Adler was sent to observe the Selma-to-Montgomery marches in Alabama of 1965. Perhaps because she was nervous on her first outing as a reporter, there is something much flatter about Adler's prose in the piece, which offers little analysis and a lot of observation. Her sentences are shorter, sometimes even terse. She was not much susceptible, either, to the stirring rhetoric of the marches. Other than expressing doubt that the marches expressed a clear demand, she limited herself to simply reporting what she saw:

> *Word came that Mrs. Viola Liuzzo had been shot. Some of the marchers went back to Selma at once. Others boarded planes for home. At the Montgomery airport exit was a permanent official sign reading, "Glad You Could Come. Hurry Back."*

The effect of the whole was curiously disconnected, aloof.

She was a good deal more confident and critical writing on the subject of generational differences. She was a bright young thing in the middle of the 1960s, but her general sense of alienation from the people around her made her suspicious of their political movements, their devotion to free love, and their antipathy to the hard stuff of living. Some called her the "East Coast's Joan Didion," but she had a more direct, less vulnerable style. Didion tended to evoke the foibles of her hippies and drifters in dialogue and scene setting, and reported quite a bit on herself and her mood. Adler was, as always, doing something more like mounting an argument, and mostly keeping her inner self out of direct view while doing so:

> *At the moment, however, there is a growing fringe of waifs, vaguely committed to a moral drift that emerged for them*

*from the confrontations on the Strip and from the general
climate of events. The drift is Love; and the word, as it is
now used among the teen-agers of California (and as it
appears in the lyrics of their songs), embodied dreams of
sexual liberation, sweetness, peace on earth, equality—
and, strangely, drugs.*

That "strangely, drugs" is more revealing than Adler intends, for
in 1967 drugs should have been anything but strange to someone her
age. (She'd only just turned thirty.) As the child of refugees, she had
not had the same all-American image against which she could rebel
during the 1960s. But even as such, Adler was always standing somewhat off to the side of things, not feeling them herself. This made
her a powerful observer, of course. The accretion of detail in Adler's
Summer of Love–era pieces is often stunning, as is her ability to toss
the strangest behavior off as a matter-of-fact statement. "He began to
yodel," she writes of one young man she meets on the Sunset Strip,
as though people simply do this when instructed. But she had trouble
making larger sense of what was happening around her. Nearly every
reporting piece she did ended on an ambivalent note. For her essay
on the Sunset Strip, she finished up at something called a Human
Be-In, at which she remarked: "There were no police around at all."

Adler would return to Mississippi to witness more civil rights
demonstrations, she'd travel to Israel to cover the Six-Day War, and
she'd go to Biafra. But in each case the problem was the same: ambivalence. Later, when she collected the pieces in a book, Adler would
see ambivalence as a recognizable phenomenon of the time she was
writing about. But even in articulating that observation, she had to
hedge herself. She'd write:

*I guess I am part of an age group that, through being
skipped, through never having had a generational voice,
was forced into the broadest possible America. Even now*

(and we are in our thirties), we have no journals we pub-
lish, no exile we share, no brawls, no anecdotes, no war,
no solidarity, no mark. In college, under Eisenhower, we
were known for nothing, or for our apathy. A center of
action seemed to have broken down in us.

Again, the woman writing this analysis was barely thirty, yet already disengaged from much of the political and social current in this country. Sometimes she almost sounded conservative about the social chaos of America in the sixties. "Our values are corny ones," she wrote without quite defining who was included in that collective pronoun, "reason, decency, prosperity, human dignity, contact, the finest, broadest possible America." Even so, the most curious thing about this analysis is that Adler so completely detached herself from the "we" she employs. Her trajectory through America had not been typical. In the 1960s, only about half of Americans even went to college; they certainly did not start writing for major national publications at twenty-two. Adler was a prodigy on the level of Dorothy Parker, writing from the beginning as she always would, her voice recognizable in those first "Talk of the Town"s on through the last pieces she published in the 1990s. But her separateness from the crowd meant she couldn't reach out and touch the broad emotional currents of America in the 1960s. She could only watch.

Perhaps this explains why, in 1968, Adler abruptly jumped the *New Yorker* ship. The *New York Times* approached her, looking for a movie critic. It had tired of fusty old Bosley Crowther, Pauline Kael's adversary. It is not clear if they thought of asking Kael herself to come over from the *New Yorker*. But Adler had been writing about film for the *New Yorker* occasionally, when Kael, or the alternating critic, Penelope Gilliatt, was out of commission. She was young, she had already made a mark for herself in criticism, and she was writing these fashionably alienated pieces about the 1960s. She must have seemed a perfect fit for the job.

If the *New York Times* was expecting an ingenue, it would not get one. Adler arrived with a sharp sense of her mission. She would not cut anyone any slack. The first review she wrote, of a German film now completely forgotten, began in the thundering register of her old books pieces, echoing her throttling of John Hersey:

Even if your idea of a good time is to watch a lot of middle-aged Germans, some of them very fat, all reddening, grimacing, perspiring, and falling over Elke Sommer, I think you ought to skip The Wicked Dreams of Paula Schultz, *because this first film of the year is so unrelievedly awful, in such a number of uninteresting ways.*

This line was so funny it ramped up expectations. It signaled a young critic hungry for blood. The next film she reviewed gave her a more familiar subject in Norman Mailer's *Wild 90*. Here Adler was back in the comfortable territory of writerly personalities. Audiences that liked Mailer, "among the most fond, forgiving, ultimately patronizing and destructive of our time," were just as likely to indulge this film as they had his other works. This was not quite a compliment, though. Adler made clear that she found Mailer's fan base a less than intellectually impressive group. For example, she could not imagine that this "permissive school, which treats Mailer as an endearing protagonist in a Peter Pan adolescent struggle to free and find himself, would ever welcome a firm, compressed and unapologetic piece of work."

As she would later be in "The Perils of Pauline," Adler seemed to be both uninfluenced by Kael—her prose in these early reviews is the terse stuff of her factual reporting—and completely in accordance with Kael's bellicose spirit. The world of Adler's movie reviews is full of accusations of pretension and sentimentality. The movies that "serious people" like, *The Graduate, In Cold Blood, Guess Who's Coming to Dinner,* are all suspect to Adler even as they are so palatable to bourgeois audiences. Her outsider status here was a boon, keeping her from feeling the pressure to follow popular tastes. It even kept her from declaring, as most film critics of this era did, a side in the auteurist/anti-auterist wars. She simply delivered her own judgments and left the systematic arguments to others.

As had happened to Kael at *McCall's*, Adler was subject in the fourteen months she was working at the *Times* to a number of challenges from the studios. The most famous one, from United Artists, was an ad pointing out that since Adler had hated many of certain popular films, the public should not listen to her:

> *Renata Adler, of The New York Times, did not like*
> In Cold Blood.
> *She had reservations about*
> The Graduate. Guess Who's Coming to Dinner? Planet
> of the Apes.
> *We're not quite sure how she felt about*
> Bonnie and Clyde.
> *The majority of other critics liked them.*
> *Most of all, the public likes them.*
> *Now she doesn't like*
> Here We Go Round the Mulberry Bush.
> *What a recommendation!*

While it's often said she was a problem for Hollywood producers from the start, in fact at first the industry felt neutral about her, as *Variety* reported in January, two weeks after she'd started. A longer article, published in March 1968, said reactions were split:

> *Both her supporters and detractors agree on one verdict: she is much more literary than cinematic in her critical stance . . . She clearly does not share the view that the director is ultimately the creator of a film. In at least six*

reviews, she didn't even mention the director's name, let alone appraise his contribution.

The people *Variety* spoke to also said they found her a better essayist than reviewer, often even enjoying her Sunday efforts at elucidating the "death cult" of films, or the appropriateness of violence in them. These efforts tended to veer from the movies themselves, though, and head for Adler's preoccupations:

> *One of the things democracy may be the system least equipped to deal with is revolution as an esthetic exercise. It is not really foreseen in any philosophy of history that a group of middle class young people, against whom the system has done no injustice whatsoever—whom the system was actually educating for positions of power— should want to bring the system down for fun.*

Adler's reviews were relentlessly serious, generally having no truck with trash. She could be devastating with a put-down, but she tried to give the good elements of a bad picture their proper due. She credited Barbra Streisand for elevating *Funny Girl*; she liked the elegantly staged ball scenes in Franco Zeffirelli's *Romeo and Juliet*, even though she thought the delivery of the whole was a little too much like *West Side Story*. When *Barbarella* came along, Adler couldn't help ranting about how movies had of late depicted women: "Maybe it is an anti-Mummy reflex, no good, decent women on the screen." She credited Jane Fonda, nonetheless, for doing what she could.

But outsiders noticed a lot of factual errors in her reviews. *Variety* reported that *Esquire* was preparing an exposé. It also reported that Darryl F. Zanuck, the head of Fox Studios, had been told by an executive that Adler had seen only half of a treacly Julie Andrews vehicle, *Star!*. Zanuck had fired off a complaint to the *Times* editor. But nothing happened until Adler quit the post at the end of February 1972. She wrote a few more pieces on the films of postrevolutionary Cuba, but after that returned to the *New Yorker*. In later interviews, she insisted she hadn't been fired, and certainly the crimes with which she'd later charge Pauline Kael suggested that Adler had simply become tired of the grind. It was good, she said, to learn to write to deadline.

After Adler left the *Times*, she wrote a few other pieces of nonfiction. The best was a long piece, published in the *Atlantic*, which took the impeachment inquiry of the Church Committee to task for its shoddy investigation of Nixon's crimes. Meticulously combing through the committee's records, she found any number of items that should have been investigated further. She ended up believing that the impeachment inquiry had become part of some sort of Nixon cover-up.

But articles like the Nixon piece seemed no longer to be what she truly wanted to do. Renata Adler had decided that what she truly wanted to do was write fiction.

Adler spent much of the 1970s ignoring journalism and writing her two novels, *Speedboat* and *Pitch Dark*, instead. Both are written in a fractured, epigrammatic style. Both feature protagonists who could be taken as stand-ins for Adler herself. Of the two, it is *Pitch Dark* that has the sound, at times, of social criticism. Adler's style in fiction is nothing like Mary McCarthy's, but she had a similar inability to keep her life out of her work. In fact, McCarthy appears in *Pitch Dark*, disguised as the character Viola Teagarden, who

> spoke with a kind of awe about what she called "my anger," as though it were a living, prized possession, a thoroughbred bull, for instance, to be used at stud, or as a man who has married a beautiful, unpredictably unpleasant woman, far richer and younger than himself, might say "my wife."

Although beautifully written, these books sometimes bear the mark of the sheer difficulty Adler had in writing them. *Speedboat* first began to appear in excerpts in the *New Yorker* in 1975. When it was published in 1976, everyone raved about it; Adler was given the prestigious PEN/Hemingway Award. It then took her another seven years to produce *Pitch Dark*, and after that she seemed to give up on fiction altogether.

She also, as befits someone who could never seem to find one subject that obsessed her wholly, took herself to Yale Law School and got a JD. Adler's mind was almost perfectly suited to operate like a lawyer's. She was already making a prosecutor's argument in her piece about new reviewing, taking apart the testimony of Podhoretz, hanging him on a single word or phrase. The orderliness of legal argument ended up inflecting "The Perils of Pauline," which also read like something of a legal brief. It was also then that her writing became combative, striving always to destroy.

Her combativeness also extended into the courts. When *Vanity Fair* was revived in the early 1980s as a passion project, it was initially intended to be a serious, intellectual publication more like the *Partisan Review* than like *People*. And Renata Adler had been hired to work on it by the editor Richard Locke. She retained her post at the *New Yorker*, but was called a "consulting editor."

The new *Vanity Fair* regime did not last long; Richard Locke was fired in April 1983, and Adler left soon after. But an article in an obscure trade journal called the *Washington Journalism Review* printed instead that she had been fired. It also said she had been dishonest with the magazine about her contributions—she published a piece of *Pitch Dark* under a pseudonym—and that she had been fired for her incompetence. Adler decided to sue the journal. She won.

Thus began the legal phase of Adler's career, in which her writings about the law began to bleed into actual events in the law. Adler became obsessed with two legal cases against the media. The first,

Westmoreland v. CBS, was a suit over a television documentary about the war in Vietnam. The documentary essentially accused former army general William C. Westmoreland of manipulating intelligence to take the United States deeper into the war. The second, *Sharon v. Time*, saw *Time* magazine sued by the Israeli military man and politician Ariel Sharon for implying in one of its articles that Sharon had been responsible for massacres in Lebanon in September 1982.

In both cases, there was little question the reporters had gotten things wrong. The facts, as reported, were shown to be incorrect. But in each of the cases the question was whether the reporters had made their errors with "actual malice," the standard required to prove libel under American law. It is an extremely difficult standard to meet. Adler argued that it ended up becoming a kind of blanket protection for the media to report falsehoods. She often seemed to sympathize with the plaintiffs in that respect:

> *Whatever their other motives may have been (pride, anger, honor, politics at home), the plaintiffs were clearly suing on principle, and that principle, in each general's mind, at least, was truth: not justice, but plain, factual truth . . . As it happens, American courts are not designed, or even, under the Constitution, permitted, abstractly to resolve issues of this sort, to decide for history what is true and false.*

Through the course of philosophical musing on this conundrum, Adler was heavily critical of the journalists in question as well, so much so that she inspired their anger. She initially published her findings on the trial in the *New Yorker* in the summer of 1986. (Under William Shawn, writers were frequently allowed to work on single articles for years while they drew a salary, an arrangement that could not be had anywhere else.) The pieces were to be collected in a book called *Reckless Disregard*. Before its scheduled publication in September, however, both *Time* and CBS put the *New Yorker* and

Renata Adler's publisher on notice of libel suits themselves. The book was held for a few months before it was released.

In the meantime, all hell broke loose in reviews of *Reckless Disregard*. Adler had raised the possibility that some journalists were slippery with their facts. So other journalists in turn focused their attention on seeing if she had made any mistakes. According to them, she had. Even a critic as predisposed to be sympathetic as the legal scholar Ronald Dworkin, writing in the *New York Review of Books*, praised Adler's general perspicacity, but also wrote that

> *she too often surrenders to the very journalistic vices she excoriates.* Reckless Disregard *is marred by the same one-sided reporting, particularly in its account of Westmoreland, and its coda displays the same intransigence in the face of contrary evidence, that we would rightly condemn in the institutional press.*

Ultimately Adler's reputation came out of the affair rather marred. The fact-checkers at the *New Yorker* claimed she had snowed them.

Yet the furor *Reckless Disregard* inspired did not apparently lessen Adler's appetite for a fight. Things had suddenly gotten worse for her, because William Shawn—the man who stood by her through many of her controversies, up to and including the hullabaloo about her *Reckless Disregard* pieces—had been fired. The *New Yorker* had been purchased by the Condé Nast company in 1985, and its owner, S. I. Newhouse, had decided it was time for a change. No longer would the *New Yorker* be home to so many long and potentially boring articles, he thought, if only it had a different editor.

What Newhouse did not anticipate was the staff revolt that followed Shawn's firing. Newhouse did not abide by Shawn's condition that he be allowed to name his successor. He instead hired an outside person, Robert Gottlieb, a longtime editor at the Alfred A. Knopf publishing house, to helm the revitalized magazine. Petitions were exchanged, staff meetings held, and for a time it looked as though the *New Yorker* might implode under the strain of the transition. But ultimately it did not lose many of its writers. Many of them could not have found a home for their works elsewhere.

Adler had a particularly negative reaction to this shake-up. She was outraged at the presumption of Newhouse, and especially upset that Shawn had been given such shoddy treatment. And she did not think Gottlieb an adequate replacement. She found him "comically incurious." He wanted to change the art. He brought in Adam Gopnik, whose "meaching" personality Adler could not abide:

> *I had learned over the course of conversations with Mr. Gopnik that his questions were not questions, or even quite soundings. Their purpose was to maneuver you into advising him to do what he would, in any case, walk over corpses to do.*

In 1999, a decade after all these events occurred, Adler wrote a book about them she called *Gone: The Last Days of the "New Yorker."* Something of an intellectual memoir, it paired unsavory portraits of certain *New Yorker* staffers with excessive praise for others. It began with a long critique of two other *New Yorker* memoirs, by Lillian Ross and Ved Mehta, that Adler had read and found insufficiently representative of the atmosphere of serious regard for writing she felt Mr. Shawn had cultivated.

Ask just about any *New Yorker* staff people of the era, and they will bring up various objections to the book. Again, Adler made a few mistakes, mostly on the order of misspelling names. One staffer told me she also thought Adler had not been around the *New Yorker* offices enough at the time described to know what was really going on. But probably the best way to look at *Gone* is not as a strict history of the dissolution of William Shawn's *New Yorker*, but rather as a personal intellectual biography of someone who could never have been the writer she was, or become the force that she was, at a different sort of magazine. *Gone* is an angry book, motivated by betrayal. And at times, it seems even the book's critics, including Robert Gottlieb himself, didn't have the heart to completely dismiss Adler's feelings of betrayal:

> *To a large extent this book is an explosion of pain and anger from someone caught up in the dynamic of a highly dysfunctional family—what must have hurt most is that there was no place in it for a daughter.*

Gone was a turning point in Adler's career. All her writing life, she had been on the offensive, and fairly confident that even if she failed she had somewhere to land softly. Suddenly she had attacked the most prestigious magazine in America. Even those who still liked her disagreed with her. And some, who were plainly looking to curry favor with the new *New Yorker* editors, decided it was finally time to well and truly attack Adler herself.

As Adler later pointed out, her book was covered by the *Times* in no fewer than eight separate articles over the course of January 2000. The first four were just about the *New Yorker*. The second four concerned one tossed-off line in the book about Judge John Sirica, who had presided over the Watergate trials. Adler had written that "contrary to his reputation as a hero, Sirica was in fact a corrupt, incompetent, and dishonest figure, with a close connection to Senator Joseph McCarthy and clear ties to organized crime."

Sirica wrote to Adler's publisher objecting to this. Then it seems he called reporters, who began calling Adler. One of them was Felicity Barringer, then the *Times* media correspondent, who began to badger Adler to reveal her sources on the Sirica allegations. Adler declined, but Barringer pressed on.

> *If I did not wish to "disclose" my "sources" to her in an interview, Barringer said, "Why don't you post it on the*

Internet?" "You post a lot of your own pieces on the Inter-
net, do you, Felicity?"

The journalist went ahead and published a piece accusing Adler
of hiding her sources anyway. The newspaper commissioned John
Dean, one of Nixon's most trusted advisers, to write his own editorial about this mysterious sentence, and suggest that Adler's source
for it had been the embittered G. Gordon Liddy. Adler was amused:

> *What was remarkable, however, was less the content of*
> *the piece than the words with which the* Times *identified*
> *its author. The caption, in its entirety, read as follows:*
>   *John W. Dean, an investment banker, is former coun-*
> *sel to President Richard M. Nixon and the author of* Blind
> Ambition.
>   *If this is the way Dean will enter history, then all the*
> Times *pieces in this peculiar episode have value.*

It turned out that when Adler finally did write her own article
about the "peculiar episode," her source for Sirica's connection to
McCarthy was his own autobiography. She also reported the connection with organized crime by tracking down the son of one of Sirica's
father's business partners. When she published her findings in the
August 2000 issue of *Harper's*, the *Times* did not issue a response.
Possibly the editors declined to correct it because of how Adler ended
her excoriation of their tactics:

> The Times, *financially successful as it may be, is a power-*
> *ful but, at this moment, not very healthy institution. The*
> *issue is not one book or even eight pieces. It is the state*
> *of the entire cultural mine shaft, with the archcensor, still*
> *in some ways the world's greatest newspaper, advocating*
> *the most explosive gases and the cutting off of air.*

This entire affair cost Adler most of her professional status. At the *New Yorker*, she was no longer a vital writer to the magazine's editor. When she called to ask if the *New Yorker* might take a piece from her about the Starr Report on Bill Clinton's affairs, then editor David Remnick said he'd had enough Monica Lewinsky pieces. She managed to get it placed in *Vanity Fair* instead.

It's a brilliant piece of work, biting into the thousand pages with appetite, the kind of lawyerly dissection of a document's own logic that had been her great strength since she gave up on fiction.

> *The six-volume Starr Report by Kenneth W. Starr to the U.S. House of Representatives—which consists, so far, of the single-volume Referral and five volumes of Appendices and Supplemental Materials—is, in many ways, an utterly preposterous document: inaccurate, mindless, biased, disorganized, unprofessional, and corrupt. What it is textually is a voluminous work of demented pornography, with many fascinating characters and several largely hidden story lines. What it is politically is an attempt, through its own limitless preoccupation with sexual material, to set aside, even obliterate, the relatively dull requirements of real evidence and constitutional procedure.*

It won a magazine award for commentary. But later the same year, the *New Yorker* severed its long contractual ties with Adler, ending her health insurance. She wrote two more pieces—one for the *New Republic* shortly before September 11, which took the Supreme Court to task, and one arguing with another *Times* mistake. But she was very much feeling ostracized, and for years felt at sea without an institution behind her like the one she'd had in the Shawn era.

"I've said it all along, in my even way: if you're at Condé Nast, and they're cutting your pieces to shreds, just hang on. Do your art in your own time, but don't quit because then you'll be out there, vulnerable. When I left the *New Yorker*, I was fair game," she told an interviewer in 2013, when her novels had been reissued and she was enjoying something of a revival. The critical consensus on the excellence of her novels had given her a newfound prominence. But the analytical viewpoint, the fierce ability to critique someone else's argument, hasn't found a similar home. Adler hasn't published a new essay since 1999.

14

Malcolm

Though Janet Malcolm's career was as tied to the *New Yorker* as Renata Adler's, she was quiet where Adler was brash, a late bloomer where Adler was a prodigy. Like Hannah Arendt, Malcolm would reach her forties before she began publishing any serious work. And her name would not really be made until she published, in 1983, a profile of a man barely anyone had heard of: a Sanskrit scholar turned psychoanalyst named Jeffrey Moussaieff Masson. He had recently been fired as the head of the Sigmund Freud Archives.

Masson was just past forty with a thick head of hair and a healthy dose of self-confidence when Malcolm interviewed him. The first time they met, as she told the story, he'd boasted of his power:

> *Almost everyone else in the analytic world would have done anything to get rid of me. They were envious of me, but I think they also genuinely felt that I was a mistake and a nuisance and a potential danger to psychoanalysis—a really critical danger. They sensed that I could single-handedly bring down the whole business—and let's face it, there's a lot of money in that business. And they were right to be frightened, because what I was discovering was dynamite.*

Malcolm was interested in the fight Masson had ignited with this dynamite, an argument over the "seduction thesis," an idea about the nature of the parent-child relationship—that it was, in a primal sense, defined by sexual attraction—that Freud later rejected and revised. But in pursuing the intellectual debate, she found herself in the company of a man who could, in her depiction of him, find no end of things to praise about himself.

Malcolm tends to convey things by implication rather than outright statement. Whenever she cast aspersions on Masson, she never did so by outright insult. She'd simply let his quotes go on and on, as above, which made Masson sound like a fool. She'd let him explain, for example, that he had gone into psychoanalysis to cure himself of "total promiscuity." He told her he'd slept with a thousand women by the time he was a graduate student, and she quoted him on it. Or she'd quote a nineteenth-century letter from Freud, talking about someone else, to inflect her account of Masson's activities: "Everything he said and thought possessed a plasticity, a warmth, a quality of importance, which was meant to conceal the lack of deeper substance."

This was relevant because Malcolm was investigating the circumstances surrounding Masson's firing. If he was grandiose and egotistical, those were relevant facts. But he was also something else: litigious. Masson would eventually sue Malcolm too, a suit that dragged on for years and ended up in the Supreme Court, on the claim Malcolm misquoted him. After two bruising trials in lower courts, in which the very nature of literary journalism was debated, Masson lost his libel claims against her.

The subtle but devastating indirectness of Janet Malcolm was a function of history and personality. She had been raised to be somewhat genteel and obedient. She was born in Prague, Czechoslovakia, in 1934, and originally named Jana Wienovera. Her family fled the country as the war came on, settling in Brooklyn, where Janet and her sister, Marie, learned English. It was not an easy process. She had a memory of "the kindergarten teacher saying, 'Good-bye, children,' at the end of the day, and my envy of the girl whose name I assumed to be Children. It was my secret hope that someday the teacher would say, 'Good-bye, Janet.'"

Her father was a psychiatrist (which no doubt influenced Malcolm's eventual interest in the discipline), and her mother was a lawyer. They managed to find work in America. He changed the family name to Winn, one much easier for Americans to pronounce. English got easier, and Janet was a good student. She ended up at the University of Michigan. She was not radically minded. She was raised, as many were in the fifties, to curry favor with men, get married, and have a family. "During my four years of college, I didn't study with a single woman professor," she told the *Paris Review*. "There weren't any, as far as I know." In this she seems sometimes to liken herself to an Alice Munro character: smart, bookish, but not particularly ambitious, and wandering into marriage because it was what was expected.

She came to a career slowly, not someone who burst out of the gates with a fully formed voice like Adler or Parker. At college, she met a young man named Donald Malcolm. Donald had ambitions of being a writer, and so did she, but her attempts were being repeatedly shot down by her creative writing teacher. When Donald Malcolm graduated and went to work for the *New Republic*, Janet Winn followed him and began to write for that magazine too. The first piece she published in 1956 was a kind of parody of a film review, written in the register of an excited teenager:

> *I went to see* Love Me Tender *last night, and I liked it enormous. Elvis Presley isn't a bit obscene or lewd; he's just different. He certainly stood out from everybody else in the picture—it takes place back in Civil War times when they didn't hardly have no rock 'n roll yet—and not only because of his singing and virileness; but also because of his acting.*

There is no way this piece was meant seriously; it ends on a wish that Marilyn Monroe should film *The Brothers Karamazov* with Elvis as a star because it would be just *"great."* The humor might be a little lost on a modern reader, because parody tends not to age well. But something about the young Janet Winn's wide-eyed sarcasm must have impressed someone, because within six months of publishing it, she began to write more serious film reviews for the *New Republic* on an intermittent basis. And she was not generally disposed to liking what Hollywood had on offer. She trashed Otto Preminger's *Saint Joan* for having diluted the moral complexity George Bernard Shaw had originally given to Joan of Arc's story. She disliked, too, Alexander Mackendrick's *Sweet Smell of Success*, because she found it too obvious. But she made some waves with readers when she wrote her reaction to a newly rescreened *The Birth of a Nation*, which she found not only racist but also far too devoted to a hard division between good and evil:

> *Outside the theatre, a few blocks away, a civil rights bill, if not a very good one, was being passed; and a few blocks in the other direction, a movie, called* I Was a Teenage Werewolf *was being played; but I couldn't help feeling cheerful and comfortably certain that film-wise and otherwise, we have come rather a long way.*

Readers reacted quite strongly to these strong opinions. One wrote in. He suspected Miss Winn of knowing a lot and of having great judgment, but added that "it is hard to tell about this, because Miss Winn is quite determinedly On the Side of the Angels, and her prose judgements come to us wearing The Whole Armor of God. Her standards seem *so* high." Another letter writer, Hal Kaufman, a self-professed "student of motion pictures," wrote in to correct Miss Winn too. His qualms about her were rather more wide-ranging, and delivered with a thickness of reference that pompous individuals often mistake for intelligence. The letter writer wished to inform Miss Winn that "the leading authorities everywhere have accorded the work of Griffith the highest praise." He noted that Lenin had loved the movie too. He also urged her to show more "charity" in her judgments of older films. Her reply to this was very simple:

> Mr. Kaufman is a "student of motion pictures" and I am not. How can we agree?

She was by then also turning her critical talents to books and theater. She reviewed a collection of D. H. Lawrence's letters, but nothing met with her judgment so strongly as the introduction, written by none other than McCarthy's and Arendt's old foe Diana Trilling, who was then the lead critic of the *Nation*. She ridiculed Mrs. Trilling's acidity in calling Frieda Lawrence an "awful nuisance," observing that she "aged badly" and "had no real intellect"—by pointing out that it shouldn't matter in a book of literary criticism whether a writer's wife was a terrible person.

These reviews, while not particularly memorable in themselves, track the development of a young writer's self-confidence. She started to get praise alongside the snide letters—including praise from one Norman Mailer, whose appearance on television with Dorothy Parker and Truman Capote Malcolm had chronicled for the magazine. Mailer thought she had gotten the quotes wrong in his discussion with Capote. But he also seemed to be writing in for a bit of flirting:

> One is forced to add that the Lady Winn's account was marvelously well-written and suffered only from the trifling flaw that most of the words she put in my mouth were never said by me.

Winn was by then engaged to Donald Malcolm. Donald took a job at the *New Yorker* in 1957, and she moved back to Brooklyn. For seven years after that, too busy bringing up their only daughter, Anne Olivia, she did not publish a single word.

If you ask her to tell it herself, Janet Malcolm will usually start the story of her becoming a writer at the *New Yorker*. While her daughter was small, she had to read an inordinate number of children's books, and eventually Mr. Shawn, whom she knew through her husband, suggested she write about children's literature for a December 1966 issue of the *New Yorker*. Malcolm complied perhaps more eagerly than he anticipated. She provided him with a ten-thousand-word omnibus essay summarizing and analyzing her favorites. She begins in a stodgier tone than the playful younger self of the *New Republic*:

> Our children are a mirror of belief and a proving ground for philosophy. If we bring up a child to be happy and don't care very much how he behaves, we evidently believe in man's essential goodness and in life's infinite possibilities for happiness.

On the strength of that article, Shawn asked her to do it again in 1967 and 1968. The review for 1967 was as stiff as the one for 1966, but in 1968, something moved Malcolm into the realm of reasoned argument. Midway through the piece Malcolm becomes embroiled in an argument with a physician who insists that reality should be made "less ugly" for the young.

> I don't know how Dr. Lasagna proposes to make reality less ugly, and I am not even sure that reality is uglier today than it ever was. There is more knowledge and concern about social problems today, but this does not mean that more or worse social problems exist today. Reality would have been harder to face in the days when

they hanged a child for stealing a loaf of bread, one would think. (Today they ought to hang the people who make our bread.)

She then begins to suggest it might be better to have children read "factual books" about drugs in order to prevent their use. She also recommended books about sex that were "a good deal more forthright than any published before, and they will not suit every family's notions of how the information ought to be presented." She also reviewed books about black history suitable for children, finding that many of them taught her things she did not know.

Mr. Shawn, apparently noticing a burgeoning talent, gave her a column called "About the House" to write, on art and design. Malcolm found these articles good training for learning to write. They were also her first forays into a field other than criticism. She began to report these pieces slowly, talking about the individual merchants of furniture and interior design. She also felt moved in 1970 to write something about the burgeoning women's liberation movement everyone else was talking about.

The piece was published in the *New Republic*. Her name was misspelled in the byline (as Janet Malcom). But her playful attitude had returned. She poked fun at the notion prevalent in the women's movement that the only place to find fulfillment was outside the home.

> *In any case, a woman who chooses to put her baby in someone else's care so she can pursue a career shouldn't be hypocritical about her decision and tell herself that she is doing it for the sake of the child. She is doing it for herself. She may be doing the right thing—selfish decisions are often the best decisions—but she ought to see what she is doing and be willing to pay the price in affection that parental neglect often exacts.*

There is more than a small whiff of anger about that. Its claim that the "new feminism may be an even more invidious cause of unhappiness and discontent" was a common argument at the time—Didion, in her concern about the "triviality" of the women's movement, often approached it too—but there is something uneasy about the argument. It doesn't quite track with someone who was building gradual independence as a writer, but it does fit someone who had found motherhood an enjoyable experience and didn't want to discard whatever good came of it, or whatever degree of choice she could claim for it. But she sounds nothing like the playful presence in the essays she was publishing at the *New Yorker*, which had become much more elegant, thorough streams of consciousness. When the *New Republic*'s editors asked her to reply to the angry mail that came in, she wrote a typically sarcastic response:

> *As for those that raise questions of substance, they require lengthier consideration than my baking and canning obligations permit me to give them at this time. When my Lot improves, I hope to send you another essay on some of the points at issue.*

Perhaps the unease was situational. By the time Malcolm wrote this, her husband, Donald, was seriously ill. The doctors could not figure out what was wrong with him; later Malcolm came to believe he had misdiagnosed Crohn's disease. Soon he was unable to work, and although the *New Yorker* in those days was financially generous to writers, his illness put the family under considerable strain. It soon became clear that Donald Malcolm was dying.

Malcolm continued to turn out her furniture columns faithfully once a month. Most of these were simple catalogs and descriptions of items she liked. But in March 1972, for the first time, she wandered off the pattern. For a column on modern furniture, she went to meet the artist Fumio Yoshimura, "who, as yet, is better known for his wife,

Kate Millett, than for his work." Millett, of course, was famous in 1972 because she had written a bestselling book called *Sexual Politics*, a kind of scorched-earth approach to bringing feminism into literary criticism. As Malcolm continues to describe the encounter with Yoshimura, she keeps getting distracted by Millett. The conversation eventually turns to women's liberation.

> *I remarked that parents here are afraid that boys who don't like sports will grow up to be homosexuals. "A fate worse than death," Kate Millett murmured without looking up from her mail. Kate Millett's removal of herself from the conversation, I later realized, was an expression of tact rather than of incivility.*

At this point Malcolm couldn't seem to help herself; the piece instead turned into an interview of Millett, whom she kept referring to by her full name.

> *The allusive, ironic, academic tone of* Sexual Politics *is entirely absent from Kate Millett's conversation . . . Kate Millett's sculptures all look alike and like Kate Millett. They have a square-cut, blocky, strong, optimistic character.*

This is the first appearance of the kind of Janet Malcolm reportage that would make her both revered and controversial. She made herself a character in this short story of an interview, began to build the "I" she would later tell everyone was untrustworthy, a kind of necessary trick. For example: readers probably didn't know, at the time, that they were reading an interview of a great feminist by a great skeptic regarding feminism, but one who had obviously already read Millett's book.

In the last year of her husband's life—Donald Malcolm would die in September 1975—perhaps suspecting she needed to build an even firmer career for herself, Janet Malcolm began to branch out into a newish art that interested her: photography. She did not then read the work of Susan Sontag, which was being slowly published in the *New York Review of Books*. She would not do that until the 1980s.

But before any of that, she reviewed first a book about Alfred Stieglitz for the *New Yorker*, and then a retrospective of the work of Edward Weston for the *Times*. She was careful and a bit prone to jargon in the Weston review. It was in the end an audition to be the *New York Times*' photography critic. The *Times* offered her the job, but William Shawn told her she could be the *New Yorker*'s photography critic instead.

When she published her photography essays as a collection, *Diana and Nikon*, in 1980, Malcolm wrote it had taken her some time to find her groove. "Rereading these essays," she wrote, "makes me think of someone trying to cut down a tree who has never done it before, isn't strong, has a dull axe, but is very stubborn." She eventually began to get the hang of it in 1978, she thought, with an essay, "Two Roads," that explored the snapshot properties of photography. She began to talk of photographs in moral terms, the same ones that had served Sontag so well. In this way of looking at things, she could more easily convey what she found so disturbing about so many of the photographs:

> The [Walker] Evans book is not the anthology of grace and order it should have been. It is a book full of chaos and disorder, of ugly clutter and mess, of people with dead eyes, victims and losers crushed by the indifferent machinery of capitalism, inhabitants of a land as spiritually depleted as its soil was physically eroded.

You could also see Malcolm relaxing into the subject matter, her sentences becoming more of a pleasure to read:

Innocently opening the book Georgia O'Keeffe: A Portrait,
published by the Metropolitan Museum on the occasion of
its exhibition of the photographs, is like taking a little drive
in the country and suddenly coming upon Stonehenge.

By the time Malcolm got a handle on photography she was also becoming more and more interested in writing what were known at the *New Yorker* as "fact pieces." This was the in-house term for the long, reported pieces that were the magazine's signature product. At that point she was married again, this time to her editor at the *New Yorker*, Gardner Botsford. And she was trying to quit smoking, an activity she closely associated with the act of writing. Meanwhile, reporting would get her out into the world, where she could not interview subjects with a cigarette in hand. So she told Mr. Shawn that she thought she'd do a "fact piece." She chose as her subject family therapy. Perhaps there is Freudian insight to be had here, since her father was a psychiatrist. But this marriage of Malcolm as a writer and psychoanalysis as a subject was a perfect, unforgettable match.

Psychoanalysis had been around, of course, for almost a century by the time Malcolm began writing about it. But in the 1970s, when she began writing about psychiatry, it was not a popular approach. Psychopharmacology was on the rise; magazines made repeated reference to "Mother's Little Helper," Valium. The feminist movement mostly abhorred psychoanalysis, seeing in Freud's ideas (like "penis envy") the basis for the fundamental repression of women. But therapy itself was growing in popularity, though its heyday wouldn't come until the late 1980s and 1990s in America. The books of the existential psychotherapist Rollo May, which connected the ideas of existential philosophers to clinical practice, were enormously popular, especially among the cultural elite that might subscribe to the *New Yorker*. And all that was enough to spark curiosity about the subject.

Malcolm opened her explorations of modern psychiatric practice with a piece on family therapy, called "The One-Way Mirror," which

pointed out that in fact the practice upset most previous psychoana-
lytical thinking. By adding more people to the equation, therapists
became more confrontational, more strategic, and it was impossible
to maintain confidentiality. Malcolm treated all of this with a skeptical
eye, but she also let the family therapist speak for himself and, as a
result, make himself sound somewhat like a salesman in a cheap suit:

> Family therapy will take over psychiatry in one or two
> decades, because it is about man in context. It is a ther-
> apy that belongs to our century, while individual therapy
> belongs to the nineteenth century. This is not a pejorative.
> It is simply that things evolve and change, and during any
> historical period certain ways of looking at and respond-
> ing to life begin to crop up everywhere. Family therapy
> is to psychiatry what Pinter is to theater and ecology is
> to natural science.

The piece is not quite written as criticism of psychoanalysis as a
whole. That was the fate that would await Malcolm's next reporting subject, a typical therapist she called Aaron Green (not his real name). Malcolm used her extensive interviews with Green as a pretext for mounting
a critique of psychoanalysts and psychoanalysis generally. In short,
she analyzed *him*. Even his therapist's couch came up for comment:

> The empty couch looked out on the room with a mean-
> ingful air. "I'm not any old shabby foam-rubber sofa," it
> seemed to say, "I am the couch."

This delicate touch (and characteristic interest in the comedic
possibilities of a subject's interior décor) reveals something important
about Malcolm's technique. While it is a critical perspective, it isn't
a cruel one. Malcolm is illustrating a problem and making certain
judgments about the solution to it, but she is more, as one reviewer

explained, "mischievous." While Aaron Green is at turns silly and anxious, he is also quite sympathetic. Under Malcolm's questioning he gradually comes around to admitting that even his attraction to the profession at all has the quality of a flaw in his psychology:

> *I was attracted to psychoanalytic work precisely because of the distance it would create between me and the people I treated. It's a situation of very comfortable abstinence.*

Malcolm continues to catalog the vaguenesses and hypocrisies of this "impossible profession": the way the duration of therapy seems to get longer and longer; the fact that what a patient will likely get from psychoanalysis is not a cure, but rather "transference," the phenomenon in which patients redirect to their relationships with their therapists the very feelings and desires retained from childhood that they came to therapy in the first place to solve. Malcolm saw most of these problems as institutionalized by psychoanalytic training institutes, which therapists themselves came to see as a kind of surrogate parent. The training, she gently points out, insists that good psychoanalysts themselves should be extensively analyzed.

But she doesn't quite turn Green into a caricature of himself. He seems hapless, confused, and quite possibly in need of a different job. But not malevolent.

Put together in a book called *Psychoanalysis: The Impossible Profession*, Malcolm's profile of Aaron Green drew raves from every corner. Nearly every American, it seemed, had tried out psychoanalysis at one point in the 1970s, then given it up in disgust, confused at what it was supposed to do for the patient. Malcolm's piece spoke so beautifully of its paradoxes that every reviewer, even the psychoanalysts, seemed enthralled.

Emboldened, she set out on a second project related to psychoanalysis. This was to be another long profile of a psychoanalyst. But this time, instead of mining Manhattan's opulent selection of therapists, Malcolm found Jeffrey Moussaieff Masson. Masson's "dynamite" was in the unpublished letters between Freud and Wilhelm Fliess, one of Freud's disciples. Masson promptly told newspapers that in these letters he'd discovered that Freud had not really abandoned what was known as the "seduction thesis." The seduction thesis in its original form had held that childhood sexual experiences, often seduction by a parent, were the source of most patient neuroses. When Freud dropped it in 1925, he explained that he had come to understand that when patients described such experiences, they were often describing not a literal truth, but a psychic one. If Masson was correct, it meant Freud originally had been correct to suspect that child sexual abuse—as contemporary mores would recognize it—had been at the heart of most psychological disorders.

Malcolm became interested in Masson because of this claim, and she decided to call him up. Masson was a good talker, and he had a flair for revealing sentences. Over the course of several days of interviews, some of which Malcolm taped and others she recorded in handwritten notes, he told her about his marriages. He told her about his affairs. He told her that Anna Freud and his other mentors had their doubts about him. "I was like an intellectual gigolo," she quoted him as saying, from her notes. "You get your pleasure from him, but you don't take him out in public." Evidently Masson was ready to meet his public, because he was preparing to write a book about the truth he claimed he had found in the Freud-Fliess correspondence. Both Anna Freud and the man who had gotten him the Sigmund Freud Archives job in the first place, Kurt Eissler, told Malcolm they believed Masson was misreading the letters.

It was this siege from his former comrades that seems to have led Masson to decide Malcolm counted as a kind of friend. He knew throughout their encounters that she planned to write about what he told her. But still he was prepared to detail, for hours, his sexual activities, his grudges within the profession, and the various elements of his robust sense of self-worth for Malcolm. Much of the resulting piece she published consisted of long block quotations from him, which read as disquisitions alternating between Masson's reading of Freud and the number of women he slept with. A typical passage:

> *Do you know what Anna Freud once said to me? She said, "If my father were alive today, he would not want to become an analyst." I swear, those were her words. No wait. This is important. I said that to her. I said, "Miss Freud, I have the feeling that if your father were alive today he would not become an analyst," and she said, "You are right."*

Though these long quotations appeared as uninterrupted soliloquies, Malcolm had actually often cobbled them together from different portions of her interviews—a practice Masson later took issue with in the court cases.

Almost all readers of the resultant articles, "Trouble in the Archives," presumed that Malcolm was deliberately turning Masson into a buffoon, destroying his credibility. Even a fan as intelligent and discerning as the critic Craig Seligman has called Malcolm's work on Masson "a masterwork of character assassination." It is undoubtedly true that no one walks away from reading *In the Freud Archives*—the title of the book Knopf later published of these articles—thinking Jeffrey Mousaieff Masson is an upstanding citizen. Even Malcolm, at the end, speaking to one of the analysts involved in the affair, had a bad read on Masson: "I wonder if he ever cared about anything."

But this seems to me to be a slight misreading of Malcolm's intent. Subsequent controversy over the book—we'll get to that in a moment—revealed that, with some exceptions, almost all of what she quoted from Masson was reflected in her tapes and notes. She had, from that perspective, simply delivered the goods that Masson had given her. He insisted, over the course of subsequent litigation, that some of these quotes were fabricated and others lifted from context, but not all of them were. A simple diagnosis of "character assassination" would imply that there was no such cooperation between reporter and subject here.

Whether Malcolm had an obligation to get in the way of Masson's own self-destruction turned out to be a question that would occupy the next decade of her life.

After the book appeared, Masson was furious. He wrote a letter to the *New York Times Book Review* complaining he'd been slandered. Malcolm replied sharply:

> *The portrait, in fact, is based on more than 40 hours of tape-recorded conversations with Mr. Masson, which began in Berkeley, Calif., in November 1982, during a week of interviews, and continued on the telephone over the following eight months . . . Everything I do quote Mr. Masson as saying was said by him, almost word for word. (The "almost" refers to changes made for the sake of correct syntax.)*

Masson eventually filed a libel suit for 10.2 million dollars. Of that, 10 million dollars was for punitive damages. It was an absurd sum. As numerous commentators pointed out over the course of the litigation—which, sadly for Malcolm, stretched over a decade— Masson kept having to change the details of his charge. In his initial complaint, he listed statements that he had indeed said on tape. Malcolm was able to play them back.

But there were a few sticking points. One was the "intellectual gigolo" phrase, which could not be found on the tapes. Another was the fact that Malcolm had altered some of the quotes, though Malcolm defended this in a letter to the *New York Times Book Review* by explaining that she thought to delete certain of Masson's more extravagant claims. This made the matter a thorny one for the courts. As in the case of *Hellman v. McCarthy*, the problem became not so much about whether Malcolm might ultimately prevail in the litigation, as she did, but what it might cost her while the dispute was ongoing.

In 1987, Masson's initial suit was dismissed. "I should have known, having written his portrait, that Masson wouldn't give up so easily," Malcolm said later. But she decided to put her energies into a new project.

The opening line of *The Journalist and the Murderer*, which originally appeared in three parts in the *New Yorker* in 1989, is famous. "Any journalist who is not too stupid or too full of himself knows that what he does is morally indefensible," Malcolm wrote. This sentence lit a fuse. Many people never seem to have read the book that follows. The first time I saw Malcolm in person, it was twenty years after she'd published that sentence and she was on a high platform at the New Yorker Festival talking about her work. A young man in the crowd got up and questioned her angrily about it. She was silent a moment before she answered: "Well, it was a bit of rhetoric, you see." The young man clearly did not really see.

This was only a small preview of what happened when Malcolm published her extensive study of a dispute that had arisen between the journalist Joe McGinniss and the murderer Jeffrey MacDonald. McGinniss had contracted with MacDonald for exclusive access to him and his defense lawyers during his 1979 trial for murdering his family. MacDonald agreed, clearly thinking he'd scored a coup. McGinniss was famous for having written a book called *The Selling of the President 1968*, which had unflatteringly portrayed the Nixon campaign's attempts to make the candidate more, well, personable. McGinniss had garnered quite a bit of respect as a result.

Unfortunately for MacDonald, by the end of the trial McGinniss had decided he was guilty of the crimes he committed. The book that resulted from their arrangement, a nonfiction potboiler called *Fatal Vision*, was a giant bestseller, but it claimed MacDonald was a psychopath who had killed his entire family in cold blood. A murderer scorned, MacDonald subsequently sued McGinniss, saying he had deliberately misled MacDonald about the nature of the project. And by most journalistic standards, McGinniss had indeed crossed a line.

MacDonald could point to letters, for example, in which McGinniss appeared to be reassuring his source that he thought his conviction a grave injustice.

Malcolm's introduction to her account of all this continued:

> *He is a kind of confidence man, preying on people's vanity, ignorance or loneliness, gaining their trust and betraying them without remorse. Like the credulous widow who wakes up one day to find the charming young man and all her savings gone, so the consenting subject of a piece of nonfiction learns—when the article or book appears—his hard lesson.*

Because this paragraph was told from the perspective of the betrayed subject, many who read the piece immediately assumed Malcolm was mounting an indictment of journalism. Journalists love nothing more than to talk about journalism. And by 1989, when Malcolm's articles appeared, the ranks of journalism were mostly stuffed with would-be Woodwards and Bernsteins, convinced that theirs was the craft that could truly take on power. As a result, many felt Malcolm had injured their honor. An exceptionally long hailstorm of criticism ensued.

"Miss Malcolm appears to have created a snake swallowing its own tail: she attacks the ethics of all journalists, including herself, and then fails to disclose just how far she has gone in the past in acting the role of the journalistic confidence man," yelled one *New York Times* columnist, who also falsely charged Malcolm with admitting to "fabrications." Christopher Lehmann-Haupt, one of the leading book critics, accused her of exonerating MacDonald by excoriating McGinniss. An injured *Chicago Tribune* columnist looked around his newsroom and saw "fellow workers recording politicians' doings, reporting breakthroughs in medicine . . . Can anyone tell me what is so wrong with any of those standard-fare journalistic chores?"

Malcolm did have her defenders. David Rieff stuck up for her in the *Los Angeles Times*. He pointed out that there was very little in Malcolm's position that departed from Joan Didion's widely celebrated phrase: "Writers are always selling somebody out." Nora Ephron, who'd befriended Malcolm sometime before, gave an interview to the *Columbia Journalism Review*: "What Janet Malcolm was saying was so reasonable I was astonished anyone took issue with it," she said. "I believe that to be a good journalist you have to be willing to complete the transaction Janet describes as betrayal." This is not an attitude so far from Phoebe Ephron's "Everything is copy," after all. The flip side is that sometimes people don't want to *be* copy.

(Jessica Mitford, the noted muckraker who had also exposed the death industry back in 1963, and was a from a family of sisters one might have called "sharp" women too, chimed in alongside Nora Ephron: "I thought Malcolm's articles were marvelous.")

The other theme of the coverage was the identification of the similarities between what had just happened between Masson and Malcolm and the situation she had analyzed in *The Journalist and the Murderer*. Masson, sensing an opportunity to reopen the story, told a *New York* magazine reporter that he read the first part of the piece to be an open letter to himself, a kind of confession of Malcolm's sins. He had continued to appeal the dismissal of his suit, going all the way to the Supreme Court. There, Justice Anthony Kennedy ordered that Masson be granted a new trial on his claims. Masson would ultimately lose that trial, in 1994, after the jury found that Malcolm was careless, but did not act with "reckless disregard." A juror told the *New York Times* that "Masson was too honest. He opened himself up, and he just showed his true colors. She painted him. And he didn't like it."

Later, Malcolm said she kind of understood why people threw so many stones at her:

Who hasn't felt pleasure in the fall of the self-styled mighty? That it was a New Yorker *writer who was being dragged through the mud only added to the wicked joy. At that time, the magazine was still wrapped in a fluffy cocoon of moral superiority that really got up the noses of people who worked at other publications. I didn't help myself by behaving the way writers at the* New Yorker *thought they ought to behave when approached by the press: like little replicas of the publicity-phobic William Shawn. So instead of defending myself against the false accusations Masson made in interview after interview, I maintained my ridiculous silence.*

That silence wasn't total. While Masson's appeals were ongoing, *The Journalist and the Murderer* appeared as a book, and Malcolm wrote a new afterword for it. In that afterword she denied that her troubles with Masson were being refracted through the McGinnis-MacDonald dispute. She said that in fact she had begun to pity Masson because he was once again being used by journalists, who were calling him for quotes they could use to attack her, and then dropping him again.

Another thing she did in this afterword was to defend the notion of editing quotes. This was an accusation at issue in the lawsuit: Masson claimed that by moving sentences around, and changing their order, Malcolm had exceeded the bounds of her rights as a journalist. She defended the practice with an argument she would make several more times in her life as a writer: that writing from the "I" was always unreliable:

Unlike the "I" of autobiography, who is meant to be seen as a representation of the writer, the "I" of journalism is connected to the writer only in a tenuous way—the way, say, that Superman is connected to Clark Kent. The journalistic "I" is an overreliable narrator, a functionary to whom crucial tasks of narration and argument and tone

*have been entrusted, an ad hoc creation, like the chorus
of Greek tragedy. He is an emblematic figure, an embodi-
ment of the idea of the dispassionate observer of life.*

This invitation to distrust even the writer herself is a small skel-
eton key not just to Malcolm's own work, but to that of nearly every
person in this book. It added something to the robust first person
that had been built down through the century from Rebecca West to
Didion and Ephron: a certain degree of uncertainty. The experience
of reading a Malcolm text is always to linger in that sense of uncertainty, both about the nominal subject—was McGinniss really that
bad; was Masson an idiot?—and about exactly what new kind of sly
trick the narrator might be pulling on us.

In Malcolm, there's always an added level of meaning like that,
some sleight of hand. Much as a psychoanalyst induces patients to
examine and analyze their habitual reactions and feelings, Malcolm
provoked an emotional response that made many journalists rethink
some of what they knew about their profession.

After all, the furor over *The Journalist and the Murderer* did
very little except prove the thesis Malcolm was trying to advance.
The topic of the book is journalism, writ large. The argument is
that subjects will always feel betrayed by what some other person
writes about them. "Journalism" did indeed feel betrayed by Malcolm's assessment of it. By a stroke of luck things did come around;
The Journalist and the Murderer is now taught in most journalism
schools. As Malcolm herself will tell you if you ask her, in the end
she was proved right.

All of Malcolm's subsequent work has been marked by *The Journalist
and the Murderer*'s preoccupations. Everywhere she looked, she found
stories that didn't match up. She wrote about trials for murder (in
Iphigenia in Forest Hills) and for corporate malfeasance (in *The Crimes*

of Sheila McGough) with an eye to the dueling stories each side of the room tells in those settings, and their seemingly irreconcilable inconsistences. She wrote about the artist David Salle in a piece that consists, as its title claims, of "Forty-One False Starts," and thereby seemed to be questioning the usefulness of writing journalism at all. Regarding narratives she expresses a skepticism very like Didion's—a doubter's view of the stories we tell ourselves—in her examinations of the people we charge to tell us the stories in the first place: writers, artists, thinkers.

But probably the best example of that is *The Silent Woman*, a book-length *New Yorker* article on the life of Sylvia Plath, her husband Ted Hughes, and the biographers who tried to understand the truth of their history together. Plath had been a precocious poet and prose writer, publishing widely in her twenties, though never becoming particularly famous. She eventually moved to England, married the poet Ted Hughes, and had two children. She published one book of poetry, but continued to feel professionally frustrated. Then, in 1963, after Hughes had left her for another woman, Plath committed suicide. A couple of years after her death, her searing book of so-called confessional poetry, *Ariel*, was published to great acclaim. Her novel, *The Bell Jar*, also posthumously published, became a classic too. And that was when the trouble began.

Plath's posthumous admirers came to believe that they had a unique insight into the suffering that led to her suicide. And they blamed Ted Hughes for it. There was some justification for his bad reputation. In the last months of Plath's life, when he left her for the other woman, Plath had to survive in a strange country with no family other than two very young children. Her subsequent spectral-feminist stardom, as the author of *Ariel*, had meant that a great deal of ire was directed his way. Subsequently, he and his sister, Olwyn, became very guarded and careful about who they would allow to write Plath's biographies, which they could control by way of controlling the permission to quote from her unpublished work.

Malcolm's interest in the whole case was piqued by a biographer they had let in, Anne Stevenson. Malcolm said she had known Stevenson at the University of Michigan.

She had once been pointed out to me on the street: thin and pretty, with an atmosphere of awkward intensity and passion about her, gesticulating, surrounded by interesting-looking boys. In those days, I greatly admired artiness, and Anne Stevenson was one of the figures who glowed with a special incandescence in my imagination.

Stevenson's Plath biography, *Bitter Fame*, had however come under serious attack. Olwyn Hughes was thanked profusely in a conspicuous author's note, and it indicated that Hughes had been able to see, comment on, and request changes to the manuscript before it was published. This was seen as an assault on Stevenson's integrity as a biographer, as it's thought a biography will be more objective if the estate does not see the manuscript before publication. Malcolm, too, decided she had qualms about the book, but hers were of a different order altogether. She found herself resenting the pose of judiciousness that as a biographer Stevenson was ordered to take. Compared with the people who got to speak from their own experiences of Plath in the book—one of these witnesses truly hated Plath—Stevenson, constrained by this necessity to carefully weigh the evidence, was boring.

Such a preference for the stronger voices of personal experience led Malcolm down a path of sympathy with both Hughes and his sister. She found letters Hughes had written to some of the chief players in the saga, angrily complaining of the way they'd transformed his experience into "official history—as if I were a picture on a wall or some prisoner in Siberia." Malcolm found that argument compelling, and says so, even as she also finds so many of the characters of this story—the other people with claims to personal witness of Plath's personality—questionable in their motives. The book ends on the total destruction of the claims of what could be called one of the key witnesses in the Plath case. I won't tell you who; you should read the book for yourself. Malcolm's point, again, is that you don't quite need to trust anyone, don't need to answer to anyone's assertions of fact with what she has called, in two different contexts, "bovine equanimity."

But along the way, Malcolm makes a small disclosure about herself. She goes to visit the critic Al Alvarez, who had been one of Plath's last friends. He first chats amiably to her about parties at Hannah Arendt's in the fifties, then goes on to explain that Plath had been far too "big" a woman for him to be attracted to:

> *I saw what he was getting at, and it made me uncomfortable. As Alvarez had flatteringly mistaken me for someone who might have been invited to Hannah Arendt's parties in the fifties (I doubt whether I even knew who Hannah Arendt was then), so he now distressingly mistook me for someone who could listen without a pang to his discussion of women he didn't find attractive. I felt like a Jew who is tacitly included in an anti-Semitic conversation because nobody knows he's Jewish.*

There is a hint of explicit feminism here, of explicit dissatisfaction with the way men talk about women, even to other women. It was a theme that took quite some time to emerge in Malcolm's work. She had come around gradually to feminism after writing that long critique in the 1970s. She also made a number of women writer friends. Malcolm even knew Sontag a little, though not well. In a short note to Sontag in 1998, when Sontag had become ill again, she wrote: "At lunch I made a mess of saying what I will have a stab at saying here, which is how distressed I am about what you have to endure, how deeply I admire you, and how grateful I am to you for writing 'Illness As Metaphor.'"

But like Didion, Malcolm would become friends with Nora Ephron and come to feel a deep connection with her work, particularly her essays. Feminism was one of their perennial subjects. Late in Ephron's life, the two of them had been part of a book club, one that reread *The Golden Notebook* just to see what it was all about.

And in her travels as a journalist and critic, she seemed to have noticed something about the way the world responded to smart, capable, and insightful women. In 1986, Malcolm published "A Girl of the Zeitgeist," her profile of Ingrid Sischy, completed amid the initial Masson lawsuit. One of its motifs is the way a serious-minded woman keeps trying to make her way among the naysaying of a bunch of serious-minded men. At one point, Sischy tells Malcolm about a man she once met at a lunch, a man who was not very interested in Sischy because of what she looked like. Malcolm immediately imagines herself to be just like that man:

> *I had formed the idea of writing about her after seeing Artforum change from a journal of lifeless opacity into a magazine of such wild and assertive contemporaneity that one could only imagine its editor to be some sort of strikingly modern type, some astonishing new female sensibility loosed in the world. And into my house had walked a pleasant, intelligent, unassuming, responsible, ethical young woman who had not a trace of the theatrical qualities I had confidently expected and from whom, like the politician at the lunch, I had evidently turned away in disappointment.*

The expectations women have for each other, the way we all size each other up, have so many hopes for each other and so many moments, too, of disappointment: that is the nature, apparently, of being a woman who thinks, and talks about thinking, in public.

Afterword

I n writing this book I had a great deal of time to reflect on what, exactly, people meant when they called these women sharp. Many offered the word as a compliment, but there was a slight sense of terror underlying it. Sharpness, after all, cuts. The longer I thought about it, the more convinced I became that there was a fantasy afoot when these women were called sharp or mean or Dark Ladies or whatever other vaguely ominous-sounding label people wanted to apply to them. The fantasy held that they were destructive and dangerous and mercurial, as though intellectual life were a kind of gothic novel.

These women were nothing of the kind. They were not always right, but they were not wrong more often than they should have been, and sometimes they were very, very right. The difficulty is that people have trouble with women who aren't "nice," who do not genuflect, who have the courage to sometimes be wrong in public.

These women also tended not to make themselves palatable to the one movement that might have recognized that conundrum. "I am not a feminist," Mary McCarthy told a San Francisco crowd a couple of years before she died. But then she walked it back.

Exceptional women in my generation certainly profited I suppose—without thinking of it that way—from the fact that women in general were rather looked down upon. So if [men] found one they didn't look down upon, they

raised her up a bit higher than she might have deserved.
I'm enough of a feminist not to like the kind of praise that
says, "She has the mind of a man." I always hated that.

It's not considered very sisterly to believe one stands out from the pack. I thought about that often over the course of researching this book. By necessity, I ran into quite a lot of people who wanted to cut these women out of history precisely because they took advantage of their talents, and did so without turning those talents to the explicit support of feminism. It is viewed as an unforgivable lapse.

The most famous version of that accusation came from Adrienne Rich, Sontag's old rival. When Rich read Arendt's *The Human Condition*, one of the last books Arendt completed, she was both intrigued and disappointed:

> *To read such a book, by a woman of large spirit and great erudition, can be painful, because it embodies the tragedy of a female mind nourished on male ideologies. In fact, the loss is ours, because Arendt's desire to grasp deep moral issues is the kind of concern we need . . . The power of male ideology to possess such a female mind, to disconnect it as it were from the female body which encloses it and which it encloses, is nowhere more striking than in Arendt's lofty and crippled book.*

This was fair enough, insofar as Arendt was steadfastly against feminism until her dying day. She had almost nothing to say about gender, far less than all the other women in this book. She could be biting in her disdain for the feminists of her time. A professor of mine, one of her last students, tells a story of once going up with her in an elevator. My professor, Jennifer Nedelsky, was wearing a button from the Chicago Women's Liberation Union. Arendt looked at her, looked at the button, and pointing at it, said in her thick German accent: "This is not *serious*."

Parker, West, Sontag, Kael, Ephron, and Malcolm were all more comfortable with the label, though they wavered. Parker wasn't exactly a suffragette. Sontag got in that argument with Rich herself over the "simple-minded" failings of feminism. Kael tried to make a feminist argument about *The Group*, and the piece was killed, after which point she seems to have abandoned women's liberation entirely. Didion would later walk back her essay against women's liberation in an interview, claiming, "That piece was about a specific moment in time." Malcolm too, now describes herself as a feminist, despite the critique she once wrote in the *New Republic*.

All through this book I have been trying to point out that there is room, in this deep ambivalence about and even hostility toward feminism, to take away a feminist message. Feminism is, yes, supposed to be about sisterhood. But sisters argue, sometimes to the point of estrangement. It is not only commonality that defines us. If we have learned anything from the debates about intersectionality, it is that the experience we call "being a woman" is deeply inflected by race, class, and other sociological markers.

It is also inflected by individual personality. Some of us are not naturally prone to fall in line the way a movement generally demands. Some of us are the types who stand on the outside of things, who can't help being the person who asks, "But *why* must it be this way?"

"When you are all alone it is hard to decide whether being different is a blemish or a distinction," Arendt once wrote of Rahel Varnhagen. "When you have nothing at all to cling to, you choose in the end to cling to the thing that sets you off from others." She argued for the notion that it was a distinction, and she was right.

You can speak only in the voice you have been given. And that voice has a tenor and inflection given to you by all the experience you have. Some of that experience will inevitably be about being a woman. We're all stuck with each other, stuck with the history of those who've preceded us. You might make your own way, but you always do it in the streams and eddies forded by others, no matter how much you may personally like or dislike them, agree or disagree with them, wish that you were able to transcend this whole situation.

That was certainly a lesson every woman in this book had to learn.

Note on Sources

A great many books went into the making of this one. Direct quotations are attributed in the endnotes. But this book could not have been written without the work of prior biographers. They were integral to assembling the chronology of this book, and I stand on all their shoulders. I list the biographies and secondary sources I relied on in constructing the chronology of this book in the selected bibliography, whether or not they are directly quoted in the book.

Because I was examining these women's personas as laid out in their writing, I worked mostly from their published texts. I did look at letter collections and on occasion did my own archival research, fumbling around for the light switches on certain issues that other biographers hadn't fully explored.

Although I did not set out to report anything like a thorough biography for any of these women, I was lucky enough to briefly interview Janet Malcolm in 2014, and to meet Renata Adler at a presentation I gave about my research in 2015. Certain things they said and did in those encounters are threaded into this book.

Selected Bibliography of Secondary Sources

Valerie Boyd, *Wrapped in Rainbows: The Life of Zora Neale Hurston* (Simon and Schuster, 2004).

Carol Brightman, *Writing Dangerously: Mary McCarthy & Her World* (Clarkson Potter, 1992).

Richard Cohen, *She Made Me Laugh: My Friend Nora Ephron* (Simon & Schuster, 2016).

Tracy Daugherty, *The Last Love Song: A Biography of Joan Didion* (St. Martin's, 2015).

Lorna Gibb, *The Extraordinary Life of Rebecca West* (Counterpoint, 2014).

Victoria Glendinning, *Rebecca West: A Life* (Knopf, 1987).

Robert Gottlieb, *Avid Reader: A Life* (Farrar, Straus and Giroux, 2016).

Anne Heller, *Hannah Arendt: A Life in Dark Times* (New Harvest, 2015).

Dorothy Herrmann, *With Malice Toward All: The Quips, Lives and Loves of Some Celebrated 20th-Century American Wits* (Putnam, 1982).

John Keats, *You Might As Well Live: The Life and Times of Dorothy Parker.* (Simon & Schuster, 1970).

Brian Kellow, *Pauline Kael: A Life in the Dark* (Penguin, 2011).

Frances Kiernan, *Seeing Mary Plain: A Life of Mary McCarthy* (Norton, 2000).

David Laskin, *Partisans: Marriage, Politics, and Betrayal Among the New York Intellectuals* (University of Chicago Press, 2000).

Marion Meade, *Dorothy Parker: What Fresh Hell Is This?* (Penguin, 1989).

Nancy Milford, *Zelda: A Biography* (Harper Perennial, 2001).

Virginia Lynn Moylan, *Zora Neale Hurston's Final Decade* (University Press of Florida, 2012).

BIBLIOGRAPHY

Carl Rollyson, *Rebecca West: A Life* (Scribner, 1996).

Carl Rollyson and Lisa Paddock, *Susan Sontag: The Making of an Icon* (Norton, 2000).

Daniel Schreiber, *Susan Sontag: A Biography* (Northwestern University Press, 2014).

Reuel K. Wilson, *To the Life of the Silver Harbor* (University Press of New England, 2008).

Ben Yagoda, *About Town: The "New Yorker" and the World It Made* (Da Capo, 2001).

Elisabeth Young-Bruehl, *Hannah Arendt: For the Love of the World*, 2nd ed. (Yale University Press, 2004).

Notes

Chapter One: Parker

1 **All her men graduates, ever after:** Frank Crowninshield, "Crowninshield in the Cubs' Den," *Vogue*, September 15, 1944.

2 **There was no need:** "The Wonderful Old Gentleman," in *Collected Stories* (Penguin Classics, 2002).

3 **There was no money:** "The Art of Fiction No. 13: Dorothy Parker," interview with Marion Capron, *Paris Review*, Summer 1956.

3 **need of money:** Ibid.

3 **Guess I have:** Photocopies of several notes from Parker's childhood are available in Marion Meade's papers at Columbia University.

4 **Edward Bernays:** See Larry Tye, *The Father of Spin: Edward L. Bernays and the Birth of Public Relations* (Picador, 1998).

4 **For women we intend:** "In *Vanity Fair*," *Vanity Fair*, March 1914.

5 **I don't call Mrs. Brown:** "Any Porch," *Vanity Fair*, September 1915.

6 **plain . . . not chic:** "The Art of Fiction No. 13: Dorothy Parker."

7 **brevity is the soul:** From a section on *Vogue* patterns, October 1, 1916, 101. Captions in *Vogue* were never signed, but the examples used here are those that scholars believe to have been Parker's.

7 **There is only one thing:** "The Younger Generation," *Vogue*, June 1, 1916.

7 **So odd a blend:** Alexander Woollcott, *While Rome Burns* (Grosset and Dunlap, 1934), 144.

8 **a horde of wraps and sofa pillows:** "Why I Haven't Married," *Vanity Fair*, October 1916 (as Dorothy Rothschild).

8 **infrequent chairs:** "Interior Desecration," *Vogue*, April 15, 1917 (as Dorothy Rothschild).

9 **a sad one for the groom:** "Here Comes the Groom," *Vogue*, June 15, 1917.

10 **So there you are:** "A Succession of Musical Comedies," *Vanity Fair*, April 1918.

10 **dog's life:** "Mortality in the Drama: The Increasing Tendency of Our New Plays to Die in Their Earliest Infancy," *Vanity Fair*, July 1918.

10 **costume the show-girls:** "The Star-Spangled Drama: Our Summer Entertainments Have Become an Orgy of Scenic Patriotism," *Vanity Fair*, August 1918.

10 **bichloride of mercury:** "The Dramas That Gloom in the Spring: The Difficulties of Being a Dramatic Critic and a Sunny Little Pollyanna at the Same Time," *Vanity Fair*, June 1918.

11 **we behaved extremely badly:** "The Art of Fiction No. 13: Dorothy Parker."

11 **anti-Semitic remarks by the hotel's proprietor:** See "Inside Stuff," *Variety*, April 5, 12, 1923.

12 **I wasn't there very often:** "The Art of Fiction No. 13: Dorothy Parker."

12 **Just a bunch of loudmouths:** Quoted in Dorothy Herrmann, *With Malice Toward All: The Quips, Lives and Loves of Some Celebrated 20th-Century American Wits* (Putnam, 1982).

12 **theirs was an attitude of superiority:** O. O. McIntyre, "Bits of New York Life," *Atlanta Constitution*, October 29, 1924.

13 **Miss Burke:** "The Oriental Drama: Our Playwrights Are Looking to the Far-East for Inspiration and Royalties," *Vanity Fair*, January 1920.

14 **It was the greatest act of friendship:** "The Art of Fiction No. 13: Dorothy Parker."

14 **a very young critic named Edmund Wilson:** See Edmund Wilson, *The Twenties* (Douglas and McIntyre, 1984), 32–34.

14 **I did not find them:** Ibid., 44–45.

14 **on an equal basis:** Ibid., 47–48.

15 **Her girlish ways:** "The Flapper," *Life*, January 26, 1922.

15 **There are the Boy Authors:** "Hymn of Hate," *Life*, March 30, 1922.

16 **makes us feel very old:** Heywood Broun, "Paradise and Princeton," *New York Herald Tribune*, April 11, 1920.

16 **Rosalind rested:** "Once More Mother Hubbard," *Life*, July 7, 1921.

17 **If she didn't like something:** Nancy Milford, *Zelda: A Biography* (Harper Perennial, 2001), 66.

17 **a sexual affair between Scott and Parker:** See Scott Donaldson, "Scott and Dottie," *Sewanee Review*, Winter 2016.

17 **I like girls like that:** "What a 'Flapper Novelist' Thinks of His Wife," *Baltimore Sun*, October 7, 1923.

18 **an armed services edition:** See, e.g., Maureen Corrigan, *So We Read On: How the Great Gatsby Came to Be and Why It Endures* (Little, Brown, 2014).

18   **Almost anyone you know:** Sterling North, "More Than Enough Rope," *Poetry*, December 1928.

19   **A kind of burlesque:** Edmund Wilson, "Dorothy Parker's Poems," *New Republic*, January 19, 1927.

19   **Let's face it, honey:** "The Art of Fiction No. 13: Dorothy Parker."

19   **edged and acrid style:** Wilson, "Dorothy Parker's Poems."

20   **Razors pain you:** "Résumé," *Enough Rope* (Boni and Liveright, 1926).

20   **an incompleted dogfight:** "Constant Reader," *New Yorker*, October 29, 1927.

21   **To celebrate in borrowed cadence:** Ernest Hemingway, "To a Tragic Poetess," in *Complete Poems* (University of Nebraska Press, 1983).

22   **His is, as any reader knows:** "Reading and Writing," *New Yorker*, October 29, 1927.

23   **roughly equivalent numbers:** Ben Yagoda, *About Town: The "New Yorker" and the World It Made* (Da Capo, 2001), 77.

23   **goddam women schoolteachers:** James Thurber, *The Years with Ross* (Harper Perennial, 2000), 4–5.

23   **the affair between Margot Asquith and Margot Asquith:** "Constant Reader," *New Yorker*, October 22, 1927.

24   **The Constant Reader columns:** Joan Acocella, "After the Laughs," *New Yorker*, August 16, 1993.

24   **literary Rotarians:** "Constant Reader," *New Yorker*, February 8, 1928.

24   **I *wanted* to be cute:** "The Art of Fiction No. 13: Dorothy Parker."

25   **sophisticated talk:** La Mar Warrick, "Farewell to Sophistication," *Harper's*, October 1, 1930.

25   **Men like a good sport:** "Big Blonde," *Bookman*, February 1929.

26   **This is instead of telephoning you:** The telegram is dated June 28, 1945, and an image of it is widely available on the Internet. See, e.g., "I can't look you in the voice," *Letters of Note* (June 17, 2011) at http://www.lettersofnote.com/2011/06/i-cant-look-you-in-voice.html.

27   **Well, I did saunter:** "NY Pickets Parade Boston Streets in Bus," *New York Herald Tribune*, August 12, 1927.

28   **I am not a member:** "Incredible, Fantastic . . . and True," *New Masses*, November 25, 1937.

29   **I don't think:** *New Masses*, June 27, 1939.

29   **As for me:** "The Art of Fiction No. 13: Dorothy Parker."

30   **traces of the unique genius:** Rebecca West, "What Books Have Done to Russia," *New York Herald Tribune*, October 28, 1928.

Chapter Two: West

31 **he is the Old Maid among novelists:** "Marriage," *Freewoman*, September 19, 1912.

32 **I wonder about the women:** Ibid.

33 **Poor child:** Letter to Letitia Fairfield, April 18, 1910, quoted in *Selected Letters of Rebecca West*, ed. Bonnie Kime Scott (Yale University Press, 2000).

34 **shabby Prospero:** *The Fountain Overflows* (New York Review Books, 2003), 85.

34 **a prison stay:** See Lorna Gibb, *The Extraordinary Life of Rebecca West* (Counterpoint, 2014), 36.

34 **there is something definite about a dog:** "I Regard Marriage with Fear and Horror," *Hearst's International*, November 1925, collected in *Woman as Artist and Thinker* (iUniverse, 2005).

35 **Christabel Pankhurst, Who Is Rich:** This headline appeared in the *Los Angeles Times* on December 2, 1906.

35 **One felt:** "A Reed of Steel," in *The Post-Victorians*, ed. W. R. Inge (Ivor Nicholson and Watson, 1933).

36 **blonde and pretty:** BBC Radio interview with Anthony Curtiss, December 21, 1972, quoted in Gibb, *Rebecca West*, 41.

37 **several skins:** V. S. Pritchett, "One of Nature's Balkans," *New Yorker*, December 21, 1987.

37 **This is most damping:** Letter to the editor by Rebecca West, *Freewoman*, March 14, 1912.

37 **a little high voice:** Rebecca West on Wells, 1CDR 0019053, at Yale's Beinecke Library, cited in Gibb, *Rebecca West*, 48.

37 **curious mixture:** H. G. Wells, *H. G. Wells in Love: Postscript to an Experiment in Autobiography* (Faber and Faber, 1984), 94–95.

38 **During the next few days:** Letter from Rebecca West to H. G. Wells, circa March 1913, in *Selected Letters of Rebecca West*.

39 **For though my lover:** "At Valladolid," *New Freewoman*, August 1913.

39 **men often turn willy nilly:** "The Fool and the Wise Man," *New Freewoman*, October 1913.

41 **I hate domesticity:** Letter from Rebecca West to Sylvia Lynd, circa 1916, in *Selected Letters of Rebecca West*.

42 **There is now no criticism in England:** "The Duty of Harsh Criticism," *New Republic*, November 7, 1914.

42 **the woman H. G. Wells calls:** This advertisement appeared in the *New York Times* on November 7, 1914.

42 **extravagant ecstasies of the fanatic:** "The Duty of Harsh Criticism."

43 **He splits hairs:** "Reading Henry James in Wartime" *New Republic*, February 27, 1915.

44 **One can learn nothing of the heroine's beliefs:** *Henry James* (Nisbet and Co, 1916).

44 **rather metallically bright:** *Observer*, July 23, 1916.

44 **Very young women:** Fanny Butcher, "Rebecca West's Insulting Sketch of Henry James," *Chicago Tribune*, December 2, 1916.

44 **so austerely veracious:** Lawrence Gilman, "The Book of the Month," *North American Review*, May 1918.

45 **It falls short:** Quoted in *Living Age*, August 18, 1922.

45 **But for her wit:** "Fantasy, Reality, History," *Spectator*, September 21, 1929.

45 **George Bernard Shaw's war speeches:** "Mr. Shaw's Diverted Genius," *New Republic*, December 5, 1914.

45 **the strains of Dostoevsky:** "Redemption and Dostoevsky," *New Republic*, June 5, 1915.

45 **Dickens's earlier biographers:** "The Dickens Circle," *Living Age*, January 18, 1919.

45 **tedious and unauthentic:** "Notes on Novels," *New Statesman*, April 10, 1920.

46 **Feminism has not invented:** "Women of England," *Atlantic*, January 1, 1916.

46 **Mrs. Gattenrigg:** *Westminster Gazette*, June 23, 1923.

46 **constant disturbance:** Letter from Rebecca West to Winifred Macleod, August 24, 1923, quoted in Gibb, *Rebecca West*, 85.

46 **egotism:** Letter from Rebecca West to Winfred Macleod, November 2, 1923, Lilly Library, quoted in Gibb, *Rebecca West*, 85.

47 **in the field of the novel:** "Rebecca West Explains It All," *New York Times*, November 11, 1923.

47 **The woman of 30:** Ibid.

47 **dazzle the eye with richness:** "Impressions of America," *New Republic*, December 10, 1924.

48 **beyond all belief slovenly:** Letter from Rebecca West to Winifred Macleod, November 2, 1923, in *Selected Letters of Rebecca West*.

48 **we are all disappointed in you:** Letter from Rebecca West to Gordon Ray, Pierpont Morgan, undated, quoted in Gibb, *Rebecca West*, 88.

49 **I wish he'd turn his mind:** "Rebecca West: The Art of Fiction No. 65," interview with Marina Warner, *Paris Review*, Spring 1981.

50 **Rebecca is a cross:** *The Diary of Virginia Woolf, Volume Four (1931–1935)* (Mariner Books, 1983), 131.

50 **hair light and straight:** *Black Lamb and Grey Falcon: A Journey Through Yugoslavia* (Penguin Classics, 2007), 403.

50   **sharp-nosed:** *A Train of Powder* (Viking, 1955), 78.

50   **I've aroused hostility:** "Rebecca West: The Art of Fiction No. 65."

50   **a dull giraffe:** From a notebook in the Tulsa archive, quoted in Gibb, *Rebecca West,* 116.

51   **not even among his own caste:** "A Letter from Abroad," *Bookman,* April 1930.

51   **intelligent fawn eyes:** Anaïs Nin, *Incest,* from *"A Journal of Love": The Unexpurgated Diary of Anaïs Nin, 1932–1934* (Harvest, 1992), entry for April 27, 1934, 323.

51   **wanting to shine:** Anaïs Nin, *Fire,* from *"A Journal of Love" The Unexpurgated Diary of Anaïs Nin* (Harvest, 1995), entry for August 12, 1935, 130.

53.   **Masterful albeit somewhat rambling:** Gibb, *Rebecca West,* 183.

53   **exactly like all Aryan Germans:** *Black Lamb and Grey Falcon,* 37.

54   **I will believe that the battle of feminism:** Ibid., 124.

54   **they wrote down:** Ibid., 59.

54   **most brilliantly objective:** Katharine Woods, "Rebecca West's Brilliant Mosaic of Yugoslavian Travel," *New York Times,* October 26, 1941.

54   **the only book I have read since the war:** Joseph Barnes, "Rebecca West in the Great Tradition," *New York Herald Tribune,* October 26, 1941.

55   **live to some extent on what we can grow:** "Housewife's Nightmare," *New Yorker,* December 14, 1941.

55   **This crisis has revealed cats:** "A Day in Town," *New Yorker,* January 25, 1941.

56   **he was a tiny little creature:** "The Crown Versus William Joyce," *New Yorker,* September 22, 1945.

56   **An old man told me:** "William Joyce: Conclusion," *New Yorker,* January 26, 1946.

57   **so plainly mad:** *A Train of Powder,* 83.

57   **There is a similarity:** *The Meaning of Treason* (Macmillan and Company, 1952), 305.

58   **extremely good-looking:** "'Shoulder to Shoulder,'" *New York Times,* October 21, 1975.

58   **If one is a woman writer:** Letter from Rebecca West to Emanie Arling, March 11, 1952, quoted in Gibb, *Rebecca West,* 198.

Chapter Three: West & Hurston

59   **blasted to bits:** "So. Carolina Man Lynched in Cruel Mob Orgy," *Los Angeles Sentinel,* February 20, 1947.

59   **ripped his heart:** "Lynch Mob Rips Victim's Heart," *New York Amsterdam News,* February 27, 1947.

60   **sheer nonsense to pretend:** "Opera in Greenville," in *A Train of Powder,* 88.

60   developed a great hostility: Ibid., 82.

60   a plea for the extension: Ibid., 109.

60   There's a law: Ibid., 99.

61   rejoicing at a salvation: Ibid., 112.

61   Gilbert and Sullivan troupe: The details of Hurston's history here are drawn from Valerie Boyd, *Wrapped in Rainbows: The Life of Zora Neale Hurston* (Simon and Schuster, 2004).

62   I am too busy sharpening: *Pittsburgh Courier*, May 12, 1938.

62   incisive and full-dress stories around Negroes: "What White Publishers Won't Print," *Negro Digest*, April 1950.

63   a flaming sword: "Ruby McCollum Fights for Life," *Pittsburgh Courier*, November 22, 1952.

64   lines she previously used: See Virginia Lynn Moylan, *Zora Neale Hurston's Final Decade* (University Press of Florida, 2012).

Chapter Four: Arendt

65   overcome by fear: "Shadows," in *Letters, 1925–1975: Martin Heidegger and Hannah Arendt*, ed. Ursula Lutz, trans. Andrew Shields (Harcourt, 2004).

65   protective third person: Elisabeth Young-Bruehl, *Hannah Arendt: For the Love of the World*, 2nd ed. (Yale University Press, 2004), 50.

65   More likely: "Shadows" in *Letters, 1925–1975*.

67   Ah, death is in life: Quoted in Young-Bruehl, *Hannah Arendt*, 40.

67   human experience and understanding: Daniel Maier-Katkin, *Stranger from Abroad: Hannah Arendt, Martin Heidegger, Friendship and Forgiveness* (Norton, 2010), 27.

68   The rumor about Heidegger: "Heidegger at 80," *New York Review of Books*, October 21, 1971.

68   I will never be able: Letter from Martin Heidegger to Hannah Arendt, February 10, 1925, in *Letters: 1925–1975*.

68   The demonic struck me: Letter from Martin Heidegger to Hannah Arendt, February 27, 1925, in *Letters: 1925–1975*.

70   potential murderer: Letter from Hannah Arendt to Karl Jaspers, July 9, 1946, in *Correspondence: 1926–1969*, ed. Lotte Kohler and Hans Saner, trans. Robert and Rita Kimber (Harvest, 1992).

70   The problem, the personal problem: "What Remains? The Language Remains: A Conversation with Günter Gaus," in *Hannah Arendt: The Last Interview and Other Conversations*, trans. Joan Stumbaugh (Melville House, 2013), 18.

71   Arab harem girl: Young-Bruehl, *Hannah Arendt*, 77.

71 loving is that act: Translated by Arendt Center from Gunther Anders, *Die Kirschen-schlacht*, available at: http://hac.bard.edu/news/?item=4302.

71 Do not forget: Letter from Hannah Arendt to Martin Heidegger, circa 1929, in *Letters, 1925–1975*, 51.

72 The thing which all my life: *Rachel Varnhagen: The Life of a Jewish Woman* (Harvest, 1974), 3.

72 It was never my intention: *Varnhagen*, xv.

73 astonishing: Seyla Benhabib, "The Pariah and Her Shadow: Hannah Arendt's Biography of Rahel Varnhagen," *Political Theory*, February 1995.

73 This sensitivity is a morbid exaggeration: *Varnhagen*, 214.

74 The modern reader will scarcely: Ibid., xviii.

75 It just doesn't look good: "What Remains?," 5.

76 immediate shock: Ibid., 8–9.

76 Whoever wants to call this: Letter from Martin Heidegger to Hannah Arendt, circa winter 1932–33, in *Letters, 1925–1975*.

76 What am I supposed to do: "What Remains?," 10.

77 I shall never: Ibid., 19.

78 Marx simply wanted: Letter from Hans Blücher to Hannah Arendt, July 29, 1948, in *Within Four Walls: The Correspondence Between Hannah Arendt and Heinrich Blücher, 1936–1968*, ed. Lotte Kohler, trans. Peter Constantine (Harcourt, 1996), 93–95.

79 dual monarchy: Young-Bruehl, *Hannah Arendt*, xi.

79 Such an existence: "Walter Benjamin," in *Men in Dark Times* (Houghton Mifflin Harcourt, 1995), 176.

80 The book made a great impression on me: Letter from Walter Benjamin to Ger-shom Scholem, February 20, 1939, in *The Correspondence of Walter Benjamin, 1910–1941*, ed. Gershom Scholem and Theodor W. Adorno, trans. Manfred R. Jacobson and Evelyn M. Jacobson (University of Chicago Press, 1994), 596.

80 I am very worried about Benji: Quoted in Howard Eiland, *Walter Benjamin: A Critical Life* (Harvard University Press, 2014).

80 Unlike the class of the intellectuals: "Walter Benjamin," 181.

81 One day earlier: Ibid., 192.

82 faces a small bay: Quoted in Gershom Scholem, *Walter Benjamin: The Story of a Friendship* (New York Review Books, 2003), 283.

82 The kind of happiness: "Theses on the Philosophy of History," in *Illuminations: Essays and Reflections* (Schocken Books, 1969), 254.

83 In the first place: "We Refugees," in *The Jewish Writings*, ed. Jerome Kohn and Ron Feldman (Schocken, 2007), 265.

83   a quiet and modest way of vanishing: "We Refugees," 268.

85   beer fiddle: Letter from Heinrich Blücher to Hannah Arendt, July 26, 1941, in *Within Four Walls*, 65.

85   A lecture on philosophy: "French Existentialism," *Nation*, February 23, 1946.

86   The conviction that everything: *The Origins of Totalitarianism* (Harvest, 1973), viii.

87   Totalitarian solutions: Ibid., 459.

88   Rose Feitelson: Young-Bruehl, *Hannah Arendt*, 250.

88   monumental but extraordinarily readable book: "People Are Talking About," *Vogue*, May 1951.

89   flatteringly mistaken: Janet Malcolm, *The Silent Woman* (Vintage, 1995), 50.

89   that Weimar Republic flapper: William Barrett, *The Truants: Adventures Among the Intellectuals* (Doubleday, 1983), 103.

89   Hannah Arrogant: See Anne Heller, *Hannah Arendt: A Life in Dark Times* (New Harvest, 2015), 25.

89   vital to my life: Alfred Kazin, *New York Jew* (Knopf, 1978), 195.

90   The theoretical analysis: Dwight Macdonald, "A New Theory of Totalitarianism," *New Leader*, May 14, 1951.

90   I've read your book, absorbed: Letter from Mary McCarthy to Hannah Arendt, April 26, 1951, in *Between Friends: The Correspondence of Hannah Arendt and Mary McCarthy, 1949–1975* (Harcourt Brace, 1995).

Chapter Five: McCarthy

92   She stood in what I later recognized: Eileen Simpson, "Ode to a Woman Well at Ease," *Lear's*, April 1990, quoted in Frances Kiernan, *Seeing Mary Plain: A Life of Mary McCarthy* (Norton, 2000), 223.

92   How can you say this to me: Young-Bruehl, *Hannah Arendt*, 197.

93   Her indiscretions were always open and forthright: Elizabeth Hardwick, "Mary McCarthy in New York," *New York Review of Books*, March 26, 1992.

94   Reading was forbidden us: *Memories of a Catholic Girlhood* (Harcourt, Brace & Company, 1957), 61.

94   I reject the whole pathos: *The Company She Keeps* (Harcourt, Brace & Company, 1942), 263.

95   could not treat your life-history: Ibid., 194.

95   I can see myself married: *Memories of a Catholic Girlhood*, 16.

95   A sense of artistic decorum: *The Company She Keeps*, 264.

95   versed in clockwork obedience: *Memories of a Catholic Girlhood*, 102.

95   If I could not win fame by goodness: Ibid., 111.

96 **There went the girl:** Ibid., 121.

96 **cold, empty gambler's mood:** Ibid., 111.

96 **There was a scent of the seminarian:** Hardwick, "Mary McCarthy in New York."

96 **She presented herself:** Quoted in Kiernan, *Seeing Mary Plain*, 119.

97 **People celebrate one member:** Diana Trilling, *The Beginning of the Journey* (Harcourt Brace, 1993), 350–51.

97 **Why can't you be like:** *The Company She Keeps*, 276.

97 **later, I gather:** *How I Grew* (Harvest Books, 1987), 56.

98 *Moby-Dick* **was way over my head:** Ibid., 61.

98 **a slight sense of being stuffed:** Ibid., 78.

98 **score some pretension:** "The Vassar Girl," *Holiday*, 1951, reprinted in *On the Contrary* (Noonday, 1961), 196.

99 **Vassar Girls, in general:** *The Group* (Harcourt Brace, 1963), 30.

99 **One of the most discouraging things:** Elinor Coleman Guggenheimer, quoted in Kiernan, *Seeing Mary Plain*, 67.

99 **I found her remarkable and intimidating:** Lucille Fletcher Wallop, quoted in Kiernan, *Seeing Mary Plain*, 67.

99 **About college:** Letter from Mary McCarthy to Ted Rosenberg, November 1, 1929, quoted in Kiernan, *Seeing Mary Plain*, 69.

100 **One by one:** "Two Crystal-Gazing Novelists," *Con Spirito*, February 1933, quoted in Kiernan, *Seeing Mary Plain*, 81.

101 **I'm not starving:** "My Confession," in *On the Contrary*, 80.

101 **megaphone for the Communist Party:** Adam Kirsch, "What's Left of Malcolm Cowley," *City Journal*, Spring 2014.

101 **For the first time:** *Intellectual Memoirs 1936–1938* (Harcourt Brace Jovanovich, 1992), 9.

101 **It should never be taken:** "Coalpit College," *New Republic*, May 2, 1934.

101 **It is hard to believe:** "Mr. Burnett's Short Stories," *Nation*, October 10, 1934.

102 **There are but two qualities:** "Pass the Salt," *Nation*, January 30, 1935.

102 **On the whole:** "Our Critics, Right or Wrong, Part I," *Nation*, October 23, 1935.

103 **Literature stirs in him:** "Our Critics, Right or Wrong, Part III," *Nation*, November 20, 1935.

103 **the curious internal warfare:** "Our Critics, Right or Wrong, Part IV," *Nation*, December 4, 1935.

103 **Oh, Mary McCarthy and Margaret Marshall:** John Chamberlain, "Books of the Times," *New York Times*, December 12, 1935.

103 **The girls remind us:** F. P. Adams, "The Conning Tower," *New York Herald Tribune,* December 13, 1935.

104 **perspicacious:** "Our Critics, Right or Wrong, Part V," *Nation,* December 18, 1935.

104 **To marry a man:** *How I Grew,* 267.

104 **A kind of political hockey:** "My Confession," in *On the Contrary,* 78.

105 **They made me feel petty and shallow:** Ibid., 86.

105 **The mark of the historic:** Ibid., 77.

105 **Jeweled lady-authors:** Ibid., 100.

105 **she was no good on abstract ideas:** Isaiah Berlin, quoted in Kiernan, *Seeing Mary Plain.*

106 **certain doubt of orthodoxy:** "My Confession," in *On the Contrary,* 102.

106 **pungently, harshly, drivingly:** "Philip Rahv (1908–1973)," in *Occasional Prose* (Harcourt, 1985), 4.

106 **He wasn't a particularly nice man:** Isaiah Berlin, quoted in Kiernan, *Seeing Mary Plain,* 121.

106 **a pretty brutal guy:** Interview of Dwight Macdonald by Diana Trilling, *Partisan Review,* 1984, in *Interviews with Dwight Macdonald,* ed. Michael Wreszin (University Press of Mississippi, 2003).

106 **sympathetic insight . . . tenderness:** "Philip Rahv (1908–1973)," in *Occasional Prose,* 4.

106 **ukase on her behalf:** *Theatre Chronicles, 1937–1962* (Farrar, Straus and Giroux, 1963), ix.

108 **a kind of viscous holy oil:** "Theatre Chronicle," *Partisan Review,* June 1938.

108 **punctuated [their writing] with pauses:** "Theatre Chronicle," *Partisan Review,* March–April 1940.

108 **purely and simply:** "Theatre Chronicle," *Partisan Review,* April 1938.

108 **The character of Dorothy Parker:** "Wartime Omnibus," *Partisan Review,* Spring 1944.

108 **her dumpy appearance:** *How I Grew,* 16.

108 **He was heavy, puffy, nervous:** Ibid., 260.

109 **I greatly liked talking to him:** *Intellectual Memoirs,* 97.

109 **two tyrants:** David Laskin, *Partisans: Marriage, Politics, and Betrayal Among the New York Intellectuals* (University of Chicago Press, 2000), 88.

110 **Suffice it to say:** Reuel K. Wilson, *To the Life of the Silver Harbor* (University Press of New England, 2008), 53.

111 **It was true:** *The Company She Keeps* (Harcourt Brace & Company, 1942), 84.

111 **At bottom, she was contemptuous:** Ibid., 112.

112 **I was at Exeter:** George Plimpton, quoted in Kiernan, *Seeing Mary Plain*, 181.

112 **a splendid thing, poetic, clever and new:** Letter from Vladimir Nabokov to Edmund Wilson, May 6, 1942, included in *Dear Bunny, Dear Volodya: The Nabokov-Wilson Letters, 1940–1971*, ed. Simon Karlinsky (University of California Press, 2001).

112 **This was a feminist heroine:** Pauline Kael, quoted in Kiernan, *Seeing Mary Plain*, 181.

113 **Its satire is administered:** William Abrahams, "Books of the Times," *New York Times*, May 16, 1942.

113 **a gift for delicate malice:** Review by Lewis Gannett, *New York Herald Tribune*, May 15, 1942.

113 **Clever and wicked:** Malcolm Cowley, "Bad Company," *New Republic*, May 25, 1942.

113 **poor biography:** *The Company She Keeps*, 194.

113 **detect her own frauds:** Ibid., 223.

113 **Miss McCarthy has learned:** Cowley, "Bad Company."

114 **I don't think that she ever wrote anything else:** Lionel Abel, quoted in Kiernan, *Seeing Mary Plain*, 180.

114 **She was aware:** "The Weeds," in *Cast a Cold Eye* (Harcourt Brace & Company, 1950), 35.

115 **And he was really quite mad:** Mary McCarthy, in *Contemporary Authors*, New Revision Series, vol. 16 (Gale, 1984), quoted in Kiernan, *Seeing Mary Plain*, 208.

116 **There was a period:** Margaret Shafer, quoted in Kiernan, *Seeing Mary Plain*, 267.

116 **like a brilliant harpy:** "People Are Talking About," *Vogue*, July 1947.

116 **deeply serious:** Alfred Kazin, "How to Plan Your Reading," *Vogue*, July 1947.

117 **The whole story is a complete fiction:** "The Art of Fiction No. 27: Mary McCarthy," *Paris Review* (Winter–Spring 1962).

117 **brusque and out-of-sorts:** *The Oasis* (Harcourt Brace, 1949), 39.

117 **The woman is a thug:** William Barrett, *The Truants: Adventures Among the Intellectuals* (Doubleday, 1982), 67.

117 **constitutes a gross infringement:** Letter from H. William Fitelson to Robert N. Linscott, May 3, 1949, in the Mary McCarthy Papers at Vassar.

118 **The inner circle is too small:** Donald Barr, "Failure in Utopia," *New York Times*, August 14, 1949.

118 **We think so much alike:** Letter from Hannah Arendt to Mary McCarthy, March 10, 1949, reprinted in *Between Friends*.

119 **his Marxist assurance:** Letter from Mary McCarthy to Hannah Arendt, August 10, 1954, reprinted in *Between Friends*.

119   **burlesque philosophers:** Letter from Mary McCarthy to Hannah Arendt, August 20, 1954, reprinted in *Between Friends*.

120   **I hear that Saul:** Letter from Mary McCarthy to Hannah Arendt, October 11, 1966, reprinted in *Between Friends*.

120   **These people get worse:** Letter from Hannah Arendt to Mary McCarthy, October 20, 1965, reprinted in *Between Friends*.

Chapter Six: Parker & Arendt

122   **Listen, I can't:** Marion Meade, *Dorothy Parker: What Fresh Hell Is This?* (Penguin, 1988), 699.

123   **Lolita:** "Lolita," *New Yorker*, August 27, 1955.

123   **had read *Lolita* and disliked it:** See Galya Diment, "Two 1955 Lolitas: Vladimir Nabokov's and Dorothy Parker's," *Modernism/Modernity*, April 2014.

124   **The late Robert Benchley:** "Book Reviews," *Esquire*, May 1958.

124   **His long body:** "Book Reviews," *Esquire*, September 1959.

125   **His publishers admit:** "Book Reviews," *Esquire*, June 1959.

125   **deadly monotony of days and nights:** Harry Hansen, "The 'Beat' Generation Is Scuttled by Capote," *Chicago Tribune*, February 1, 1959.

125   **Miss Parker, who is no longer (if in fact she ever were):** Janet Winn, "Capote, Miller, and Miss Parker," *New Republic*, February 9, 1959.

126   **brings back all my faith:** "Book Reviews," *Esquire*, December 1962.

126   **To write about art now:** "New York at 6:30 p.m." *Esquire*, November 1964.

127   **walked through the mob, alone:** Details here are drawn from Christine Firer Hinze, "Reconsidering Little Rock: Hannah Arendt, Martin Luther King Jr., and Catholic Social Thought on Children and Families in the Struggle for Justice," *Journal of the Society of Christian Ethics*, Spring/Summer 2009.

127   **It certainly did not require too much:** "Reflections on Little Rock," *Dissent*, Winter 1959, 50.

128   **discrimination is as indispensable a social right:** Ibid., 51.

128   **We publish [this piece] not because we agree with it:** Ibid., 46.

129   **At first one thinks:** Melvin Tumin, "Pie in the Sky..." *Dissent*, January 1959.

129   **Olympian authority:** "The World and the Jug," in Ralph Ellison, *Shadow and Act* (Random House, 1964), 108.

129   **I believe that one of the important:** Ralph Ellison, quoted in Robert Penn Warren, *Who Speaks for the Negro?* (Random House, 1965), 343.

130   **Your remarks seem to me so entirely right:** Letter from Hannah Arendt to Ralph Ellison, July 29, 1965, cited in Young-Bruehl, *Hannah Arendt*, 316.

131 **She also wrote to James Baldwin:** "Letter from a Region in My Mind," *New Yorker*, November 17, 1962.

131 **frightened . . . gospel of love:** Letter from Hannah Arendt to James Baldwin, November 21, 1962, available at http://www.hannaharendt.net/index.php/han/article/view/95/156.

131 **At least one black scholar:** Kathryn T. Gines, *Hannah Arendt and the Negro Question* (Indiana University Press, 2014), 5.

Chapter Seven: Arendt & McCarthy

132 **I would never be able to forgive myself:** Letter from Hannah Arendt to Karl Jaspers, December 2, 1960, in *Correspondence: 1926–1969*.

133 **I never killed a Jew:** *Eichmann in Jerusalem* (Penguin, 1963), 22.

133 **very tempted:** Letter from Hannah Arendt to William Shawn, August 11, 1960, quoted at http://www.glennhorowitz.com/dobkin/letters_hannah_arendt-william_shawn_correspondence1960-1972.

134 **I myself had no hatred:** *Eichmann in Jerusalem*, 30.

134 **Is this a textbook case:** Ibid., 51–52.

135 **sympathizing with Eichmann:** Michael A. Musmanno, "Man with an Unspotted Conscience," *New York Times*, May 19, 1963.

135 **point-by-point refutations:** Letter to editor of the *New York Times* by Robert Lowell, June 23, 1963.

135 **the whole truth was that:** *Eichmann in Jerusalem*, 125.

136 **a deep effect on her:** Hilberg claimed that Arendt owed a huge debt to him and believed she had plagiarized his work. See Nathaniel Popper, "A Conscious Pariah," *Nation*, March 31, 2010.

136 **undoubtedly the darkest chapter:** *Eichmann in Jerusalem*, 117.

136 **cruel and silly:** Ibid., 12.

137 **in place of the monstrous Nazi:** Norman Podhoretz, "Hannah Arendt on Eichmann: A Study in the Perversity of Brilliance," *Commentary*, September 1, 1963.

137 **If a man holds a gun:** Lionel Abel, "The Aesthetics of Evil: Hannah Arendt on Eichmann and the Jews," *Partisan Review*, Summer 1963.

137 **unimaginably inappropriate:** Letter from Gershom Scholem to Hannah Arendt, June 22, 1963, reprinted in "Eichmann in Jerusalem: An Exchange of Letters Between Gershom Scholem and Hannah Arendt," *Encounter*, January 1964.

138 **soul:** See, for example: "Don't tell anybody, is it not proof positive that I have no 'soul'?" in Letter from Hannah Arendt to Mary McCarthy, June 23, 1964, in *Between Friends*.

138 I indeed love "only" my friends: Letter from Hannah Arendt to Gershom Scholem, July 24, 1963, in "An Exchange of Letters."

138 infect[ed] those segments: Letter from Hannah Arendt to Karl Jaspers, October 20, 1963, in *Correspondence: 1926–1969* (Harcourt Brace, 1992), 523.

138 part of the political campaign: Letter from Hannah Arendt to Mary McCarthy, September 20, 1963, in *Between Friends*.

138 What surprises and shocks me most of all: Ibid.

139 George Arliss playing Disraeli: Saul Bellow, quoted in Kiernan, *Seeing Mary Plain*, 354.

140 no one in the know likes the book: Letter from Robert Lowell to Elizabeth Bishop, August 12, 1963, in *Words in Air: The Complete Correspondence Between Elizabeth Bishop and Robert Lowell*, ed. Thomas Travasino and Saskia Hamilton (Farrar, Straus and Giroux, 2008), 489.

140 The flat praise and the faint dissension: Elizabeth Hardwick, "The Decline of Book Reviewing," *Harper's*, October 1959.

141 first serious piece of science fiction: Mary McCarthy, "Déjeuner sur l'herbe," *New York Review of Books*, February 1, 1963.

141 obsession with public success: Gore Vidal, "The Norman Mailer Syndrome," *Nation*, October 2, 1960.

141 She was letting herself: Norman Mailer, quoted in Kiernan, *Seeing Mary Plain*, 189.

142 I confess I enjoyed it enormously: Letter from Mary McCarthy to Hannah Arendt, September 28, 1962, in *Between Friends*.

142 simply not a good enough woman: Norman Mailer, "The Mary McCarthy Case," *New York Review of Books*, October 12, 1963.

143 What I want to say is Congratulations: Letter from Elizabeth Hardwick to Mary McCarthy, August 3, 1963, in the Mary McCarthy Papers at Vassar.

143 I find it strange that people: Letter from Mary McCarthy to Hannah Arendt, October 24, 1963, in *Between Friends*.

144 I am very sorry about the parody: Letter from Elizabeth Hardwick to Mary McCarthy, November 20, 1963, in the Mary McCarthy Papers at Vassar.

144 Fred, who was exquisitely polite: Gore Vidal, quoted in Kiernan, *Seeing Mary Plain*, 525.

144 I love you for taking all these pains: Letter from McCarthy to Katharine White, quoted in Kiernan, 524.

145 Oh poor girl, really: Letter from Elizabeth Bishop to Pearl Kazin, February 22, 1954, in *One Art: Letters Selected and Edited by Robert Giroux* (Farrar, Straus and Giroux, 1994), 288–89.

Chapter Eight: Sontag

146   **a picaresque anti-novel:** Daniel Stern, "Life Becomes a Dream," *New York Times*, September 8, 1963.

146   **reductio ad absurdum:** *As Consciousness Is Harnessed to Flesh*, ed. David Rieff (Farrar, Straus and Giroux, 2012), 237.

146   **I just finished Miss Sonntag's [sic] novel:** Letter from Hannah Arendt to Farrar, Straus & Giroux, August 20, 1963, quoted in Carl Rollyson and Lisa Paddock, *Susan Sontag: The Making of an Icon* (Norton, 2000), 73.

147   **When I last watched her at the Lowells':** Letter from Mary McCarthy to Hannah Arendt, December 19, 1967, in *Between Friends*.

147   **"the imitation me":** Susan Sontag, quoted in Kiernan, *Seeing Mary Plain*, 537.

147   **I hear you're the new me:** Morris Dickstein, quoted in Sheelah Kolhatkar, "Notes on Camp Sontag," *New York Observer*, January 10, 2005.

147   **Mary McCarthy's grin:** *As Consciousness*, 8.

148   **Because you smile too much:** This anecdote is retold in Kiernan, *Seeing Mary Plain*, 538.

148   **Mary McCarthy can do anything with her smile:** *As Consciousness*, 10.

148   **I realize I misspelled your name:** Letter from Mary McCarthy to Susan Sontag, August 11, 1964, in the Mary McCarthy Papers at Vassar.

149   **I still weep in any movie:** "Project for a Trip to China," *Atlantic Monthly*, April 1973.

149   **All I can think of is Mother:** *Reborn: Journals and Notebooks 1947–1963* (Farrar, Straus and Giroux, 2008), 5.

149   **I felt I was slumming in my own life:** "Pilgrimage," *New Yorker*, December 21, 1987.

150   **hadn't understood any of the essays:** See Daniel Schreiber, *Susan Sontag: A Biography* (Northwestern University Press, 2014), 22.

150   **lesser-known Handel operas:** Terry Castle, "Desperately Seeking Susan," *London Review of Books*, March 17, 2005.

150   **a writer who had never mattered to me:** "Susan Sontag: The Art of Fiction No. 143," interview by Edward Hirsch, *Paris Review*, Winter 1995.

151   **Have you read *Nightwood?*:** Interview with Harriet Sohmers Zwerling, November 30, 2015, available at http://lastbohemians.blogspot.com/2015/11/harriet-sohmers-zwerling-ex-nude-model.html.

151   **My concept of sexuality is so altered:** *Reborn*, 28.

152   **You can imagine what that did to me:** "Susan Sontag: The Art of Fiction No. 143."

153 **Our investigations thus far:** Wilhelm Stekel, *The Homosexual Neurosis* (Gotham Press, 1922), 11.

153 **He needs all his money to keep from going to jail:** Letter from Susan Sontag to "Merrill," undated, but found in journal near entry for March 23, 1950, quoted in Alice Kaplan, *Dreaming in French: The Paris Years of Jacqueline Bouvier Kennedy, Susan Sontag, and Angela Davis* (University of Chicago Press, 2014).

153 **I marry Philip with full consciousness:** *Reborn*, 60.

153 **Talked for seven years:** *As Consciousness*, 362.

154 **Whoever invented marriage:** *Reborn*, 79.

154 **emotional totalitarian:** Ibid., 138.

154 **no one to talk to about it:** Joan Acocella, "The Hunger Artist," *New Yorker*, March 6, 2000.

154 **It took me nine years:** *In America* (Picador, 1991), 24.

155 **I replied, "Yes, I'm going to":** Interview with Marithelma Costa and Adelaide López, in *Conversations with Susan Sontag*, ed. Leland A. Pogue (University of Mississippi Press, 1995), 227.

155 **light her cigarettes as she typed:** Sigrid Nunez, *Sempre Susan: A Memoir* (Atlas, 2011), 87.

155 **shrewd, serene, housewifely confidence:** Donald Phelps, "Form as Hero," *New Leader*, October 28, 1963.

155 **Mary used to do it:** "Susan Sontag: The Art of Fiction No. 143."

156 **no one's interested in fiction, Susan:** Ellen Hopkins, "Susan Sontag Lightens Up," *Los Angeles Times*, August 16, 1992.

156 **Many things in the world:** "Notes on 'Camp,'" *Partisan Review*, September 1964.

156 **Camp is a form of regression:** "Not Good Taste, Not Bad Taste—It's 'Camp,'" *New York Times*, March 21, 1965.

157 **every kind of perversion is regarded as avant-garde:** Letter from Philip Rahv to Mary McCarthy, April 9, 1965, in Mary McCarthy Papers at Vassar.

157 **It's embarrassing to be solemn and treatise-like about Camp:** "Notes on 'Camp.'"

158 **too obviously queer, too revealing of her sexuality:** See Terry Castle, "Some Notes on Notes on Camp," in *The Scandal of Susan Sontag*, ed. Barbara Ching and Jennifer A. Wagner-Lawlor (Columbia University Press, 1999), 21.

158 **the revenge of the intellect on art . . . an erotics of art:** "Against Interpretation," *Evergreen Review*, December 1964.

159 **either history-making or a daring sham:** "Sontag and Son," *Vogue*, June 1966.

159 **a sharp girl:** Kevin Kelly, "'A' for Promise, 'F' for Practice," *Boston Globe*, January 30, 1966.

159 **Susan Sontag is hardly a likable person:** Geoffrey A. Wolff, "Hooray for What Is There and Never Mind Reality," *Washington Post*, February 5, 1966.

160 **Agnès Varda's sleek bob:** Camera Three interview, circa fall 1969, available at https://vimeo.com/111098095.

160 **the kind of ultra-chic occasion:** Letter from Lila Karpf to Susan Sontag, November 22, 1966, quoted in Schreiber, *Susan Sontag*, 133.

160 **the Natalie Wood of the U.S. avant-garde:** Robert Phelps, "Self-Education of a Brilliant Highbrow," *Life*, January 1, 1966.

161 **Miss Sontag has been undone as a novelist:** Gore Vidal, "The Writer as Cannibal," *Chicago Tribune*, August 10, 1967.

161 **Susan Sontag would be ugly, or at least plain:** Beatrice Berg, "Susan Sontag, Intellectuals' Darling," *Washington Post*, January 8, 1967.

161 **I must not quote her:** Carolyn Heilbrun, "Speaking of Susan Sontag," *New York Times*, August 27, 1967.

162 **A legend is like a tail:** James Toback, "Whatever You'd Like Susan Sontag to Think, She Doesn't," *Esquire*, July 1968.

162 **Sue. Suzy Q.:** Howard Junker, "Will This Finally Be Philip Roth's Year?" *New York*, January 13, 1969.

162 **I've always been touched by your personal charm:** Letter from Philip Roth to Susan Sontag, January 10, 1969, in the Susan Sontag Archive at UCLA.

163 **Today's America:** "What's Happening in America: A Symposium," *Partisan Review*, Winter 1967.

163 **sweet young thing:** William F. Buckley, "Don't Forget—'Hate America' Seems to Be the New Liberal Slogan," *Los Angeles*, March 20, 1967.

163 **Alienated Intellectual:** Lewis S. Feuer, "The Elite of the Alienated," *New York Times*, March 26, 1967.

164 **made miserable and angry:** "Trip to Hanoi," *Esquire*, February 1978.

164 **a patient in psychoanalysis:** Frances FitzGerald, "A Nice Place to Visit," *New York Review of Books*, March 13, 1969.

165 **an American has no way of incorporating Vietnam:** *Trip to Hanoi* (Farrar, Straus and Giroux, 1969), 87.

165 **I confess that when I went to Vietnam:** Mary McCarthy, "Report from Vietnam I: The Home Program," *New York Review of Books*, April 20, 1967.

165 **do the work of a careful ethnologist:** FitzGerald, "A Nice Place to Visit."

165 **I was really dumb in those days:** Susan Sontag, quoted in Kiernan, *Seeing Mary Plain*, 594.

165 **Interesting that you too were driven:** Letter from Mary McCarthy to Susan Sontag, December 16, 1968, in Susan Sontag Archives at UCLA.

166　My "I" is puny, cautious, too sane: *Reborn*, 168.

166　last year's literary pin-up: Herbert Mitgang, "Victory in the Ashes of Vietnam," *New York Times*, February 4, 1969.

166　I'm assuming you've read mine: Letter from Mary McCarthy to Susan Sontag, December 16, 1968, in Susan Sontag Archives at UCLA.

166　I don't write essays anymore: Leticia Kent, "What Makes Susan Sontag Make Movies?" *New York Times*, October 11, 1970.

167　a cross between Hannah Arendt and Donald Barthelme: *As Consciousness*, 340.

167　had difficulty relating: For a thorough accounting of this development and its recurrence as a cyclical phenomenon in feminism, see, e.g., Susan Faludi, "American Electra," *Harper's*, October 2010.

168　dull cow . . . battle-ax: Norman Mailer, "The Prisoner of Sex," *Harper's*, March 1971.

168　Norman, it is true that women find that: See *Town Bloody Hall* (1979) dir. D. A. Pennebaker and Chris Hegedus.

168　Where did you get that idea?: Leticia Kent, "Susan Sontag Speaks Up," *Vogue*, August 1971.

169　They should whistle at men in the streets: "The Third World of Women," *Partisan Review*, Spring 1973.

169　They are a grammar: *On Photography* (Dell, 1978), 3.

170　A way of certifying experience: Ibid., 9.

170　Assume that we are born to die: "How to Be an Optimist," *Vogue*, January 1975.

170　the way women are taught: "A Woman's Beauty: Put-Down or Power Source?," *Vogue*, April 1975.

170　feminists would feel a pang: "Fascinating Fascism," *New York Review of Books*, February 6, 1975.

171　Since I'm a feminist too: Interview with the *Performing Arts Journal*, 1977, in *Conversations with Susan Sontag*, ed. Leland Pogue (University Press of Mississippi, 1995), 84.

171　My body is invasive, colonizing: From David Rieff, *Swimming in a Sea of Death* (Simon and Schuster, 2008), 35. Rieff did not include this journal entry in *As Consciousness*.

171　opaque to myself: Ibid.

172　I wasn't in the slightest detached: Interview with Wendy Lesser, 1980, in *Conversations with Susan Sontag*, 197.

172　cancerphobes: *Illness as Metaphor* (Vintage, 1979), 22.

173　a disturbing book: Denis Donoghue, "Disease Should Be Itself," *New York Times*, July 16, 1978.

173   **Nostrils flaring:** Castle, "Desperately Seeking Susan."

Chapter Nine: Kael

175   **reviewing a novel for the paper:** See letter from Robert Silvers to Pauline Kael, August 28, 1963, in the Pauline Kael Papers at Lilly Library, Indiana University at Bloomington.

175   **As a group:** Draft of *The Group* review, in the Pauline Kael Papers, quoted in Brian Kellow, *Pauline Kael: A Life in the Dark* (Penguin, 2011).

176   **I wonder, Mrs. John Doe:** Undated (circa 1962–1963) broadcast on KPFA radio, Berkeley, California, available online at https://www.youtube.com/watch?v=sRhs-jKei3g.

178   **It was not out of guilty condescension:** Pauline Kael, "'Hud': Deep in the Divided Heart of Hollywood," *Film Quarterly*, Summer 1964.

178   **The place is cluttered up:** Letter from Pauline Kael to Rosenberg, February 28, 1942, quoted in Kellow, Pauline Kael, 29.

179   **The Chaplin of *Limelight*:** *City Lights*, Winter 1953, reprinted in *Artforum*, March 2002, 122.

180   **When I was a kid:** Interview with the *Los Angeles Reader*, 1982, in *Conversations with Pauline Kael*, ed. Will Brantley (University Press of Mississippi, 1996), 76.

180   **Pauline, let's start positively:** See *Ed and Pauline*, dir. Christian Brando (2014).

181   **I would like to talk about the collapse:** Ibid.

181   **Welles not only teases:** Ibid.

182   **For 5½ years:** "Owner and Employe [sic] Feud over 'Art'; Guess Who Has to Take Powder?" *Variety*, November 16, 1960.

182   **fifty-nine thousand dollars in back wages and profits:** "Wife Wants Artie Operators 'Wages,'" *Variety*, May 31, 1961.

183   **It began to seem like *True Confession*:** "Fantasies of the Art House Audience," *Sight and Sound*, Winter 1961.

184   **There is, in any art:** "Is There a Cure for Film Criticism?" *Monthly Film Bulletin*, Spring 1962.

185   **the second premise of the *auteur* theory:** Andrew Sarris, "Notes on the Auteur Theory in 1962," *Film Culture*, Winter 1962–63.

185   **The smell of a skunk:** "Circles and Squares," *Film Quarterly*, Spring 1963.

186   **Pauline acted as if I were a great menace:** Quoted in Kellow, *Pauline Kael*, 78.

186   **What's the matter?:** Ibid. This entire story is drawn from Kellow. *Pauline Kael*, 78.

187   **Were we to infer:** "Movie vs. Kael," *Film Quarterly*, Autumn 1963.

187   **why that offensive, hypocritical, "alas":** Ibid.

187 **I've always been a little surprised:** Interview with Allen Barra in the *San Francisco Bay Guardian*, August 28, 1991, in *Conversations with Pauline Kael*, 135.

187 **charges her with careerism:** See Kellow, *Pauline Kael*, 78.

187 **Despite your implacable harassment of me:** Letter from Dwight Macdonald to Pauline Kael, November 27, 1963, in Pauline Kael Papers, Lilly Library, quoted in Kellow, *Pauline Kael*, 70.

188 **rather fruitless to care:** Letter from Elizabeth Hardwick to Pauline Kael, September 14, 1963, in the Pauline Kael Papers, Lilly Library.

188 **Too hard on her personally:** Letter from Susan Sontag to Pauline Kael, October 25, 1963, in the Pauline Kael Papers, Lilly Library.

188 **Pauline was deaf to feminism:** Karen Durbin, quoted in Kellow, *Pauline Kael*, 174.

189 **Not being used to the role:** "The Making of *The Group*," in *Kiss Kiss Bang Bang* (Little Brown, 1968), 97.

189 **My job is to show him:** Kellow, *Pauline Kael*, 91.

189 **one of her books:** This would be *Kiss Kiss Bang Bang*.

190 **Susan Sontag published an extraordinary essay:** Pauline Kael, *I Lost It at the Movies* (Dell, 1965), 17.

190 **disclaims ideas:** See Sontag, *Against Interpretation*, 229.

191 **she is the sanest, saltiest, most resourceful:** Richard Schickel, "A Way of Seeing a Picture," *New York Times*, March 14, 1965.

191 **we respond most and best to work:** "Circles and Squares."

191 **the destructive emotionality:** Geoffrey Nowell-Smith, Review of *I Lost It at the Movies*, *Sight and Sound*, Summer 1965.

192 **Whom could it offend?:** "The Sound of . . ." in *Kiss Kiss Bang Bang*, 177.

192 **Miss Kael became more and more critical:** "Sez McCall's Stein: Kael Pans Cinema Profit Motives," *Variety*, July 20, 1966.

193 **How do you make a good movie in this country:** "Bonnie and Clyde," *New Yorker*, October 21, 1967.

194 **deliberately crude:** Interview with Marc Smirnoff for Oxford American, Spring 1992 in *Conversations with Pauline Kael*, 155.

195 **getting a letter from an eminent *New Yorker* writer:** Ibid., 156.

195 **Your picture on the dust cover:** Letter from Louise Brooks to Pauline Kael, May 26, 1962, quoted in Kellow, *Paulin Kael*.

195 **Zest but No Manners:** See *Variety*, December 13, 1967.

196 **shouldn't need to tear a work apart:** "Trash, Art, and the Movies," *Harper's*, February 1969.

198 **shallow masterpiece:** "Raising Kane," *New Yorker*, February 20, 1971.

199　**shallow work, a shallow masterpiece:** Mordecai Richler, "The Citizen Kane Book," *New York Times*, October 31, 1971.

199　**just a lot of people telling jokes:** "The Art of Fiction No. 13: Dorothy Parker."

199　**Orson Welles is not significantly diminished:** Andrew Sarris, "Films in Focus," *Village Voice*, April 1, 1971.

200　**I support her war:** Kenneth Tynan, "The Road to Xanadu," *Observer*, January 16, 1972.

200　**crying in his lawyers' office:** See Barbara Leaming, *Orson Welles: A Biography* (Limelight Editions, 2004), 476.

200　**Mankiewicz's contribution:** Peter Bogdanovich, "The Kane Mutiny," *Esquire*, October 1972.

201　**Marvelous as Mankiewicz's script was:** "Raising Kael," interview with Hollis Alpert in the *Saturday Review*, April 24, 1971, in *Conversations with Pauline Kael*, 13.

202　**the E. B. White elf academy:** James Wolcott, *Lucking Out: My Life Getting Down and Semi-Dirty in Seventies New York* (Anchor, 2011), 67.

202　**Don't answer:** Kellow, *Pauline Kael*, 167.

202　**an arrogantly silly book:** John Gregory Dunne, "Pauline," in *Quintana and Friends* (Penguin, 2012).

Chapter Ten: Didion

203　**a princess fantasy:** Pauline Kael, "The Current Cinema," *New Yorker*, November 11, 1972.

203　**Two tough little numbers:** Dunne, "Pauline."

204　**I didn't realize then:** "Joan Didion: The Art of Nonfiction No. 1," *Paris Review*, Spring 2006.

204　**Her father, Frank:** Details about Didion's family here drawn from Tracy Daugherty, *The Last Love Song: A Biography of Joan Didion* (St. Martin's, 2015).

204　**Really?:** *Where I Was From* (Vintage, 2003), 211.

205　**nothing was irrevocable:** "Farewell to the Enchanted City," *Saturday Evening Post*, January 14, 1967, republished as "Goodbye to All That" in *Slouching Towards Bethlehem* (Farrar, Straus and Giroux, 1968).

206　**Talk to anyone whose work:** "Jealousy: Is It a Curable Illness?" *Vogue*, June 1961.

206　**I was writing pieces that I just sent out:** "Telling Stories in Order to Live," Interview on the occasion of the National Book Award, June 3, 2006, formerly available online, copy author's own files.

207　**a stunningly predictable Sarah Lawrence girl:** "Finally (Fashionably) Spurious," *National Review*, November 18, 1961.

208 **The smoke of creation rises:** "The Current Cinema," *New Yorker*, November 11, 1972.

208 **Self-absorption is general:** "Letter from 'Manhattan,'" *New York Review of Books*, August 16, 1979.

209 **What man in his forties:** Pauline Kael, "The Current Cinema," *New Yorker*, October 27, 1980.

210 **Let me lay it on the line:** "Movies," *Vogue*, February 1, 1964.

210 **possibly the only seduction ever screened:** "Movies," *Vogue*, March 1, 1964.

210 **tends to play these things:** "Movies," *Vogue*, June 1, 1964.

210 **try to pass off as sociological:** "Movies," *Vogue*, November 1, 1964.

210 **More embarrassing than most:** "Movies," *Vogue*, May 1, 1965.

211 **it is easy to Dial-a-Devotion:** "How Can I Tell Them There's Nothing Left," *Saturday Evening Post*, May 7, 1966, republished as "Some Dreamers of the Golden Dream" in *Slouching Towards Bethlehem*.

212 **We recognize these feelings:** Letter to the editor by Howard Weeks, *Saturday Evening Post*, June 18, 1966.

212 **frail, lazy and unsuited:** "The Big Rock Candy Figgy Pudding Pitfall," *Saturday Evening Post*, December 3, 1966.

213 **Some instinct, programmed by all the movies:** "Farewell to the Enchanted City."

214 **She has told me that the governor:** "Pretty Nancy," *Saturday Evening Post*, June 1, 1968.

214 **I thought we were getting along:** Nancy Skelton, "Nancy Reagan: Does She Run the State Or the Home?" *Fresno Bee*, June 12, 1968.

215 **I ask a couple of girls what they do:** "Slouching Towards Bethlehem," *Saturday Evening Post*, September 23, 1967.

215 **The majority of the flower children:** Letter to the editor by Sunnie Brentwood, *Saturday Evening Post*, November 4, 1967.

215 **one of the least celebrated and most talented:** "Places, People and Personalities," *New York Times*, July 21, 1968.

215 **Journalism by women is the price:** "Her Heart's with the Wagon Trains," *Christian Science Monitor*, May 16, 1968.

216 **Joan Didion: Writer with Razor's Edge:** See article of this title in the *Los Angeles Times*, August 2, 1970.

216 **Slouching Towards Joan Didion:** See article of this title in *Newsday*, October 2, 1971.

216 **a creature of many advantages:** Alfred Kazin, "Joan Didion, Portrait of a Professional," *Harper's*, December 1971.

217   some of the guys are going out: *The Year of Magical Thinking* (Vintage, 2006), 111.

217   My husband switches off the television set: "A Problem of Making Connections," *Life*, December 9, 1969.

218   very New England: "The Women's Movement," *New York Times*, July 30, 1972.

219   enslaved because she persists: Didion was quoting from Wendy Martin, ed. *The American Sisterhood: Writings of the Feminist Movement from Colonial Times to the Present* (Harper and Row, 1972).

219   this litany of trivia: "The Women's Movement."

220   The impulse to find solutions: "African Stories," *Vogue*, October 1, 1965.

220   Isn't it interesting: Susan Brownmiller, letter to the editor, *New York Times*, August 27, 1972.

221   We tell ourselves stories: "The White Album," in *The White Album* (Farrar, Straus and Giroux, 1979), 11.

222   all the day's misinformation: Ibid., 142.

222   I used to wonder how Pauline Kael: "Hollywood: Having Fun," *New York Review of Books*, March 22, 1973.

223   A possible reason: Letter to the editor, *New York Review of Books*, April 19, 1973.

223   Self-absorption is general: "Letter from 'Manhattan.'"

224   Oh, wow: "They'll Take Manhattan," *New York Review of Books*, October 11, 1979.

224   Donner Party: Wolcott, *Lucking Out*, 61.

225   all the elements in the puzzle: "Love and Death in the Pacific," *New York Times Book Review*, April 22, 1984.

225   a special kind of practical information: *Salvador* (Vintage, 2011), 17.

227   The narrative is made up: "Insider Baseball," *New York Review of Books*, October 27, 1988.

Chapter Eleven: Ephron

229   The first day: *Heartburn* (Knopf, 1983), 3.

230   be the heroine of your life: Commencement address to Wellesley College, 1996, available online at http://www.wellesley.edu/events/commencement/archives/1996commencement.

230   frail and tiny and twinkly: "Dorothy Parker" in *Crazy Salad and Scribble Scribble* (Vintage, 1972), 168.

231   to see if it was good enough: See Henry Ephron, *We Thought We Could Do Anything* (Norton, 1977), 12–13.

231   If I haven't raised you: Eulogy for Phoebe Ephron, printed as "Epilogue," in *We Thought We Could Do Anything*, 209.

231   **She was not doctrinaire:** Ibid., 211.

232   **One day she wasn't an alcoholic:** "The Legend," from *I Remember Nothing* (Random House, 2010), 37.

232   **She knew, I think, that she was dying:** "Epilogue," in *We Thought*, 210.

233   **strictly infantile:** Bosley Crowther, "The Screen," *New York Times*, December 20, 1944.

233   **P.S. I'm the only one in my class:** Henry and Phoebe Ephron, *Take Her, She's Mine* (Samuel French, 2011), 18.

233   **Tempest of Mirth:** Thomas R. Dash, "Bringing Up Father Theme Yields Tempest of Mirth," *Women's Wear Daily*, December 26, 1961.

233   **told interestingly:** "Take Her, She's Mine," *Variety*, November 29, 1961.

233   **Writers are always selling somebody out:** Preface to *Slouching Towards Bethlehem*, xiv.

234   **It would never have crossed my mind:** "Journalism: A Love Story," in *I Remember Nothing*.

235   **I feel bad:** "Dorothy Schiff and the *New York Post*," *Esquire*, April 1, 1975.

235   **People who are drawn to journalism:** Introduction to *Wallflower at the Orgy* (Bantam, 2007), 18.

236   **she'd never marry if she read too much:** *New York Post*, September 23, 1967.

236   **As in let them read schlock:** "Dorothy Schiff and the *New York Post*."

237   **I think she's a spider:** A clip of this interview appears in *Everything Is Copy*, dir. Jacob Bernstein (2016).

237   **more devoted to language than to people:** Meg Ryan, interview, in *Everything Is Copy*, dir. Jacob Bernstein (2016).

237   **Twenty-five years ago, Howard Roark laughed:** "A Strange Kind of Simplicity," *New York Times*, May 5, 1968.

237   **I also got letters asking me:** "Dick Cavett Reads Books," *New York Times*, June 2, 1968.

238   **a saucy, snoopy, bitchy man:** Review of *Do You Sleep in the Nude? New York Times*, July 21, 1968.

238   **lunch is two hours out there:** "Where Bookmen Meet to Eat," *New York Times*, June 22, 1969.

238   **ten thousand dollars a year before 1974:** Interview with Michael Lasky, *Writer's Digest*, April 1974, reprinted in *Nora Ephron: The Last Interview and Other Conversations* (Melville House, 2015).

238   **something a little embarrassing:** "Women's Wear Daily Unclothed," *Cosmopolitan*, January 1968, reprinted in *Wallflower at the Orgy*.

239 **She is demonstrating:** "Helen Gurley Brown Only Wants to Help," *Esquire*, February 1970, reprinted as "If You're a Little Mouseburger, Come with Me. I Was a Mooseburger and I Will Help You," in *Wallflower at the Orgy*.

239 **the little princess:** Joan Didion, "Bosses Make Lousy Lovers," *Saturday Evening Post*, January 30, 1965.

240 **forgave Ephron:** *Nora Ephron: The Last Interview*.

240 **kitsch killed:** "Mush," *Esquire*, June 1971.

241 **There are times:** Introduction to *Wallflower at the Orgy*.

241 **Why not use a Band-Aid:** "Some Words About My Breasts," *Esquire*, May 1972.

243 **Writing a column on women in *Esquire*:** "Women," *Esquire*, July 1972.

243 **If I could know for sure:** Alix Kates Shulman, *Memoirs of an Ex–Prom Queen* (Knopf, 1972), 17.

243 **an ugly girl in America:** "On Never Having Been a Prom Queen," *Esquire*, August 1972.

244 **It's her baby, damn it:** "Miami," *Esquire*, November 1972.

245 **blood, birth and death:** "Vaginal Politics" in *Crazy Salad*.

245 **I think that piece:** Interview with Joan Didion by Christopher Bollen, *V*, available online at http://www.christopherbollen.com/archive/joan_didion.pdf.

246 **a deodorant for the external genital area:** "Dealing with the uh, Problem," *Esquire*, March 1973.

246 **Once I tried to explain to a fellow feminist:** "On Never Having Been a Prom Queen."

246 **recurring ironies of this movement:** "Truth and Consequences," *Esquire*, May 1973.

247 **Dashiell Hammett used to say:** "A Star Is Born," *New York Magazine*, October 1973.

248 **As near as possible:** Quoted in "Guccione's Ms. Print," *New York*, October 29, 1973.

248 **As one journalist put it:** "Women: The Littlest Nixon," *New York*, December 24, 1973.

249 **full of nonsense:** See, e.g., "The Legend," in *I Remember Nothing*, 37.

249 **You can be malevolent:** This clip appears in *Everything Is Copy*.

250 **You can write the most wonderful piece:** Jurate Karickas, "After Book, Friends No More," *Atlanta Constitution*, August 3, 1975.

250 **there are certain magazines:** *Nora Ephron: The Last Interview*.

251 **We decided to get married on Sunday:** Peter Stone, "Nora Ephron: 'I Believe in Learning the Craft of Writing,'" *Newsday*, December 5, 1976.

251 **We meet outside a Chinese restaurant:** "The Story of My Life in 5,000 Words or Less," in *I Feel Bad About My Neck* (Knopf, 2006).

251 **When you slip on a banana peel:** Ibid., 86.

252 **Nora is a much classier person:** Jesse Kornbluth, "Scenes from a Marriage," *New York Magazine*, March 14, 1983.

Chapter Twelve: Arendt & McCarthy & Hellman

253 **HEINRICH DIED:** Telegram from Hannah Arendt to Mary McCarthy, November 1–2, 1970, reprinted in *Between Friends*.

253 **I am now sitting:** Letter from Hannah Arendt to Mary McCarthy, November 22, 1970, reprinted in *Between Friends*.

254 **The first time I heard her:** "Saying Good-By to Hannah," *New York Review of Books*, January 22, 1976.

255 **on her bare shriveled arms:** Letter from Mary McCarthy to Ben O'Sullivan, February 26, 1980, in the Mary McCarthy Papers at Vassar.

256 **The only one I can think of:** *The Dick Cavett Show*, October 17, 1979, quoted in Kiernan, *Seeing Mary Plain*, 673.

256 **reckless:** Irving Howe, quoted in Kiernan, *Seeing Mary Plain*, 674.

256 **with that smile of hers:** Jane Kramer, quoted in Kiernan, *Seeing Mary Plain*, 674.

256 **I guess I never thought of you:** Dick Cavett, "Lillian, Mary and Me," *New Yorker*, December 16, 2002.

257 **I haven't seen her:** "Miss Hellman Suing a Critic for $2.25 Million," *New York Times*, February 16, 1980.

257 **They are both splendid writers:** Norman Mailer, "An Appeal to Lillian Hellman and Mary McCarthy," *New York Times*, May 11, 1980.

257 **my unspecialized study of apocryphism:** Martha Gellhorn, "Guerre de Plume," *Paris Review* , Spring 1981.

258 **It was quite a while:** Nora Ephron, introduction to *Imaginary Friends* (Vintage, 2009).

Chapter Thirteen: Adler

260 **Mr. Shawn felt:** Lili Anolik, "Warren Beatty, Pauline Kael, and an Epic Hollywood Mistake," *Vanity Fair*, February 2017.

261 **Now, *When the Lights Go Down*, a collection:** "The Perils of Pauline," *New York Review of Books*, August 14, 1980.

262 **depressing, vengeful, ceaseless tirade:** Letter from Matthew Wilder to the editor, *New York Review of Books*, February 5, 1980.

262 **the staff critics I know:** John Leonard, "What Do Writers Think of Reviews and Reviewers?" *New York Times*, August 7, 1980.

262 **I'm sorry that Ms. Adler:** *Time*, July 27, 1980.

263 **as assertively and publicly 'private':** Jesse Kornbluth, "The Quirky Brilliance of Renata Adler," *New York*, December 12, 1983.

263 **thin, rather Biblical-looking:** Letter from Mary McCarthy to Carmen Angleton, August 29, 1961, quoted in Kiernan, *Seeing Mary Plain*, 499.

264 **I was surprised:** Quoted in Kiernan, *Seeing Mary Plain*, 500.

264 **His book begins:** Review of John Hersey's *Here to Stay*, *Commentary*, April 1963.

264 **included a coloring book:** "Talk of the Town," *New Yorker*, December 8, 1962.

265 **In literary criticism, polemic is short-lived:** "Polemic and the New Reviewing," *New Yorker*, July 4, 1964.

266 **After the Second World War:** Ibid.

266 **To Miss Arendt's quiet, moral, rational document:** "Comment," *New Yorker*, July 20, 1963.

266 **If anyone was . . . sitting adoringly:** *Gone: The Last Days of the "New Yorker"* (Simon and Schuster, 1999), 82.

266 **strict parent:** Interview with Christopher Bollen, *Interview*, August 14, 2014.

267 **did not care for Ms. Sontag:** *Gone*, 33.

267 **It's not that Hannah Arendt:** Adler said this during a Q&A for a lecture given on the research in progress for this book at the New York Institute for the Humanities in November 2015.

267 **First, "everyone I know" occurs fourteen times:** "Polemic and the New Reviewing," *New Yorker*, July 4, 1964.

268 **Though I may have read things:** Irving Kristol, "On Literary Politics," *New Leader*, August 3, 1964.

269 **Word came that Mrs. Viola Liuzzo:** "Letter from Selma," *New Yorker*, April 10, 1965.

269 **East Coast's Joan Didion:** Jesse Kornbluth, "The Quirky Brilliance of Renata Adler," *New York*, December 12, 1983.

269 **a growing fringe of waifs:** "Fly Trans Love Airways," *New Yorker*, February 25, 1967.

270 **He began to yodel:** Ibid.

270 **I am part of an age group:** Introduction to *Toward a Radical Middle: Fourteen Pieces of Reporting and Criticism* (Dutton, 1971).

272 **Even if your idea of a good time:** "A Teutonic Striptease," *New Yorker*, January 4, 1968.

272 **among the most fond:** "Norman Mailer's Mailer," *New York Times*, January 8, 1968.

273 **Renata Adler, of the *New York Times*, did not like:** This advertisement was quoted by the court in *Adler v. Condé Nast Publications, Inc.*, 643 F. Supp. 1558 (S.D.N.Y. 1986).

273 **Both her supporters and detractors:** Lee Beauport, "Trade Making Chart on Renata Adler; but Some Like Her Literary Flavor," *Variety*, March 6, 1968.

274 **One of the things democracy may be:** "How Movies Speak to Young Rebels," *New York Times*, May 19, 1968.

274 **Maybe it is an anti-Mummy reflex:** "Science + Sex = Barbarella," *New York Times*, October 12, 1968.

275 **learn to write to deadline:** Interview with Christopher Bollen, *Interview*, August 14, 2014.

275 **spoke with a kind of awe:** *Pitch Dark* (NYRB Classics, 2013), 5.

277 **Whatever their other motives:** Renata Adler, *Reckless Disregard: Westmoreland v. CBS et al.; Sharon v. Time* (Knopf, 1986).

278 **she too often surrenders:** Ronald Dworkin, "The Press on Trial," *New York Review of Books*, February 26, 1987.

278 **claimed she had snowed them:** See Robert Gottlieb, *Avid Reader: A Life* (Farrar, Straus and Giroux, 2016), 220.

279 **comically incurious:** *Gone*, 203.

280 **an explosion of pain and anger:** Robert Gottlieb, "Ms. Adler, the *New Yorker*, and Me," *New York Observer*, January 17, 2000.

280 **contrary to his reputation:** *Gone*, 125.

280 **If I did not wish to "disclose" my "sources":** "A Court of No Appeal," *Harper's*, August 2000.

282 **The six-volume Starr Report:** "Decoding the Starr Report," *Vanity Fair*, February 1999.

282 **I've said it all along:** Rachel Cooke, "Renata Adler: 'I've Been Described as Shrill. Isn't That Strange?'" *Guardian*, July 7, 2013.

Chapter Fourteen: Malcolm

284 **Almost everyone else in the analytic world:** *In the Freud Archives* (Knopf, 1983), 35.

285 **Everything he said and thought:** Ibid., 133

285 **the kindergarten teacher saying:** "Janet Malcolm: The Art of Nonfiction No. 4," interview with Katie Roiphe, *Paris Review*, Spring 2011.

286 **I went to see:** "A Star Is Borne," *New Republic*, December 24, 1956.

287 **Outside the theatre:** "Black and White Trash," *New Republic*, September 2, 1957.

287 **it is hard to tell about this:** Letter to the editor by James F. Hoyle, *New Republic*, September 9, 1957.

288 **the leading authorities everywhere:** Letter to the editor by Hal Kaufman, *New Republic*, September 30, 1957.

288 **awful nuisance:** "D. H. Lawrence and His Friends," *New Republic*, February 3, 1958.

288 **One is forced to add:** Letter to the editor by Norman Mailer, *New Republic*, March 9, 1959.

289 **Our children are a mirror of belief:** "Children's Books for Christmas," *New Yorker*, December 17, 1966.

289 **I don't know how Dr. Lasagna:** "Children's Books for Christmas," *New Yorker*, December 14, 1968.

290 **In any case, a woman who chooses:** "Help! Homework for the Liberated Woman," *New Republic*, October 10, 1970.

291 **As for those that raise questions of substance:** "No Reply," *New Republic*, November 14, 1970.

291 **who, as yet, is better known for his wife:** "About the House," *New Yorker*, March 18, 1972.

293 **Rereading these essays:** Preface to *Diana and Nikon* (Aperture, 1997).

293 **The [Walker] Evans book:** "Slouching Towards Bethlehem, Pa.," *New Yorker*, August 6, 1979.

294 **Innocently opening the book:** "Artists and Lovers," *New Yorker*, March 12, 1979.

295 **Family therapy will take over:** "The One-Way Mirror," *New Yorker*, May 15, 1978.

295 **The empty couch:** *Psychoanalysis: The Impossible Profession* (Knopf, 1977), 47.

296 **mischievous:** Joseph Adelson, "Not Much Has Changed Since Freud," *New York Times*, September 27, 1981.

296 **I was attracted to psychoanalytic work:** *Psychoanalysis*, 110.

297 **an intellectual gigolo:** Ibid., 41.

298 **what Anna Freud once said to me:** Ibid., 38.

298 **a masterwork of character assassination:** https://www.salon.com/2000/02/29/malcolm/.

298 **I wonder if he ever cared:** Ibid., 163.

299 **The portrait, in fact:** Letter to the editor by Janet Malcolm, *New York Times*, June 1, 1984.

299 **numerous commentators:** See, e.g., Robert Boynton, "Who's Afraid of Janet Malcolm?" *Mirabella*, November 1992, available at http://www.robertboynton.com/articleDisplay.php?article_id=1534.

300 **I should have known:** "Janet Malcolm: The Art of Nonfiction No. 4."

300 **Any journalist who is not too stupid:** *The Journalist and the Murderer* (Vintage, 1990), 3.

300 **Well, it was a bit of rhetoric:** I remember this remark from Malcolm's appearance with Ian Frazier at the New Yorker Festival on September 30, 2011.

301 **He is a kind of confidence man:** *The Journalist and the Murderer*, 3.

301 **Miss Malcolm appears:** Albert Scardino, "Ethics, Reporters, and the *New Yorker*," *New York Times*, March 21, 1989.

301 **fellow workers recording politicians' doings:** Ron Grossman, "Malcolm's Charge Turns on Itself," *Chicago Tribune*, March 28, 1990.

302 **David Rieff stuck up for her:** David Rieff, "Hoisting Another by Her Own Petard," *Los Angeles Times*, March 11, 1990.

302 **What Janet Malcolm was saying:** Nora Ephron in the *Columbia Journalism Review*, July 1, 1989.

302 **I thought Malcolm's articles were marvelous:** Jessica Mitford in the *Columbia Journalism Review*, July 1, 1989.

302 **confession of Malcolm's sins:** John Taylor, "Holier Than Thou," *New York*, March 27, 1989.

302 **Masson was too honest:** David Margolick, "Psychoanalyst Loses Libel Suit Against a New Yorker Reporter," *New York Times*, November 3, 1994.

302 **Who hasn't felt pleasure:** "Janet Malcolm: The Art of Nonfiction No. 4."

303 **then dropping him again:** "The Morality of Journalism," *New York Review of Books*, March 1, 1990.

303 **Unlike the "I" of autobiography:** *The Journalist and the Murderer*, 159–60.

305 **Forty-One False Starts:** See article of that title in the *New Yorker*, July 11, 1994.

306 **She had once:** *The Silent Woman: Sylvia Plath and Ted Hughes* (Vintage, 1995), 13.

306 **official history:** Letter from Ted Hughes, quotes in *The Silent Woman*, 53.

307 **I saw what he was getting at:** Ibid., 48.

307 **At lunch I made a mess:** Letter from Janet Malcolm to Susan Sontag, dated October 3, 1998, in the Susan Sontag Archive at UCLA.

308 **I had formed the idea of writing:** "A Girl of the Zeitgeist," *New Yorker*, October 20, 27, 1986.

Afterword

309 **Exceptional women in my generation:** Speech given by Mary McCarthy at City Arts and Lectures, San Francisco, October 1985, quoted in Kiernan, *Seeing Mary Plain*, 710.

310 **To read such a book:** Adrienne Rich, "Conditions for Work: The Common World of Women," in *On Lies, Secrets and Silence* (Norton, 1979).

311 **simple-minded:** Adrienne Rich and Susan Sontag, "Feminism and Fascism: An Exchange," *New York Review of Books*, March 20, 1975.

311 **That piece was about:** Interview with Christopher Bollen, undated, available online at http://www.christopherbollen.com/archive/joan_didion.pdf.

311 **When you are all alone:** Arendt, *Varnhagen*, 218.

Index